FOREWORD

This book, by a psychiatrist, is written for lawyers. But it is a thoroughly good read and will prove fascinating to lay people.

The psychiatrist/author is eminently qualified in the field. He has been working in public psychiatry since 1962, is a distinguished scholar and lecturer and has served with a large number of public organisations concerned with mental health.

The legal profession and the judiciary, at which the book is primarily aimed, will be well advised to read it and have it available for reference. Utilisation of psychiatric evidence and concepts in legal proceedings is increasing exponentially with the growth in the range of problems which the legal system is required to address and to attempt to resolve, with the range of injuries and grievances which the legal system is authorised to redress, and with the ingenuity of psychiatrists in developing new legal markets for their wares. Examples of these phenomena include:

- Equal opportunity tribunals which may consider claims of sexual discrimination and victimisation in the workplace alleged to have resulted in the victims suffering from disorders such as "hypertension", "depression", and stress related physical problems.

- Recognition, the strength and degree of which waxes and wanes with the climate of the times, of conditions such as "RSI" and various types of post-traumatic stress disorders.

- Involvement of psychiatrists in disputes over wills, with the expert psychiatrist purporting to be able to assess the testator's capacity to make the will using only written historical material.

- Growing recognition that the prevalence of intellectual disability and mental disorder in New South Wales prisons has been vastly underestimated in the past, leading to concerns that people with such disabilities suffer prejudice and other disadvantages when subjected to court processes, prompting calls for reforms in those processes which would give greater scope for the expertise of psychiatrists and psychologists.

- An apparent increase in reliance on defences to criminal charges requiring psychiatric expertise to prove them, such as diminished responsibility and mental illness. (For example, in New South Wales, in December 1991, there were 86 forensic patients contained within its prisons and psychiatric hospitals, or living in the community on conditional release, whereas by December 1992 there were 98. The rate is continuing to increase).

- More psychiatrists than ever before are taking up "forensic psychiatry" as their specialty. With an increase in the supply has come an increase in the use of that service.

This long overdue text explains, in a clear and illuminating manner, the language and concepts of psychiatry, and the limitations of psychiatric expertise in providing possible answers to questions in dispute before the traditional courts and the growing range of judicial and quasi-judicial commissions, inquiries, tribunals and boards which comprise our modern legal system.

Psychiatry in Court will not be limited in its effect to the better utilisation of the science of psychiatry by lawyers, on behalf of their clients, with the sole objective of bringing the decision-maker round to a point of view consistent with the client's interest. It could well have a broader impact than that, one which inures to the benefit of the community as a whole. For in many quarters the expert is on trial.

One of the many solutions proposed to the difficulty that expert testimony generally, and psychiatric expert testimony in particular, presents to the law, as proposed by Ian Freckleton in *The Trial of the Expert*, is the development of a:

> consciousness on the part of all involved with the legal system that clear-cut answers frequently cannot be given by experts . . . [This] should lead to a more critical attitude towards the testimony they give, and accordingly, the deleterious consequences of the testimony of the odd expert whose theories or techniques are unreliable will be reduced. Similarly, the development of standard procedures to which experts are expected to adhere in coming to their conclusions will serve to reduce the communication gap between lay person and expert witness in the court room.[1]

Psychiatry in Court will assist in increasing the "consciousness", and reducing the "communication gap", to which Ian Freckleton refers. Dr Shea brings to bear a refreshing scepticism about the value and limitations of the "science" in which he is manifestly so deeply expert. He quite unabashedly proclaims that "psychiatry is not a science at all". His conclusions about predictions of dangerousness are salutary, particularly in light of the attention paid by the tabloid press, and our fearless and so-called investigative television journalists, to gruesome homicides: "Psychiatrists are especially poor at predicting dangerousness, except for . . . short term predictions".

Dr Shea goes on to give this advice:

1. In the courtroom psychiatrists should resist being drawn into making predictions about the dangerousness of mentally disordered people. They should limit themselves to providing the court with as much clinical

information as they can . . . and leave the question of dangerousness for the court to decide.

2. Lawyers, in turn, should refrain from asking psychiatrists specific questions about dangerousness. They should respect the fact that dangerousness is not "a medical or psychological concept", that psychiatrists have no particular expertise in this area and that their track record in predicting dangerousness is, on the available evidence, poor.

Some of the problems alluded to by Dr Shea are under active consideration by law reformers in Australia and overseas. He refers to the fact that:

Of the forensic psychiatric reports that are commissioned, only a percentage is actually presented in court. Given the nature of the adversarial system, this is also not surprising. If a lawyer asked for a report on a client and it turned out to be unhelpful to the case, or, even worse, unfavourable, a likely outcome is that the report would simply be filed away and a new one commissioned.

Freckelton discusses some of the tentative solutions, which have been raised before law reform bodies, and in some cases endorsed, and in others, rejected. But perhaps something even more radical than what has already been considered, and rejected, might be required. Along with the monarchy, the traditional legal profession and traditional court processes are being put under the microscope by people who want a more appropriate response to contemporary societal problems and aspirations than has been thrown up by English constitutional and legal history. Dr Shea, having addressed issues posed by the adversarial system in areas where psychiatric expertise is required, expresses doubt as to whether change is even remotely possible, but nevertheless makes some suggestions, including:

- increased use of court appointed experts;

- employment of expert assessors;

- giving of group expert evidence; and

- pre-trial consultation between forensic psychiatrists.

While serious consideration and immediate adoption of one or other of these alternatives seems a long way off, the vigour with which politicians, alarmed at the growing cost and inaccessibility of traditional court processes as a solution to disputes and problems (such as the appropriate disposition of a mentally ill person who has caused the death of another), are attacking the issue, may well induce a climate in which something radical, and better, is achieved. Dr Shea's book will enhance and focus the debate.

Dr Shea's is a challenging and provocative book, which refuses to take for granted the assumptions about psychiatry, the significance of mental illness to crime, and the appropriate management of mental illness, which people who have given up thinking and are simply content routinely to practise what they know, are prone to make. Sympathisers of the anti-psychiatry movement should not be deterred from reading it by dint of the fact that Dr Shea recently ran a large psychiatric hospital. He is unsparing in his assessments of his own profession, stating that:

> The personality of the psychiatrist may have an effect on the conclusions reached.
>
> "[An] individual with strong but unrecognised feelings towards people in authority may completely fail to detect similar feelings in a patient, or may perhaps detect them yet overlook their significance for his personality and illness" [quoting Maddison].

Finally, to turn to the judiciary, the book challenges the assumptions upon which the claims of mental illness or the claims of mental disorder are usually treated in the criminal courts. Dr Shea points out what would probably be obvious to a lay person, namely, that:

> [T]here is no doubt whatever that if a mentally disordered person commits a crime there can be a causal relationship between the two. There is also no doubt whatever that the causal relationship cannot simply be assumed. It must be established . . . [T]he simple co-existence of two sets of phenomena - criminal behaviour and mental disorder - especially for the first time, does not establish a causal relationship. Simply because a person with a depressive disorder or hebephrenic schizophrenia steals something from a shop, this does not necessarily mean that the symptoms of the disorder are the cause of the behaviour. They may be. They may not be. If they are they may be the sole cause or they may be just one of several causes operating together. In the past, some courts have found it convenient to routinely equate co-existence with causality. . . A closer analysis of the assumed relationship between the disorder and the crime may lead to different conclusions.

Judges are not contained in a monastic environment after hours, to be wheeled into court, minds devoid of all general knowledge about matters commonplace and technical, of all experience, and of all their individual perceptions of human behaviour, to decide cases entirely with reference to the evidence, expert or otherwise, put before them. Each judge has in his or her mind a data bank of experience, recollections, knowledge and, dare I say, prejudice and misconception, gained from previous experience. As an antidote, this book of Dr Shea's should be read by every judge who sits on cases requiring an understanding of the human mind, because of its comprehensive and readily understandable common-sense approach to psychiatry and the law.

Robert Hayes
President, Mental Health Review Tribunal,
Sydney,
April, 1993.

FOREWORD TO THE SECOND EDITION

I once had the honour of escorting two Korean experts in forensic psychiatry on a visit to the medium security psychiatric unit at Morisset Hospital, near Newcastle NSW. Their English was excellent, their knowledge of Australia impressive. But what exactly was the law in this State, they insisted, with regard to mentally disordered offenders? I did my best and they nodded politely, but the conversation palled during the 90 minute trip on the freeway. It was with a quiet desperation that I handed them over to Peter Shea, the author of this book. Could he help them?

He stood in front of a whiteboard and picked up a green felt pen. Twenty minutes later, the board was covered in a neat outline of a difficult subject, the visitors were delighted and, without a skerrick of shame, I confess to having learned much that day.

A good teacher writes a clear book. This one is written by a psychiatrist for lawyers, usually a Sisyphean task. Its purpose is to describe the scope and limitations of psychiatric evidence in court. In the first edition of the book, Dr Shea took us to the top of the hill with easy grace and without incident. In this edition he has rolled a bigger boulder. The chapters on psychopathy and on dangerousness have been expanded to evaluate recent advances in our knowledge of these controversial subjects. He has added a section on a much-discussed symptom (repressed memories) and a chapter on the most important psychiatric disorder in civil litigation (post-traumatic stress disorder). He has highlighted the changes in psychiatric classification which have been made in the fourth edition of the *Diagnostic and Statistical Manual of the American Psychiatric Association* (DSM-IV) and in the tenth edition of the *International Classification of Diseases* published by the World Health Organisation (ICD-10).

Dr Shea is well aware of the vagaries of much psychiatric evidence in court. In typically succinct style, he writes:

> It is a waste of time pursuing the fine details of psychiatric diagnosis in court. . .
> Instead of a diagnostic label what you need to know about (for forensic purposes)
> are the person's symptoms, the short and long term effects of those symptoms on
> the person's behaviour and lifestyle, the degree of impairment the symptoms
> produce, both individually and in concert, and whether or not anything can be done
> about any of those things.

As the luckless recipient of one of those unanswerable queries favoured by judges ("Doctor, could you explain for the benefit of the court what Dr X meant when she said in evidence. . .") I hope that the barristers who read this book press the paragraph above upon every expert witness they call.

Psychiatric evidence deserves scrutiny and challenge. Rather than laying about him with the broadsword approach favoured by Ziskin and Faust,[2] Dr Shea dissects with a rapier. At the end of a satisfying read, I was reminded of the aphorism of my friend and bibliophile Dr Richard Travers. "In fact" he said as I clutched a precious first edition he had found for me, "most books are firsts. But a really valuable book goes into another edition". And here it is.

Robert Finlay-Jones
Professor of Forensic Psychiatry, University of New South Wales
April, 1996

NOTES

1 Freckleton, I, *The Trial of the Expert, A Study of Expert Evidence and Forensic Experts*, Melbourne: Oxford University Press, 1987.

2 Ziskin, J and Faust, D, *Coping with psychiatric and psychological testimony* (5th ed), Marina del Rey: Law and Psychology Press 1994.

CONTENTS

FOREWORD   iii
INTRODUCTION   xi

SECTION A – The Language of Psychiatry   **1**

1   THE CLASSIFICATION OF PSYCHIATRIC DISORDERS   2
2   THE MAJOR SCHOOLS OF PSYCHIATRY   11
3   SCHIZOPHRENIA   27
4   DEPRESSIVE DISORDERS   45
5   PSYCHOPATHY   61
6   POST-TRAUMATIC STRESS DISORDER   78

SECTION B – The Assessment   **89**

7   THE PSYCHIATRIST AND THE PERSON BEING ASSESSED   90
8   THE ASSESSMENT PROCESS   102

SECTION C – The Connection Between Mental Disorder and Criminal Behaviour   **117**

9   MENTAL DISORDER AND CRIMINAL BEHAVIOUR   118

SECTION D – Dangerousness   **141**

10   THE CONCEPT OF DANGEROUSNESS   142
11   THE RELATIONSHIP BETWEEN MENTAL DISORDER AND
     DANGEROUSNESS   149
12   THE PREDICTION OF DANGEROUSNESS   155

CONCLUSION   164

BIBLIOGRAPHY   170

INDEX   182

ACKNOWLEDGMENTS

First, I would like to acknowledge the invaluable contributions, over the years, of the many friends, colleagues and students who have shared my interest in the problems that exist (and that, given the nature of the two disciplines, will undoubtedly continue to exist) at the interface between psychiatry and the law. I would especially like to thank the students in my forensic psychiatry classes at the Institute of Criminology for their challenging, perceptive and insightful comments and questions and for their input into the debate.

I am also hugely indebted to the patients and relatives with whom I have had the pleasure of working for over 30 years in a variety of settings. The rich and varied clinical experiences that we have shared have been both personally satisfying and professionally enlightening. Without them this monograph could not have been written.

I must also express my gratitude to the staff at both Rozelle and Gladesville hospitals, especially John Kennedy-Gould and Chris Crumlin, whose dedication, enthusiasm and support ensured that the forensic rehabilitation services that were developed at both hospitals at a time when I was privileged to administer them, were of world class standard.

Finally, my thanks to Mark Findlay for inviting me to contribute to this monograph series and to Liz Schwaiger for helping me to put it all together.

Peter Shea
April 1993

For this second edition I must add my gratitude to the staff of the Medium Security Unit at Morisset Hospital, of which I have been Director since August 1993. Institutional forensic psychiatry at this level is governed by a constantly changing (and challenging) mix of clinical, administrative and political issues. Directing the Unit has been an incomparable learning experience. My thanks also to Liz Halley for her invaluable assistance in organising the new edition.

PS
April 1996

INTRODUCTION

Naomi T . . . says she believes in Satanism, thinks the notorious murderer Charles Manson is a hero, listens to 'death metal music' and hears voices telling her to kill people. She stabbed a man through his heart, killing him, while she was out on bail after stabbing two brothers a few months earlier, a court was told. . . Last week, a jury found her guilty of the murder of Steven H . . . 23, of Blacktown, on November 29 last year. During submissions on sentence yesterday, a psychiatrist called by the defence . . . said he was 'convinced that this girl is psychotic', giving her the defence of diminished responsibility. A psychiatrist called by the prosecution . . . said [the] interpretations of the voices she claimed she heard were not, in his opinion, delusional or psychotic.[1]

Two expert witnesses, two different opinions. This is not an uncommon situation in court even when the matter being discussed is something a lot more tangible than the state of a person's mind. Burrows, an English physician who specialised in the field of mental illness and was sometimes called upon to give evidence in court, commented upon this problem as long ago as 1828:

I own that I have felt something akin to shame, when I have heard men of education not only delivering the most conflicting testimony, but supporting distinctions in insanity that never had existence except in their own inventive imaginations.[2]

Rollin, an English psychiatrist, gives a personal account of how it feels to be involved in such an adversarial situation:

The prisoner in the dock in a recent trial at the Old Bailey stood accused of a particularly brutal murder. Medical opinions were divided: the defence had put forward a plea of diminished responsibility which the prosecution had rejected. There was to be a fight. In the adversarial process which followed the lawyers were in their natural element; but for the two doctors, one representing each side (I was a witness for the prosecution), it was an embarrassing, if not humiliating experience, irrespective of which side won. Leading counsel for the prosecution began his opening speech to the jury. At one point he changed the tone of his voice and with great deliberation warned, 'In this country we have trial not by doctors, but by juries', a warning he was to repeat in the same ominous tones in his closing speech.[3]

It is not surprising that such conflict should occur. In any trial both sides want to present the best possible case. If one side is going to present expert evidence to support their case then the only options open to the other side are to attempt to discredit such evidence through rigorous cross-examination[4] or to present a contrary point of view using their own expert witness or witnesses.

Of the forensic psychiatric reports that are commissioned, only a percentage are actually presented in court. Given the nature of the adversarial system, this is also not surprising. If a lawyer asked for a report on a client and it turned out to be unhelpful to the case or, even worse, unfavourable, a likely outcome is that the report would simply be filed away and a new one commissioned. The cost of an unfavourable report, however, is not necessarily a complete waste as the preparation of the report precludes the psychiatrist involved from being used by the other side to support their case.

Of the reports that are presented, some are accepted, in whole or in part, and may assist the court to reach a decision about such matters as the mental state of the accused at the time of the offence and, hence, the guilt (or lack of guilt) of the accused; whether there is a case for diminished responsibility; the sentence that should be imposed; and the disposal of the accused. Other reports are rejected. Others are ignored. As Rollin points out, in the trial of the "Yorkshire Ripper":

> The opinion of 12 men and women on the Clapham omnibus was preferred to the unanimous opinion of no fewer than four experienced psychiatrists. Forensic psychiatry was itself on trial and rightly or wrongly, was found sadly wanting.[5]

And as Mr Sergeant Shee pointed out in his direction to a jury in 1863:

> You are not to be deprived of the exercise of your common sense because a gentleman (Dr Harrington Tuke) comes from London and tells you scientific sense.[6]

The use and usefulness of forensic psychiatric evidence has in fact been the subject of dispute for a long time. Henry Maudsley commented on "the dispute between lawyers and doctors"[7] in 1874, and the dispute has resurfaced periodically in the literature since that time.[8]

Part of the dispute relates to the different technical meanings that lawyers and psychiatrists ascribe to key concepts. As Miller points out:

> It is ironic that the law and mental health professions, two of the disciplines most concerned with the meaning of language, should have so much difficulty in agreeing on the meaning of many of the key concepts and phrases in their ongoing dialogue about how best to deal with the mentally ill. Unfortunately, a number of 'catchwords' have entered the legal-clinical dialogue, becoming in practice a sort of shorthand but frequently serving to interfere with, rather than to facilitate, effective interdisciplinary communication.

> Both professions use the various terms with approval; but as they have very different meanings to each, the apparent agreement in fact serves as an obstacle to collaboration, and it is confusing to those [such as members of courts and legislatures] who must arbitrate disagreements between the two groups.[9]

Another part of the dispute relates to the opposition to psychiatry in general raised by the anti-psychiatry movement.[10]

The focus of this book is the third aspect of the dispute — the use and usefulness of the language of psychiatry itself. In the opinion of the author, psychiatric evidence has a valuable but limited part to play in certain court proceedings. However, its value to the court and whether or not the court ultimately accepts or rejects it should depend upon its intrinsic worth and not, as it so often does, upon the status and reputation of the psychiatrist concerned and the manner in which he or she stands up under cross-examination. Like all evidence, the worth of psychiatric evidence is a matter for the court to determine in the circumstances of each particular case. This means, however, that the court has to be capable of understanding (a) exactly what it is that the psychiatrist is trying to tell the court about the accused and (b) the limitations of the language and the concepts that the psychiatrist is using. It is with these two matters — the interpretation and the limitations of psychiatric evidence — that this book is concerned.

There are two sorts of psychiatric reports that may be presented in court. There are those that begin by stating that the person concerned has a mental illness. They go on to consider whether or not the mental illness has any connection with the criminal activity of which the person is accused. In and around these two pieces of basic information may be found information about the supposed cause of the mental illness, its treatment and its prognosis.

The second type of report may not identify the presence of a mental illness but it may purport to explain or to demonstrate, given the person's background and upbringing, and their personal, social and economic circumstances, why they may have committed the crime.

Each type of report has its problems and these problems need to be explored.

The first set of problems centre around the diagnostic label itself and the assumption that because the label exists there must be a commonly agreed upon definition which everybody understands and accepts and that has some relevance for treatment and prognosis. There are a number of reasons why this is not the case. These are discussed in Section A.

The second set of problems concerns the practical difficulties of garnering accurate information about the state of the accused's mind at the time the crime was committed. As it is most unlikely that the psychiatrist would have been present at the time of the crime, he or she must rely upon what the accused can remember, what they are prepared to say and what the witnesses to the crime, if any, have to say. Some of the problems here are the interval between the crime and the assessment and what has happened to the accused in the interim; the length of time available for the assessment; the expectations of the accused; role play; observer variation; and the differences between forensic examinations and routine psychiatric examinations. These are discussed in Section B.

The third set of problems arise from two assumptions. The first is that because a mental illness was present at the time of the crime there is a necessary connection between the two. This is something that courts sometimes take for granted. The fact is that there may or may not be a connection. If such a connection is thought to exist, then its nature needs to be demonstrated, not simply assumed. Unfortunately this is not always easy to do. One thing, however, is certain — the simple coexistence of two sets of phenomena, especially for the first time, does not establish a causal relationship.

The second assumption is that a person's upbringing can be used to explain why they committed a crime. The history given is usually a combination of some of the following elements — a disturbed family, a broken family, parental neglect, emotional deprivation, physical abuse, sexual abuse, difficulty in forming interpersonal relationships, difficulties at school including learning difficulties, drug or alcohol abuse from an early age, a difficult marriage, inability to get a job, repeated job losses, and so on. The questions that have to be asked however are: How selective is the history taking? Why haven't other people from the same or similar backgrounds committed a crime? And if a causal connection between the person's background and the crime can be demonstrated to the court's satisfaction, how should it be treated — as an explanation or an excuse? The problems arising from these two assumptions are dealt with in Section C.

The fourth set of problems are the question of dangerousness, the prediction of dangerousness and the psychiatrist's role in this. These are dealt with in Section D.

Although they may not admit to it readily in court, most psychiatrists are aware of the limitations of the language and the concepts they use. This book is written for the non-psychiatrist, for the lawyers, judiciary and lay people who may have to assess the value of very complicated and sometimes, unfortunately, very technical psychiatric evidence without any background or training in psychiatry. If it does nothing more than direct people to ask the right questions the book will have achieved its purpose.

Introduction to the second edition

The first edition of this book was published two years ago. At the time of its publication several reviewers suggested additional topics that needed to be included (such as post-traumatic stress disorder and Hare's work on psychopathy). In 1993 and 1994 two major textbooks on forensic psychiatry were published (Gunn and Taylor's *Forensic Psychiatry. Clinical, Legal and Ethical Issues* and the second edition of Faulk's *Basic Forensic Psychiatry*). In 1994 the DSM-IV appeared, along with a major American textbook on forensic psychiatry (Rosner's *Principles and Practice of Forensic Psychiatry*). As well, over the past two years, there have been major developments in a number of areas, such as risk assessment and management (through the work of Monahan and his colleagues) and new and controversial topics (such as repressed memories and abuse syndromes) have received a great deal of publicity and attention in both the journals and the popular press. When the time came to reprint the book it was obvious that a new edition was needed. In spite of the changes to the book, however, its general thrust remains the same. Forensic psychiatric evidence is frequently misunderstood, misused and abused in court. Part of this is the fault of psychiatrists who present their evidence without informing the court of its limitations. Part of it is the fault of the legal system which has often used psychiatric evidence inappropriately, sometimes deliberately for its own purposes, sometimes through ignorance, sometimes as a matter of convenience. Part of it is the fault of the law-makers and politicians who have failed to address the difficult and contentious issues that a succession of reports and advisers have informed them exist at the interface between psychiatry and the law. The time for addressing these issues is long overdue. In this book I have attempted to delineate and clarify the issues, believing that education and debate are the first steps in producing change.

This book is not an anti-psychiatry tract. I do not agree, for example, with Ziskin that "no credence can be given to any psychiatrist's assertion, no matter how sincerely felt, to the effect that psychiatric assessments have any reasonable probability of being correct".[11] It is not a question of correctness. There is no "correct" explanation for any form of human behaviour, normal or abnormal. All explanations of human behaviour are based upon theories, not facts. Multiple and often conflicting theories of human behaviour may exist at any point in time. Old theories are regularly discarded (or sometimes obstinately clung to) as new theories emerge. Today's firmly held beliefs quickly become tomorrow's intellectual garbage. In each particular case it is up to the court to determine the value it will assign to the explanations proffered by any particular psychiatrist. This, of course, is something that courts do regularly. What they do not do regularly is base their determination on a rigorous assessment of the theoretical constructs underlying the psychiatrist's explanation. Nor do they regularly take into account the problems of the language of psychiatry, the deficiencies of the assessment and reporting process, and the precise nature of the relationship, if any, between the postulated mental state or mental disorder of the accused and the behaviour in question. There is no reason why psychiatric evidence should not be subjected to the same rigorous examination and cross-examination as any other form of evidence. This can only occur, however, if its limitations are recognised and understood.

NOTES

1   *Sydney Morning Herald* 14.11.92.

2   Burrows, G, *Commentaries on the Causes, Forms, Symptoms, and Treatment, Moral and Medical, of Insanity* (1828) p 711.

3   Rollin, H, "Nineteenth Century Doctors in the Dock" (1981) 283 *B Med J* 1176.

4   Burrows had something to say about this as well in 1828.

ridicule on the witness, and thus endeavour to turn aside the force of his evidence... It is [the medical witness's] own fault if he be entrapped into giving elaborate and fanciful descriptions of the state of his patient's mind; but he cannot always be guarded against legal subtlety (Burrows, above n 2 p 711).

5   Rollin, above n 3.

6   Id.

7   Id.

8   See for example the papers by Faust and Ziskin, Brodsky and Matarrazzo cited in Rogers, R, Bagby, R and Chow, M, "Psychiatrists and the Parameters of Expert Testimony" (1992) 15 *Int'l J L & Psychiat* 387.

9   Miller, R, "Hidden agenda and the law-psychiatry interface" (1990) Spring/Summer *J Psychiat & L* 35.

10   The term "anti-psychiatry" was introduced by a psychiatrist, David Cooper, in 1967. See Cooper, D, *Psychiatry and Anti-Psychiatry* (1970). The most clearly expressed of Cooper's objections to traditional psychiatry is contained in a later book, first published in 1974:

> Clinical psychiatry is ... a small part of an extensive system of violence, or normalizing techniques that commence with the principal conformism-inducing instrument of the bourgeois state, the family, and run on through primary and secondary schooling and universities aiming to produce and then reproduce an endless assembly-line of identical industrious creatures who all work for some purpose which has long been lost sight of and which was never very visible in the first place anyhow... The bourgeois psychiatrist succeeds when his victim (patient) is reduced to nothing more than the wretched, forsaken condition into which the psychiatrist himself has fallen. Anti-psychiatry tries to reverse the rules of the psychiatric game as a prelude to stopping such games. (Cooper, D, *The Grammar of Living* (1976) p 55.)

Ingleby makes a similar point:

> The particular social institutions (work, the family, education, 'politics') which are supposed to provide for [human needs and demands] ... do not represent the common good, but a particular set of interests which conceal themselves behind the notion of 'economic progress'. Psychiatry, in turn, protects the efficient functioning of these institutions by converting the conflict and suffering that arises within them into 'symptoms' of essentially individual (or at best familial) 'malfunctioning'; it thus attempts to provide short-term technological solutions to what are at root political problems... Psychiatry takes on itself the responsibility for people's pain and frustration; it confiscates their problems, redefines them as 'illnesses', and (with luck) exterminates the symptoms. Come unto me, all ye who labour and are heavy laden (it says), and I will give you - oblivion. As this apparatus perfects itself, so the goal of a society truly fit for human habitation recedes further and further into the future". Ingleby, D, "Understanding 'Mental Illness'" in Ingleby, D (ed) *Critical Psychiatry* (1981) pp 44-45.

Several years before Cooper introduced the term, Szasz had raised doubts about the validity of the traditional psychiatric approach in his book *The Myth of Mental Illness*: "I submit that the traditional definition of psychiatry, which is still in vogue, places it alongside such things as alchemy and astrology, and commits it to the category of pseudo-science" (Szasz, T, *The Myth of Mental Illness* (1961) p 1).

11   Ziskin, J, *Coping with Psychiatric and Psychological Testimony*, (3rd ed, 1981), Vol 1 p 441. Cited in Marcus, E, "Psychiatric Disability Evaluations: Plaintiff and Defense Perspectives" (1986) 7/2 *American Journal of Forensic Psychiatry* 11.

SECTION A
The Language of Psychiatry

The six chapters in this section are all concerned with the language of psychiatry and its limitations. Chapter 1 looks at some of the general problems associated with the use of descriptive terms and diagnostic labels. Chapter 2 considers the theoretical constructs that lie behind the terms and labels. Chapters 3, 4, 5 and 6 look at four diagnostic categories of particular relevance to forensic psychiatry — schizophrenia, depression, psychopathy and post-traumatic stress disorder. In these chapters an historical approach is used to highlight changes in the meanings of these concepts over time.

1

THE CLASSIFICATION OF PSYCHIATRIC DISORDERS

There seems to be an inherent need for people to understand human behaviour by sorting it into categories.[1]

> Throughout the history of psychiatric classification, there . . . has been a constant oscillation between the "lumpers" and the "splitters". Sauvages, the ultimate splitter, had some 2400 categories, most of which were simply discreet symptoms. The majority of early nineteenth century French and German psychiatrists were "lumpers" who maintained the traditional four categories of psychiatric illness: manie, melancolie, frenzy, and idiotism. DSM-III and DSM-III-R were a splitter's dream and a lumper's nightmare. DSM-III-R . . . nearly doubled the number of categories that were included in the DSM-II. . . . DSM-IV has been conservative, not only "holding the line against proliferation" of new diagnoses and further splitting, but also discouraging new and untested methods of lumping.[2]

Introduction

"Mental health" and "mental illness" or "mental disorder" are impossible to define in general terms (a) because they are socially and culturally determined, and (b) because there are both subjective and objective elements involved. The result, as Zusman points out with regard to the definition of mental health, is that "There is no single definition . . . that comes anywhere near to encompassing a general professional consensus".[3]

This sums up the situation with regard to the term "mental disorder" as well. There is no general definition that is acceptable in all countries or that is applicable in all settings, and there never will be.[4] When psychiatrists talk about "mental illness" or "mental disorder" what they are usually referring to is a list of specific psychiatric syndromes. The list can be long or short depending upon the purpose for which it is being used and different psychiatrists may have different lists. The closer one gets to the forensic field, the shorter the list tends to get.[5]

Neurosis and psychosis

For many years, psychiatric disorders were divided into the "neuroses" and the "psychoses". The "neuroses" were also known as the "psychoneuroses". Sometimes the "personality disorders" were included with the "neuroses". At other times they were treated as a separate group of disorders. The "psychoses" were divided into "functional psychoses" and "organic psychoses". The functional psychoses were those for which a definite physical cause could not be determined (such as schizophrenia, mania, major depression, manic-depressive disorder and the paranoid psychoses). The organic psychoses (also known as organic mental disorders, organic brain syndromes, organic mental syndromes, acute and chronic brain syndromes, and delirium and dementia) were those in which a demonstrable physical cause was always present resulting in impairment of brain tissue. Although the organic psychoses were, and still are, listed in classifications of psychiatric disorders, they are really the province of general medicine and neurology rather than psychiatry.[6] Their presence in psychiatric classifications merely reflects the fact that many of the symptoms are mental symptoms.

Over the years the division of psychiatric disorders into neuroses and psychoses has been gradually abandoned. The original distinction was partly etiologically and partly phenomenologically based, although, except in the case of the organic psychoses, the etiology was more often assumed than known. This is discussed further in the next chapter. The type of reasoning behind the distinction can best be illustrated by referring to the American Psychiatric Association's first *Diagnostic and Statistical Manual of Mental Disorders* (the DSM–I), published in 1952. It described what it referred to as the "psychoneurotic disorders" in psychodynamic terms:

> The chief characteristic of these disorders is "anxiety" which may be directly felt and expressed or which may be unconsciously and automatically controlled by the utilisation of various psychological defense mechanisms (depression, conversion, displacement, etc). In contrast to those with psychoses, patients with psychoneurotic disorders do not exhibit gross distortion or falsification of external reality (delusions, hallucinations, illusions) and they do not present gross disorganization of the personality. Longitudinal (lifelong) studies of individuals with such disorders usually present evidence of periodic or constant maladjustment of varying degree from early life. Special stress may bring about acute symptomatic expression of such disorders.

> "Anxiety" in psychoneurotic disorders is a danger signal felt and perceived by the conscious portion of the personality. It is produced by a threat from within the personality (for example, by supercharged repressed emotions, including such aggressive impulses as hostility and resentment), with or without stimulation from such external situations as loss of love, loss of prestige or threat of injury. The various ways in which the patient attempts to handle this anxiety results in the various types of reactions listed below.[7]

The DSM–I then goes on to list seven types of psychoneurotic disorders — anxiety reaction, dissociative reaction, conversion reaction, phobic reaction, obsessive compulsive reaction, depressive reaction, and psychoneurotic reaction, other. The use of the term "reaction" is a feature of the DSM–I. It "reflected the influence of Adolf Meyer's psychobiologic view that mental disorders represented reactions of the personality to psychological, social, and biological factors".[8]

The ninth revision of the International Classification of Diseases (the ICD–9, 1977) was the last major classification to use the general headings of psychoses and neurotic disorders but it did so with the following caveats. It stated that "[psychosis] is not an exact or well-defined term"[9] and that "[the] distinction between neurosis and psychosis is difficult and remains subject to doubt. However, it has been retained in view of its wide use".[10]

The current classification of Mental and Behavioural Disorders of the World Health Organisation (the ICD–10, 1992) deliberately avoids it:

> The traditional division between neurosis and psychosis that was evident in ICD–9 (although deliberately left without any attempt to define these concepts) has not been used in ICD–10. However, the term 'neurotic' is still retained for occasional use. . . Instead of following the neurotic-psychotic dichotomy, the disorders are now arranged in groups according to major common themes or descriptive likenesses. . .
>
> 'Psychotic' has been retained as a convenient descriptive term. . . Its use does not involve assumptions about psychodynamic mechanisms, but simply indicates the presence of hallucinations, delusions, or a limited number of several abnormalities of behaviour, such as gross excitement and overactivity, marked psychomotor retardation and catatonic behaviour.[11]

So in the ICD–10 the term "psychotic" refers to specific symptoms rather than specific psychiatric syndromes.

The American Psychiatric Association's current *Diagnostic and Statistical Manual of Mental Disorders* (DSM–IV, 1994) uses the atheoretical and descriptive approach to classification first used in the DSM-III.[12] Like the ICD–10 it avoids the general division of psychiatric disorders into neuroses and psychoses.

Clinically and theoretically there are good grounds for abandoning the neurotic-psychotic dichotomy altogether. It is overly simplistic, unnecessary and does not add anything to our understanding of psychiatric disorders. It creates problems rather than solving them. A leading article in the *British Medical Journal* in 1978 illustrated some of the difficulties that arise when the neurosis-psychosis dichotomy is used:

> Schizophrenia is classed as one of the psychoses; if asked to say which symptoms were chiefly responsible for the incapacity most doctors would probably cite such conventional psychotic manifestations as delusions and hallucinations. These are certainly prominent in the acute stage, but schizophrenia is usually a chronic disorder, and a recent study suggests that in chronic schizophrenia the symptoms that cause the most handicap and present the most intractable management problems are those usually termed neurotic.
>
> Cheadle and his colleagues studied 190 schizophrenics treated for an average of 12 years mainly in the community . . . and found that worrying, social unease, tension, depression, lack of energy and irritability were far commoner than delusions and

hallucinations. More important, patients with high neurotic scores seemed to have more difficulties with work and social life than those with psychotic symptoms.[13]

Having said this, it should be noted that many psychiatrists will continue to use the terms "neurosis" and "psychosis" in their everyday work and in their reports. As Cooper points out, in a review of the DSM-IV,

> 'neurosis' [and] 'neurotic' . . . [are] some of the most hallowed terms in psychiatry. . . Many psychiatrists and other mental health workers in the USA (and in many other countries) still find them useful. . . The authors of DSM-IV should remember the warning given by the late Sir Aubrey Lewis about the tendency of some psychiatric terms to outlive their obituarists.[14]

The ICD and DSM classifications

As already indicated above, there are two major classifications of mental disorders in use throughout the world today — the ICD–10 and the DSM–IV. Both of them have their critics.[15]

The ICD–10, to give it its full title, is the International Statistical Classification of Diseases and Related Health Problems, published by the World Health Organization. Its section on mental disorders has been published separately as *The ICD–10 Classification of Mental and Behavioural Disorders* (1992). The DSM–IV is the *Diagnostic and Statistical Manual of Mental Disorders* of the American Psychiatric Association in its fourth edition published in 1994. Previous editions were published in 1952 (DSM-I), 1968 (DSM-II), 1980 (DSM-III) and 1987 (DSM-III-R). Each new edition of the ICD and DSM brings a number of changes in the classification of psychiatric illnesses, some major, some minor. The rapidity with which these changes have occurred in the past two decades has led to a mixed reaction amongst health care workers. Cooper suggests that:

> There seems to be a distinct feeling at large that we all need a period of classificatory rest and calm, during which experience can be gained and evaluations carried out. . . With luck, it is likely that many more than ten years will pass before the next major revisions are attempted.[16]

In the meantime it is important to bear in mind that neither the authors of the ICD-10 nor the authors of the DSM-IV consider that their classifications are anything more than temporary, incomplete and imperfect. As the authors of the ICD–10 point out:

> A classification is a way of seeing the world at a point in time.[17]

> [The] descriptions and guidelines [in the ICD–10] carry no theoretical implications, and they do not pretend to be comprehensive statements about the current state of knowledge of the disorders. They are simply a set of symptoms and comments that have been agreed, by a large number of advisors and consultants in many different countries, to be a reasonable basis for defining the limits of categories in the classification of mental disorders.[18]

5

No classification is ever perfect.[19]

Not all countries accept the World Health Organization classification and even those that use it for statistical purposes sometimes have alternative classifications for clinical use. Some diagnostic categories may be acceptable to one country and may even be frequently diagnosed in those countries but may be totally unacceptable to other countries. The ICD–10 note on neurasthenia highlights this problem:

> Although omitted from some classification systems, neurasthenia has been retained as a category in ICD–10, since this diagnosis is still regularly and widely used in a number of countries. Research carried out in various settings has demonstrated that a significant proportion of cases diagnosed as neurasthenia can also be classified under depression or anxiety; there are, however, cases in which the clinical syndrome does not match the description of any other category but does meet all the criteria specified for a syndrome of neurasthenia. It is hoped that further research on neurasthenia will be stimulated by its inclusion as a separate category.[20]

The DSM–IV does not have a separate category of neurasthenia. The DSM-III-R included it in its index, but this simply referred the reader to the category of dysthymia or depressive neurosis. The description of dysthymia in the DSM–III–R and the description of neurasthenia in the ICD–10 were quite different. Some of the differences between the ICD-10 and the DSM-IV will be looked at in detail in the chapters on schizophrenia, depression, psychopathy and post-traumatic stress disorder.

Diagnostic categories and labelling

Diagnostic labels must be treated with caution as they do not tell us a great deal about the person who has the disorder.

In the first place, the boundaries of diagnostic categories are not clear-cut but blurred. As the authors of the DSM–IV point out:

> In DSM-IV, there is no assumption that each category of mental disorder is a completely discrete entity will absolute boundaries dividing it from other mental disorders of from no mental disorder. There is also no assumption that all individuals described as having the same mental disorder are alike in all important ways. The clinician using DSM-IV should therefore consider that individuals sharing a diagnosis are likely to be heterogeneous even in regard to the defining features of the diagnosis and that boundary cases will be difficult to diagnose in any but a probabilistic fashion.[21]

Maddison et al make the same point:

> [Many] of the mental processes which appear on the surface in . . . a person with a schizophrenic disorder may be detected in normal people at other times and in other circumstances — notably in dreams. There are . . . no clear-cut dividing lines in psychiatry between the normal, the moderately ill and the severely ill.[22]

Secondly, and more importantly, psychiatric illness is superimposed on a person's pre-existing personality and the clinical presentation is therefore influenced by that personality.

> [No] two personalities are identical — great and obvious differences can be detected between all the members of any group of people. . . As psychiatric illness arises out of and is very much coloured by the whole personality of the patient, then every individual will have some distinctive features depending on the past habits, feelings and life experience of the patient concerned. . . This is true even in those illnesses which are related to definite brain injury and damage.[23]

Aldrich goes even further:

> Usually, it becomes progressively harder to fit a patient into a typical symptom picture as more becomes known about him; a patient who on first impression seems to be typically schizophrenic may on further exploration reveal signs of other psychotic or even neurotic reactions. When careful and painstaking diagnostic techniques are used in psychiatry, 'typical' almost becomes a synonym for 'rare'. As Fodere said, almost 150 years ago, 'When one has seen many insane people, one can recognize that there are as many (individual) differences among them as there are personalities among individuals whose minds are healthy. . . It is therefore really difficult to make up classes of diseases which would not prove fictitious'.[24]

Thirdly, psychiatrists sometimes use diagnostic labels in personal and idiosyncratic ways. Sometimes these are based on sources other than the standard classifications, for example a local classification, an experimental classification, a new classification or even an old classification revisited. Sometimes they are based on the psychiatrist's own personal views and hence are truly idiosyncratic. Examples of this are given in the chapters on schizophrenia and psychopathy.

Fourthly, the personality of the psychiatrist may have an effect on the conclusions reached.

> [An] individual with strong but unrecognised hostile feelings towards people in authority may completely fail to detect similar feelings in a patient, or may perhaps detect them yet overlook their significance for his personality and illness.[25]

Extending this, one cannot, of course, exclude the possibility that the occasional psychiatrist, like the occasional lawyer and judge, may be mentally disordered or may have suffered from some mental disorder in the past and that this, in turn, may influence their attitude towards, or their perception of, mental disorder in others.

Fifthly, a diagnosis tells us nothing about the level of impairment or disability, that is how the person who has the disorder is being affected by it. Some people have greater coping skills than others. As the DSM-IV points out: "Impairments, abilities and disabilities vary widely within each diagnostic category. . . Assignment of a particular diagnosis does not imply a specific level of impairment of disability".[26]

7

As I have pointed out elsewhere, it is precisely because of this that:

> It is a waste of time pursuing the fine details of psychiatric diagnosis in court. . . Instead of a diagnostic label what you need to know about [for forensic purposes] are the person's symptoms, the short and long term effects of those symptoms on the person's behaviour and lifestyle, the degree of impairment the symptoms produce, both individually and in concert and whether or not anything can be done about any of these things.[27]

Conclusion

Diagnostic labels are mostly shorthand ways of conveying information about individuals and their illnesses or disorders. They only work if both the person applying the label and the person interpreting the label have exactly the same understanding of what the label means. If they do not, the label has not only ceased to serve a useful purpose but it may actually contribute to the dissemination of misinformation. As Ellard puts it:

> Let us have and use diagnoses, but let us remember what they are and what they are not. They are not stations on the way to some ultimate reality; they are this year's shorthand for this year's hypotheses about the nature of things that interest us. The only thing certain about them is that they will be found wanting and will change as the years change.[28]

The DSM-IV has a special section on the "Use of DSM-IV in Forensic Settings". It describes both the problems and the inherent dangers and makes it quite clear that great caution must be applied in using DSM-IV categories and diagnoses in such settings.

> When the DSM-IV categories, criteria, and textual descriptions are employed for forensic purposes, there are significant risks that diagnostic information will be misused or misunderstood. These dangers arise because of the imperfect fit between the questions of ultimate concern to the law and the information contained in a clinical diagnosis. In most situations, the clinical diagnosis of a DSM-IV mental disorder is not sufficient to establish the existence for legal purposes of a "mental disorder", "mental disability", "mental disease" or "mental defect". In determining whether an individual meets a specified legal standard (eg for competence, criminal responsibility, or disability), additional information is usually required beyond that contained in the DSM-IV diagnosis.[29]

NOTES

1   Mack, A, Forman, L, Brown, R and Frances, A, "A Brief History of Psychiatric Classification From the Ancients to DSM-IV" (1994) 17 *Psychiatric Clinics of North America* 515.

2   Ibid p 520.

3   Zusman, J, "Primary Prevention" in Freedman, A, Kaplan, H, and Sadock, B, (eds) *Comprehensive Textbook of Psychiatry–II* (1975) p 2327.

4   Even the term "mental disorder" is problematic. The authors of the DSM-IV have problems with the word "mental":

> Although this volume is titled the Diagnostic and Statistical Manual of Mental Disorders the term mental disorder unfortunately implies a distinction between "mental" disorders and "physical" disorders that is a reductionist anachronism of mind/body dualism. A compelling literature documents that there is much "physical" in "mental" disorders and much "mental" in "physical" disorders. The problem raised by the term "mental" disorders has been much clearer than its solution, and, unfortunately, the term persists in the title of DSM-IV because we have not found an appropriate substitute. American Psychiatric Association, *Diagnostic and Statistical Manual of Mental Disorders* (4th ed; 1994) p xxi.

The authors of the ICD-10 have problems with the word "disorder":

> The term "disorder" is used throughout this classification, so as to avoid even greater problems inherent in the use of terms such as "disease" and "illness". World Health Organization, *The ICD-10 Classification of Mental and Behavioural Disorders* (1992) p 5.

5   Sometimes the list may even be reduced to a small group of psychiatric symptoms. The New South Wales *Mental Health Act* 1990, for example, defines mental illness as:

> a condition which seriously impairs, either temporarily or permanently, the mental functioning of a person and is characterised by the presence in the person of any one or more of the following symptoms:
>
> (a) delusions; (b) hallucinations; (c) serious disorder of thought form; (d) a severe disturbance of mood; (e) sustained or repeated irrational behaviour indicating the presence of any one or more of the symptoms referred to in paragraphs (a)–(d).

6   The organic mental disorders can be classified into several types depending upon whether the damage is diffuse and the impairment global (eg, due to drugs or generalised arteriosclerosis) or whether the damage is localised to a specific part or parts of the brain (eg, due to trauma or a space-occupying lesion) and the resulting impairment selective. The DSM-IV has stopped using the term "organic" in its classification for the following reasons:

> In DSM-III-R, these disorders were placed in a section entitled "Organic Mental Syndromes and Disorders". The term organic mental disorder is no longer used in DSM-IV because it incorrectly implies that "nonorganic" mental disorders do not have a biological basis. In DSM-IV, disorders formerly called "organic mental disorders" have been grouped into three sections: 1) Delirium, Dementia and Amnestic and Other Cognitive Disorders; 2) Mental Disorders Due to a General Medical Condition; and 3) Substance-Related Disorders. American Psychiatric Association, above n 4 p 123.

The ICD-10 has retained the term "organic" with the following explanation:

> Use of the term "organic" does not imply that conditions elsewhere in this classification are "nonorganic" in the sense of having no cerebral substrate. In the present context, the term "organic" means simply that the syndrome so classified can be attributed to an independently diagnosable cerebral or systemic disease or disorder. World Health Organization, above n 4 p 44.

7   American Psychiatric Association, *Diagnostic and Statistical Manual. Mental Disorders* (1952) pp 31–32.

8   American Psychiatric Association, *Diagnostic and Statistical Manual of Mental Disorders* (3rd ed, rev; 1987) p xviii.

9   World Health Organization, *International Classification of Diseases* (1977) p 177.

10	Ibid p 191.

11	World Health Organization, above n 4 p 3.

12	American Psychiatric Association, Diagnostic and Statistical Manual of Mental Disorders (3rd ed, 1980) p 7.

13	Leading Article, "Is schizophrenia a psychosis or neurosis?" (1978) *Brit Med J* 76.

14	Cooper, J, "On the Publication of the Diagnostic and Statistical Manual of Mental Disorders: Fourth Edition (DSM-IV)" (1995) 166 Brit J Psych 6.

15	Cooper, above n 14 p 4, for example, notes that "even in the United States there may be some ambivalence about DSM-IV, so those of us in other countries need to evaluate it with special care". Pathe and Mullen are trenchant critics of the DSM, referring to it as "no more than a distillate of the prejudices and power plays of a group of aging American academics, of no interest to most Europeans and only passing relevance to some Australasians". They go on to note, however, that "Lawyers are unimpressed by such disclaimers, for in law it is exactly the texts produced by the consensus of the prejudices of aging jurists which do carry the weight of authority". Pathe, M and Mullen, P, "The Dangerousness of the DSM-III-R" (1993) 1:1 *Journal of Law and Medicine* 48.

16	Cooper, above n 14 pp 7-8.

17	World Health Organization, above n 4 p vii.

18	Ibid p 2.

19	Ibid p xi.

20	Ibid p 15.

21	American Psychiatric Association, above n 4 p xxii.

22	Maddison, D, Day, P and Leabeater, B, *Psychiatric Nursing* (1965) p 151.

23	Ibid p 150.

24	Aldrich, C, *An Introduction to Dynamic Psychiatry* (1966) p 77.

25	Maddison et al, above n 22 p 151.

26	American Psychiatric Association, above n 4 p xxii.

27	Shea, P, Paper delivered to the Thirteenth Biennial Conference of District and County Court Judges of Australia (1995) p 6. With regard to the futility of "pursuing the fine details of psychiatric diagnosis in court" see Pathe and Mullen, above n 15.

28	Ellard, J, "New White Elephants for Old Sacred Cows: Some Notes on Diagnosis" (1992) 26/4 *ANZ J Psychiat* 548.

29	American Psychiatric Association, above n 4 p xxiii.

2

THE MAJOR SCHOOLS OF PSYCHIATRY

INTRODUCTION

As pointed out in the previous chapter, the authors of the DSM-III, in 1980, decided to use an atheoretical and descriptive approach rather than an aetiological one, an approach that was carried forward into the DSM-III-R and the DSM-IV. They did this for the following reasons:

> For most of the DSM-III disorders . . . the etiology is unknown [although] a variety of theories have been advanced, buttressed by evidence – not always convincing – to explain how these disorders come about.[1]

With minor exceptions, the situation remains the same today. There is no single theory that can be used to explain the origins of psychiatric disorders, although there are several theories that purport to do so. McLaren accurately sums up the present situation:

> Practitioners routinely pick and choose from three theoretical stances in their daily work, the psychodynamic, the behaviourist and the 'organic' or biological. It must be emphasised that these different approaches are not merely variations on a single theme but are radically different and, in fact, incompatible views of the same subject matter. Behaviourism specifically denies a causative role for a 'mind' in the generation of observable behaviour, if not denying it altogether, whereas for psychodynamic theories, the mental life is all. Fully articulated, an exclusively 'organic' theory of psychiatry would deny that psychological factors can cause mental disorder, although few would openly espouse such an extreme position. Faced with the unhappy choice between 'mindless' and 'brainless' psychiatry most psychiatrists opt for a theoretically vague eclecticism.[2]

It is not possible to evaluate psychiatric reports and psychiatric evidence properly without understanding something about the theoretical constructs underlying and underpinning them, especially when it comes to treatment options, as there may be several, each one grounded in the theory of a particular school. Even individual terms in psychiatric reports may have different meanings for different schools. This chapter examines the theories of the three major schools. A fourth school — the existential school — is also discussed, for even though its

11

theories are a lot less influential than those of the three major schools, they have valuable lessons for forensic psychiatry.

Theories about the causes and treatment of psychiatric disorders are not, of course, the exclusive province of Western science. Many Western and Eastern philosophies and religions have well-developed and systematised theories of their own. The type of forensic reports presented in Australian courts, however, are invariably written by people who are trained in Western scientific method and who subscribe to one or more of the schools of psychiatry that this method encompasses. It is unlikely that a report based on the theory of demonic possession and recommending exorcism as a solution would advance a client's case in an ordinary court in twentieth century Australia. Nor would a report predicated on the law of karma. Nor, for that matter, would a report recommending reflection on the thoughts of Chairman Mao. In other settings,[3] however, such explanations and recommendations may be far more acceptable than those derived from the organic, cognitive-behavioural and psychodynamic schools that provide the theoretical bases for our understanding of psychiatric disorders in the Western world, incomplete as it may be at the present time.

THE ORGANIC SCHOOL

According to the organic or biological school of psychiatry, biochemical factors, either genetic or acquired, or gross pathological change are the causes of psychiatric disorders. Their argument runs as follows:

1 All those activities that are usually considered to be part of mental life — thoughts, moods, perceptions, drives — are mediated by the nervous system and, in particular, by the brain.

2 The brain, like the rest of the body, is composed of chemicals and brain activity consists of physico-chemical interactions.

3 All mental life, both normal and abnormal, must therefore have a chemical or physico-chemical basis.

It is a fact that psychological symptoms can have physical causes. Many different types of physical illness can produce symptoms identical with those in psychiatric disorders. Hallucinations, for example, can occur in infectious diseases, in certain types of epilepsy, in drug and alcohol-induced states, as a result of brain-damage from a variety of causes and in normal people under certain conditions such as fatigue. The problem that needs to be resolved, however, is whether psychiatric syndromes, such as schizophrenia and depression, have physical causes.

The evidence that has been put forward to support the proposition that schizophrenia has an organic etiology consists of genetic evidence, biochemical evidence and anatomical evidence.

The genetic evidence derives mainly from studies of the prevalence of schizophrenia in families, and especially in twins. There are two sorts of twins.

12

Identical or monozygotic twins are derived from one ovum and one sperm. Normally, half a person's genes are derived from their mother (in the ovum) and half from the father (in the sperm). When the sperm fertilises the ovum their genetic loads are combined. This produces the first cell of the new organism. This cell divides into two, the two into four, and so on. As the cells divide some of them start to differentiate into different tissue types and an embryo is formed. In the case of identical twins, when the first cell divides into two, each of these cells, instead of staying together and forming part of the new organism, separate, and each cell then divides and goes on dividing until two embryos are formed. Because they are derived from the one fertilised ovum, they are very similar genetically. Even monozygotic twins, however, are not completely identical genetically as there may be some differences in the amount of genetic material passed on to each cell at the first split.[4]

In the case of non-identical (dizygotic) twins, two ova are produced at the same time (instead of the usual one) and each is fertilised by a different sperm. Each of the fertilised ova then develop into separate embryos. Because they derive from two ova and two sperm, they are no more alike genetically, than ordinary siblings. Identical twins are always of the same sex. Non-identical twins can be the same or different sexes.

If an illness has a genetic basis and one twin develops it, then it follows that identical twins should have a much higher chance of both developing the illness than non-identical twins. The observed frequency with which twins develop an illness with a suspected or known genetic basis is known as the concordance rate.

Early twin studies (from Luxenburger's 1928 study to Kallman's 1953 study) suggested that the concordance rate for schizophrenia was much higher in identical twins than non-identical twins. Kallman's 1953 study, for example, suggested a concordance rate of 86 per cent for identical twins and 15 per cent for non-identical twins.[5] Most of these early studies, however, had serious methodological flaws and their results can be discounted. More scientific studies began in 1941 with Essen-Moller's Swedish study, which used red blood cell groups to confirm zygosity (that is, whether the twins were really monozygotic or dizygotic), and have continued to the present. In 1992, Fuller Torrey[6] analysed the results of all the studies in which representative samples were used and zygosity was determined with reasonable certainty and found that the average concordance rate for monozygotic twins was 28 per cent, and for dizygotic twins 6 per cent. This is still a substantial difference in frequency but it suggests that genetic factors play a smaller role in producing schizophrenia than was previously thought.

Other studies have examined the frequency of schizophrenia in children born to schizophrenic parents (one or both) and raised by them, and in the children of schizophrenic mothers who have been adopted out. Unfortunately it is extremely difficult to separate out genetic effects from environmental effects in those studies.

As Tienari[7] points out, the crucial question may not be "how much . . . is due to heredity and how much to environment but rather how heredity and environment interact to influence development", a problem compounded by the fact that "the relationship between environment and development is transactional; not only is the individual influenced by the environment, but the individual also influences the environment." Tienari concludes that although "it is accepted that schizophrenia runs in families . . . whether this relates to genetic or psycho-social transmission is an unanswered question."

There are many methodological problems involved in carrying out genetic studies and no study is without them. The major hurdle, however, is the identification of the actual genetic defect in schizophrenia. Twin, family and adoptive studies may suggest a partial genetic factor, but the actual genetic defect or defects (as they may be multiple) have to be identified before the evidence can be considered to be conclusive. No studies have done this as yet.[8] In 1993, Kendler and Diehl summed up the problems in carrying out such studies as follows:

> Little is known about how genetic liability to schizophrenia is transmitted, although statistical models suggest that transmission is probably not due solely to a single major gene. Schizophrenia is clearly a complex disorder in that gene carriers need not manifest the illness (incomplete penetrance), affected individuals need not have the gene (environmental forms or phenocopies), diagnostic uncertainties cannot be avoided, and different families may carry different susceptibility genes (genetic heterogeneity).[9]

As a recent leading article in the *British Medical Journal* suggested, gene linkage studies in schizophrenia "must still be regarded as acts of faith".[10] This is not to say that some genetic defect or defects may not be eventually isolated, but even if they are the more complex problems raised by Tienari will still need resolution.

Turning now to biochemical studies, these are many and varied. A large number of biochemical abnormalities and other bodily defects have been described in studies on schizophrenia, including abnormalities in protein metabolism, carbohydrate metabolism, blood globulins, the cerebro-spinal fluid and neurotransmitters. Few of these studies have been replicated and they all suffer from methodological problems. No comprehensive theory has yet been put forward to pull all these independent observations together in a meaningful way.

The detection of various abnormalities in the brains of people with schizophrenia (mostly atrophic changes), illustrate the difficulties that beset any search for the physical causes of schizophrenia. With the development of modern sophisticated neuro-imaging techniques many brain abnormalities have been reported in schizophrenia. The significance of these, however, remains to be determined.

As Owens pointed out in a review article in 1992: "There remains no clear consensus on the pattern of abnormality associated with the schizophrenic brain, the clinical correlates of structural change or the theoretical implications".[11] Catts, however, suggests that:

> A consensus is rapidly emerging that schizophrenia results from a genetically determined neurodevelopmental anomaly [and that its] exact nature, in a particular case, will be determined by which brain system is affected at what stage of neurodevelopment.[12]

Biochemical abnormalities and anatomical abnormalities, if they could be proven to exist and to have some etiological role to play in schizophrenia, would still have to have their own origin explained. Various theories have been suggested (other than genetic ones), ranging from viral and other infections to nutritional deficiencies (especially vitamin deficiencies), food allergies, and stress. O'Reilly summarises the evidence for viral infections as follows:

> A viral hypothesis for the pathogenesis of schizophrenia has been under serious consideration for more than 70 years. . . It is possible that a viral infection is an environmental trigger for the development of schizophrenia in genetically predisposed individuals. Alternatively, persons who are genetically susceptible to viral infection may develop schizophrenia as a result of the effects of the virus on brain structure or function. . . Recent epidemiological findings, such as the excess of winter births among schizophrenic patients and the association of prenatal exposure to the influenza virus with the subsequent development of schizophrenia, have shifted the focus from the role of viral encephalopathy in adult life to the pathological effects of viral invasion of the CNS in the pre- or perinatal period. To date, attempts to detect the presence of specific viruses, including the known retroviruses, have failed.[13]

The evidence for nutritional deficiencies and food allergies is poor but cannot be discounted as psychiatrists working in this field can always point to individual cases where patients have responded to treatments based on these theories. The evidence for stress is difficult to evaluate. As Tennant points out: "The widely held view that life events can precipitate schizophrenic episodes may be supported by our own clinical impressions; it is as yet not well supported by empirical data".[14]

In depression and mania, just as in schizophrenia, evidence of genetic factors and of biochemical abnormalities has also been accumulating over the past few decades but the problems are the same as with schizophrenia. The evidence is not conclusive, all of the studies have methodological problems and there is, as yet, no overriding theory into which all the pieces of evidence fit.

There is little evidence to suggest that genetic factors or biochemical factors have any major part to play in the etiology of the psychoneuroses, the personality disorders[15] or criminality. Some studies suggest that genetic factors may have a minor role to play in them, but the evidence is far from conclusive.

THE COGNITIVE-BEHAVIOURAL SCHOOL

The cognitive-behavioural school is not really one school but several. The first arose out of the experiments of Pavlov and Skinner on animal behaviour. It was (and still is) a pure science school whose primary focus is not therapy but experimentation. When this school does become involved in therapy, it concerns itself with the elimination of specific forms of behaviour under strictly controlled experimental conditions, preferably carried out in the laboratory. As Hafner puts it, "There is no room within this framework for motivation, meaning, will or purpose."[16]

The focus of therapeutic interest is the symptom; not the person who has the symptom. Pavlov and Skinner were studying animal behaviour (dogs in the case of Pavlov and rats and pigeons in the case of Skinner) and then extrapolating their findings into theories about human behaviour. The critics of this approach and of the therapies that subsequently evolved from it argue, quite reasonably, "that research findings on animal behaviour can at best only be analogous to human behaviour and that generalisation from one to the other is specious or simplistic."[17]

As behaviourists gradually extended their involvement in the treatment of behavioural disorders in human beings, a new school arose which saw behaviourism more as an applied science than a pure science. Their focus of attention shifted from the symptom to the person who had the symptom. As Hafner explains it:

> Clinical behaviour therapists have aims and objects fundamentally different from those of pure scientists. The clinician's task is primarily to treat and his scientific endeavours are generally oriented towards evaluating and improving treatment. The clinical behaviour therapist's role as an applied scientist is almost invariably secondary to his role as a clinician.[18]

The situation became even more complicated, and the debate between the schools quite acrimonious, in the 1970s when cognitive therapy entered the field.[19] Cognitive therapy focuses on the way people think about themselves and their illnesses, on "what the client says to himself (that is, his appraisals, attributions and self-evaluations), or the self-statements and images that he emits prior to, accompanying, and following his overt behaviour,"[20] and it attempts to eradicate ways of thinking that are self-defeating and contribute to the prolongation of the illness.

If there is anything that is common to the various schools it is the belief that all behaviour is learned behaviour. Behaviourists totally reject the idea that genetic factors or psychodynamic factors influence the development of behaviour in any way. As far as behaviourists are concerned, the child is born without any innate predispositions to do anything. From the moment of birth, however, the child is exposed to a series of experiences to which he or she responds in various ways. By trial and error and through the effects of rewards and punishments, the child learns that one particular form of behaviour, that is, one particular response, is more successful, in terms of its outcome, than the others, so the successful behaviour is repeated and tested and a habit bond develops between the stimulus and response, a bond which gradually strengthens. Repetition of the stimulus then automatically elicits that response. But what is an appropriate or adaptive response to a situation at one stage of a person's life may not be appropriate at another stage. Normally, when the response ceases to be associated with the desired outcome, new responses are tested until an appropriate one is found. Screaming when hungry, for example, may be an appropriate response for a baby to make provided it gets the desired result — food. It would not be an appropriate habitual response for a hungry adult.

Sometimes, however, the habit bond is so strong that the learned behaviour persists even when it is no longer serving the needs of the individual and sometimes even when it is positively detrimental. The symptoms of psychiatric disorders are thought to be acquired in this way.

If all behaviour is learned behaviour it follows that it should be able to be unlearned. This idea led to the development of various types of behaviour therapies. Their success, however, has been limited to a narrow range of conditions (a few psychoneuroses) and certain specific abnormal behaviours for which a simple model based on learning principles can be developed.

This is not to say that the only models that have been developed are simple ones concerned with specific behaviours. Quite to the contrary. General models have been developed for very complex behaviours but their common failing is that they are overly simplistic. One example is the criminological theory of "differential association" which purports to explain criminal behaviour in individuals.[21] According to this theory, both criminal techniques and attitudes are learned through exposure to them in the intimate, social groups in which a person moves. In such groups people are exposed to ideas and attitudes that are both favourable and unfavourable to the law. If the latter predominate over the former, criminal attitudes will be adopted, criminal techniques may be learnt and criminal behaviour may result.

In spite of applications such as the above, learning theory does not contribute a great deal to our understanding of the etiology of psychiatric disorders in general; although, as Sainsbury and Lambeth suggest, it may provide "a part answer to the development of some clinical forms of neurosis".[22]

Where an understanding of learning theory is most likely to be needed in forensic work is in the evaluation of psychiatric reports containing proposed treatment plans for people with psychosexual disorders, alcohol dependency problems and compulsive gambling problems, for it is in the treatment of conditions such as these that behaviour therapy has had some limited success. The particular type of behaviour therapy most commonly used in these disorders is known as aversion therapy. This involves pairing a painful or unpleasant stimulus, either in reality or fantasy, but more commonly in reality, with the type of behaviour that one is trying to eradicate. There are a number of difficulties with this kind of therapy ranging from the ethics of its use, particularly with psychosexual disorders, to methodological problems associated with the precise control of the timing, intensity, duration and specificity of the stimulus, to observations which suggest that variables other than the aversive stimulus, such as the relationship between the patient and the therapist, contribute significantly to the outcome. There are also doubts about its long-term effectiveness. Aversion therapy is not often recommended for use but, if it is, the court should be aware of the problems associated with its use and the theory or theories underlying it.

THE PSYCHODYNAMIC SCHOOL

The psychodynamic school was founded by Sigmund Freud. Although Freud's theories have undergone a great many changes in the hands of his followers, there are certain basic concepts that have had a continuing influence to the present day. Not all psychiatrists accept them unreservedly, but many of them do and explanations of the psychoneuroses are commonly based upon them. The most important concept in this regard is Freud's theory of the unconscious.

The unconscious was not a concept that Freud invented. Its existence had been postulated by many earlier philosophers and thinkers. What Freud did was to give it a crucial role in mental life. Before Freud it had mainly been conceived of as a repository for thoughts and feelings for which there was no further conscious need or use. Freud saw it as a very large and active area of the mind into which thoughts, feelings, wishes and other mental phenomena were forced, not because they were no longer needed but because they were no longer acceptable to the conscious mind. He postulated that there was a mechanism which forced them out of consciousness and kept them out and he named it repression. Because the mental processes which are repressed remain active and dynamic, striving for discharge regardless of the consequences, the unconscious exerts a continuing influence upon the conscious part of mental life. Stafford-Clark uses the analogy of an iceberg to illustrate the influence of the unconscious:

> If everything that we know and remember is regarded as the part of the iceberg above the surface, at least seven times as much lies below the surface, and determines both the centre of gravity of the whole, and much of the movements, direction and fate of the iceberg.[23]

When repression is weak and the unconscious mental material seeking release is strong and threatens to break through the repressive barrier, other unconscious mechanisms (called "defence mechanisms") may automatically come into play to prevent this happening. To take a simplistic example, unconscious anger, which could have the potential for turning into murderous rage, can be prevented from finding its direct expression by the development of a suitable physical symptom,

18

such as paralysis of the arms. The defence mechanism involved is known as conversion.

Another related defence mechanism is known as dissociation. According to Freudian theory, what this does is suddenly remove a large part of recent memory from consciousness and place it in the unconscious, resulting in a psychological or psychogenic amnesia for some event in the person's immediate past, an event that cannot remain in consciousness because it would be too painful, too unpleasant, too threatening or too disturbing.

There is no doubt that psychogenic amnesia occurs. Well-authenticated descriptions of the condition go back to the nineteenth century. The question is whether the mechanism of dissociation explains it adequately. This is discussed further in Section B.

Suffice for the moment to say that acceptance of any psychodynamic explanation requires, first, an acceptance of the Freudian concept of the unconscious and, secondly, an acceptance of the concept of mental defence mechanisms that operate by themselves outside of consciousness. These are not facts; they are theories.

Many people have challenged the Freudian concept of the unconscious. Some deny its very existence. Others accept the idea of an unconscious but see it as being at one end of a continuous spectrum of consciousness rather than some part of mental activity that is sharply differentiated from consciousness with a life and rules of its own.[24]

Others still extend the concept of the unconscious far beyond the personal unconscious described by Freud. Jung, for example, postulated the existence of a collective unconscious containing archetypal images derived from the psychological heritage of humanity as a whole.

Apart from the unconscious, there are several other Freudian concepts that find their way into forensic reports. These include such concepts as drive theory and the division of the personality into the ibid, ego and superego.

Drive theory involves the belief that human beings are born with a number of innate biological drives, two of which — the sexual drive and the aggressive drive, but especially the sexual drive — are major determinants of human personality development. This theory has been the subject of heavy criticism since the time it was introduced. To accept it requires an act of faith, not rational judgement. The fact that human beings have biological drives that they share with lower animals does not mean that they serve an identical purpose in both. As Brown points out, biological drives might explain why humans initiate certain actions but they do not "in any way explain how, when, or even if they do these things."[25] A human being's mode of relating to the world is not innate. It is the result of a long process of socialisation and acculturation. As Brown explains:

Human behaviour cannot be understood purely in terms of the satisfaction or frustration of biological drives because the social process generates new needs which may be as powerful as or even more powerful than the original biological ones.[26]

Freud's division of personality processes into id, ego and superego processes also needs to be examined as it is sometimes used to explain psychopathy. Brown explains their development and relationship to one another as follows:

The new-born child is a seething mass of impulses or instinctual drives entirely lacking in a directing or guiding consciousness, and because of its impersonal nature this primitive mass is described as the 'id', Freud's Latinized version of Groddeck's 'das Es', the It. But since the child must come to terms with external reality a part of this primeval conglomeration sooner or later becomes separated off and differentiated as the 'ego' or self, the prime function of which is to test reality in order that the organism's reactions shall be in terms of what is, rather than uncoordinated responses or those aiming at direct and immediate satisfaction. At a still later stage of development there arises out of the need to face society's moral prohibitions the 'superego' loosely equated with 'conscience' although both more and less than this word implies. . . [The child now takes] the moral dictates of its parents, their attitudes, opinions and judgements . . . by a process of identification [into] itself. In the words of Franz Alexander: 'Parental attitudes are taken over by the personality, one part of which (that is, the superego) assumes the same attitude towards the rest as the parents did previously towards the child'.[27]

It needs to be made clear that the id, ego and superego are not entities. They are simply groups of mental processes that work together. In Freud's words:

The id and super-ego have one thing in common: they both represent the influence of the past — the id the influence of heredity, the super-ego the influence, essentially, of what is taken over from other people — whereas the ego is principally determined by the individual's own experience, that is by accidental and contemporary events.[28]

In order to understand the psychodynamic explanation of the psychopathic personality all we need know in addition to the above is that the defence mechanisms mentioned earlier operate at the ego level, that is, they are ego defence mechanisms. They are the first line of defence against the primitive drives of the id and they are reinforced by the superego which has two powerful sanctions to apply — guilt and shame — should id drives break through or even threaten to break through.

According to psychodynamic theory, the psychopathic personality suffers from deficiencies (of varying degrees) at both ego and superego levels. In a normal person when some external or internal event stimulates the arousal of drives, the ego ensures that the drive is expressed in some socially acceptable manner or, if this is not possible, that it is controlled and its immediate expression prevented. And reinforcing the ego controls are the superego controls. In the case of the psychopathic personality the ego and superego deficiencies mean that when drives are aroused immediate gratification is sought with little regard for the consequences and there is no (or little) subsequent experience of guilt or shame.

This explanation provides a useful model for describing the developmental history of the psychopathic personality. It is reasonably easy to follow, comprehensive, and, presented the right way, sounds quite plausible. There are other models available, such as those based on learning theory, including cognitive-developmental theory and social learning theory,[29] but they are not as well integrated as the psychodynamic model (especially the social learning theory model, which sees morality as being situation-specific) and they are less likely to be presented as an explanation of the psychopathic personality in court, at least by a psychiatrist. The different theories, of course, have quite different theoretical implications for treatment and prognosis (although, in practice, neither learning theory nor psychodynamic theory have so far shown that they have anything much to offer in the way of treatment possibilities at all). Acceptance of the psychodynamic model, however, means acceptance of the theory underlying it, and this includes not just the theories discussed above but also the Freudian theory of psychosexual development, including Oedipal theory, and his belief that the basic structure of the human personality is more or less complete by the age of five or six, concepts that are open to serious challenge. As Shaffer points out, "Many tests of Freudian theory have now been conducted, and most of the evidence does not support Freud's theory of moral development".[30]

The point of all this is that Freudian theory has been with us for so long that many of Freud's concepts and terms have found their way into our ordinary intellectual life and hence into common use. People think they know what terms like "ego" and "unconscious" mean even though they have undergone extensive revisions in the hands of the neo-Freudians. Familiarity with the terms means that we may accept them as fact (although often defining them in our own idiosyncratic way), rather than treating them as the theoretical constructs they are and rigorously examining them whenever they appear. One of the dangers of psychodynamic theory is that it is well systematised and can be used to explain almost any form of human behaviour. Its very versatility contributes to its plausibility. Whether or not an explanation of criminal behaviour in any terms — psychodynamic or otherwise — is accepted by the court depends upon many factors. Familiarity and plausibility should not be the overriding ones.

THE EXISTENTIAL SCHOOL

The three schools discussed above are typical examples of the application of the type of scientific method that has characterised Western thought since the time of the Renaissance. They attempt to explain the complex in terms of the more simple by breaking things down into what they assume to be their component parts and looking at these. From what they learn from examination of the parts they then build up a theory which is supposed to explain the behaviour of the organism as a whole. The existential school does not reject this approach but it does regard it as narrow, inadequate and, to some extent, misleading in that it focuses attention on pieces of human behaviour and so diverts attention from the human being who is exhibiting that behaviour. It is as if a person is looking at a large complex painting but, through tunnel-vision, is only seeing a small part of it and is then assuming that the small part they are looking at contains all the information they need to understand and appreciate the complete painting without ever seeing it as a whole. The existential therapist does not dismiss the relevance of stimulus-response relationships or of innate drives, but attempts to enlarge the focus so that they are seen in a broader perspective and from a different point of view. He or she will be more concerned with the individual experiencing the drives or making the responses than with the drives and responses themselves. As May puts it: "If, as I sit with a patient, I am chiefly thinking of the whys and hows of the way the problem came about, I will have grasped everything except the most important thing of all, the existing person".[31]

To grasp this "most important thing" what is required is, first, a "disciplined effort to clear one's mind of the presuppositions that so often cause us to see in the patient only our own theories or the dogmas of our own systems",[32] and secondly, a new approach on the part of the therapist, an approach characterised by empathy, interaction and encounter rather than detachment. The therapist has to be what Sullivan called "a participant observer".

But exactly what is it that the existential therapist is trying to grasp? In simple terms it is the meaning of existence itself and the significance of this and of life's experiences for the individual. As May puts it:

> No matter how interesting or theoretically true is the fact that I am composed of such and such chemicals or act by such and such mechanisms or patterns, the crucial question always is that I happen to exist at this given moment in time and space, and my problem is how I am to be aware of that fact and what I shall do about it.[33]

There are three problems with existential theory that inhibit its application to forensic practice. First, it does not provide a model or set of models for explaining human behaviour. It is not so much a theory as a loose synthesis or network of ideas coming together, over a long period of time, from a number of disciplines including art, literature, philosophy and religion. Secondly there is a problem with the underlying presumption that the meaning of existence, that is, the significance of being-in-the-world, to use a technical term, is a basic theme that runs through all mental life and concerns all people to some degree. Whether or not this is so is highly debatable. According to May, "rarely has the existential problem been put more simply or beautifully" than in the following passage from the seventeenth century scientist and philosopher, Blaise Pascal:

22

> When I consider the brief span of my life, swallowed up in the eternity before and behind it, the small space that I fill, or even see, engulfed in the infinite immensity of spaces which I know not, and which know not me, I am afraid, and wonder to see myself here rather than there; for there is no reason why I should be here rather than there, now rather than then.[34]

If, as May claims, this accurately expresses the basic existential problem, it is rather unlikely that such a concern is of significance to a vast number of contemporary Australians, although it may be of significance to some.

Thirdly, explanations of human behaviour in existential terms can be very hard to understand as they are likely to be couched in terms that require a sophisticated understanding of concepts drawn from philosophy, transpersonal psychology and religion, concepts that may not even have English equivalents. So it is unlikely that such explanations would be put forward in Australian courts. In spite of these problems, existential psychiatry has some valuable lessons for forensic psychiatry.

The first is the doubt it casts on the value of reductionist theories in explaining human behaviour. As pointed out above, traditional Western science attempts to explain the complex in terms of the more simple. In existential terms, the simple can only be understood in terms of the more complex, not the reverse. May illustrates this by referring to the work of Teilhard de Chardin. According to Chardin, when new forms of life evolve in the evolutionary chain, when, for example, single-celled organisms joined together to form multi-celled organisms, something new emerged, some new function or governing principle which was not previously present. Two important principles follow. The behaviour of the new organism cannot be explained fully by looking at the functions of the simpler elements, the single cells, of which it is composed. More importantly, the functions and purpose of the simpler elements forming the new organism can now only be understood in terms of the new function which has emerged. As May puts it, "every new function forms a new complexity that reorganises all the simpler elements in [the] organism".[35] Similarly in human beings. In humans there is a degree of self-consciousness, of self-awareness, of being-in-the-world, that is unique to humans and that totally alters the way that the mechanisms we share with the lower animals operate. In humans, for example, sex serves many purposes other than the preservation of the species, although it could still be argued, at one level, that the reason for the continued existence of the drive in humans is species preservation. This would not explain, however, the multiplicity of psychosexual practices that human beings engage in, or, just as importantly, choose not to engage in.

The second lesson is that there is no such thing as complete objectivity. The idea that we need to be completely detached from something in order to study it properly, has dominated Western science for several centuries. For existentialists and, indeed, for many modern scientists, such a goal is neither desirable nor achievable.

23

The 'ideal of a science which is completely independent of man (that is, completely objective) is an illusion' in Heisenberg's words. . . [The] human being who is engaged in studying . . . natural phenomena is in a particular and significant relationship to the object studied and he must make himself part of the equation.[36]

This applies equally to psychiatry. The very presence of the psychiatrist in the client-therapist encounter invariably influences the outcome of the encounter, and of any subsequent encounters, even if the psychiatrist is attempting to stay as detached as possible. When it comes to preparing a report for court, the same principle applies. Every psychiatrist is an individual and every psychiatric report will have the stamp of that individuality. One psychiatrist might have a directive approach. A second might be non-directive. One psychiatrist might elicit a great deal of information from the patient (especially if he or she is the psychiatrist helping with the case for the defence). Another might not. The data, both verbal and non-verbal, that the psychiatrist has obtained has to be sorted and organised in some way. In the process the psychiatrist will have to decide which aspects of the history and mental state examination to emphasise and which not to emphasise. The reasons behind the arrangement of material in the final report will be complex and varied and may not even be fully understood by the person writing the report. In brief, there can be no such thing as an "objective" report.

The third lesson from the existential school is the uniqueness of the individual. This refers to both the uniqueness of the normal individual, in terms of his or her experience of the world and mode of being-in-the-world, and the unique way that each individual will be affected by the experience of a psychiatric disorder. This may seem obvious but it needs to be emphasised, as a psychiatric label can acquire a meaning and significance of its own, diverting attention away from the individual to whom the label has been attached. It is easy to generalise, to say, for example, that the middle-aged woman who was caught shoplifting was depressed at the time and that this was the reason she shoplifted. Sometimes this sort of generalisation is all the court wants. It does not sit easily, however, with the known facts. The majority of people who are depressed do not shoplift and the majority of shoplifters are not in the least depressed. By emphasising the uniqueness of the individual and the uniqueness of each individual's responses to life events, including psychiatric disorders, the existential school reminds us that the linkage between supposed causes and effects, between depression and shoplifting, has to be demonstrated, not simply assumed. This will be discussed further in Section C.

CONCLUSION

On current evidence all that can be said about the causes of psychiatric disorders is that they are probably multifactorial but that, as yet, there is no way of identifying any of the factors clearly enough to establish their individual etiological significance.

NOTES

1   American Psychiatric Association, *Diagnostic and Statistical Manual of Mental Disorders* (3rd ed; 1980) at 6.

2   McLaren, N, "Is Mental Disease Just Brain Disease? The Limits to Biological Psychiatry" (1992) 26 *ANZ J Psychiat* 270.

3   See, for example, Prins, H, "Besieged by Devils — thoughts on possession and possession states" (1992) 32/3 *Med, Sci, Law* 237; Brown, L, "A Psychologist's Perspective on Psychiatry in China" (1980) 14 *ANZ J Psychiat* 21; Sainsbury, M, "Psychiatry in the People's Republic of China" (1974) 1 *Med J Aust* 669.

4   Kiloh, L, "Non-Pharmacological Biological Treatments of Psychiatric Patients" (1983) 17 *ANZ J Psychiat* 215.

5   The percentages have been rounded off.

6   Torrey, E, "Are We Overestimating the Genetic Contribution to Schizophrenia?" (1992) 18/2 *Schizophr B* 159.

7   Tienari, P, "Implications of Adoption Studies on Schizophrenia" (1992) 161 (suppl.18) *Brit J Psychiat* 52.

8   Schulz, S and Pato, C, "Advances in the Genetics of Schizophrenia: Editor's Introduction" (1989) 15/3 *Schizophr B* 361; Pato, C, Lander, E and Schulz, S, "Prospects for the Genetic Analysis of Schizophrenia" (1989) 15/3 *Schizophr B* 365; Mowry, B, and Levinson, D, "Genetic Linkage and Schizophrenia: Methods, Recent Findings and Future Directions" (1993) 27 *ANZ J Psychiat* 200.

9   Kendler, K and Diehl, S, "The Genetics of Schizophrenia: A Current, Genetic-Epidemiologic Perspective" (1993) 19/2 *Schizophr B* 261.

10 Owen, M and McGuffin, P, "The molecular genetics of schizophrenia, Blind alleys, acts of faith and difficult science" (1992) 305 *Brit Med J* 664.

11 Owens, D, "Imaging aspects of the biology of schizophrenia" (1992) 5 *Curr Op Psychiat* 6.

12 Catts, S, "A biological basis to schizophrenia: have we learnt anything?" (1995) 4 *Psyche* 2.

13 O'Reilly, R, "Viruses and Schizophrenia" (1994) 28 *ANZ J Psychiat* 226. See also King, D and Cooper, S, "Viruses, Immunity and Mental Disorders" (1989) 154 *Brit J Psychiat* 43; and O'Callaghan, E, Sham, P, Takei, N, Glover, G and Murray, R, "Schizophrenia after prenatal exposure to 1957 A2 influenza epidemic" (1991) 337 *Lancet* 1248. Against the viral theory is evidence adduced from a recent *WHO* 10-country study described by Crow as "a landmark in the epidemiology of schizophrenia", a study which "gives considerable support to the anthroparity principle - that onsets [of schizophrenia], in relation to population size and structure, are constant over time and space". What the study showed was that "In the face of substantial variation in climactic, social and industrial environment, the incidence of schizophrenia, restrictively defined, remains the same". Crow, T, "Aetiology of Schizophrenia" (1994) 7 *Curr Op Psychiat* 39.

14 Tennant, C, "Life Events and Schizophrenic Episodes" (1985) 19 *ANZ J Psychiat* 329.

15   McGuffin, P and Thapar, A, "The Genetics of Personality Disorder" (1992) 160 *Brit J Psychiat* 12.

16   Hafner, R, "Behaviour Therapy For The Neuroses: Some Conceptual And Practical Problems" (1981) 15 *ANZ J Psychiat* 288.

17   Id. Ingleby suggests that "Behaviour therapy has sought to apply to human problems a theory of learning that barely fits the albino rat". Ingleby, D, "Understanding 'Mental Illness'" in Ingleby, D (ed), *Critical Psychiatry. The Politics of Mental Health* (1981) p 39.

18   Id.

19   Eysenck, representing the pure science school, said, of cognitive theory, that it "does not even exist as a 'theory' that could be meaningfully criticised or tested; it is an aspiration, born of mentalistic preconceptions, in search of hypotheses". Eysenck, H, "Behaviour Therapy and the Philosophers" (1979) 17 *Beh'r Res & Therapy* 511.

20   Hafner, above n 16 p 289.

21   Sutherland, E and Cressey, D, *Principles of Criminology* (1960) p 77.

22   Sainsbury, M and Lambeth, L, *Sainsbury's Key to Psychiatry* (1988) p 260.

23   Stafford-Clark, D, *What Freud Really Said* (1967) p 115.

24   Mayer-Gross, W, Slater, E and Roth, M, *Clinical Psychiatry* (1960) p 22. See also Howard, C, "Amnesia" in Bluglass, R and Bowden, P (eds), *Principles and Practice of Forensic Psychiatry* (1990) p 297.

25   Brown, J, Freud and the Post-Freudians (1961) p 148.

26   Id.

27   Ibid p 28.

28   Stafford-Clark, above n 23 p 112.

29   See, for example, Shaffer, D, *Developmental Psychology* (1985) pp 558-594.

30   Ibid p 593.

31   May, R, (ed) *Existential Psychology* (1969) p 20.

32   Ibid p 21.

33   May, R, "The Origins and Significance of the Existential Movement in Psychology" in May, R, Angel, E and Ellenburger, H, (eds) *Existence. A New Dimension in Psychiatry and Psychology* (1958) p 12.

34   Ibid p 18.

35   Above n 31 p 78.

36   May, above n 33 p 26.

3

SCHIZOPHRENIA

Introduction

More has been written about schizophrenia than about any other topic in psychiatry. In spite of this it remains an enigma with a wide variety of definitions and a considerable diversity of opinion about its causes, its outcome and its treatment. As Mortimer puts it: "[In schizophrenia] few findings stand the test of time, most of the pieces of this particular jigsaw seem to be missing, and it is not easy to make sense of those that are available".[1]

Some of the symptoms that are attributed to it were first described hundreds of years ago[2] and yet, in its present form, it appears to be a disorder that sprang into prominence in the late nineteenth century, gradually changed its presentation over the first half of the twentieth century and may have started to diminish in both frequency and severity over the past few decades.[3]

It has had particular significance for forensic psychiatry because, like other major psychiatric disorders, it can provide a complete defence to a crime. If, however, it is to be used in evidence, the court should have a clear understanding of what the term means to the person using it. Unfortunately psychiatrists themselves, psychiatric textbooks and major international classifications of psychiatry all differ in the meanings they ascribe to schizophrenia. These differing meanings will be explored in this chapter as they can have profound consequences for the way the condition is conceptualised and, hence, for the court's understanding of the mental state of the accused and the outcome of the trial.

The definitional difficulties diminish as one moves from the general concept of schizophrenia as a syndrome, through its subtypes, to its symptoms. Even at the symptom level, however, definitional problems remain.

Schizophrenia — the syndrome

What is meant by the term 'schizophrenia'? Unfortunately there is no consensus on this point . . . criteria vary from country to country and from hospital to hospital.[4]

No strictly pathognomonic symptoms [of schizophrenia] can be identified.[5]

Clinical diagnoses in psychiatry have a relatively low reliability and the diagnosis of schizophrenia is no exception. Much of this unreliability is due to a diversity of diagnostic schools.[6]

As the above quotations indicate, "schizophrenia" can be defined in many ways and there is no single definition that is recognised or accepted as being the "right" one. Argument about the meaning of the term began as soon as the concept was introduced and has continued ever since. The debate started in 1896 when Emil Kraepelin, in the fifth edition of his psychiatric textbook, brought together into one syndrome a number of conditions that had previously been considered separate entities. He called the new syndrome "dementia praecox" because, unlike the other known dementias of the time, it began, characteristically, in adolescence. Kraepelin believed that it led ultimately to deterioration of the personality and that the underlying cause of the illness was some undiscovered disorder of the brain with a "specific anatomical pathology" and "a specific etiology", most probably metabolic.[7]

Eugen Bleuler, a contemporary of Kraepelin's, took Kraepelin's concept, reworked it and, in 1911, renamed it "schizophrenia".[8] Kraepelin's classification had been based primarily on the deteriorating outcome he saw as being fundamental to the disease (which distinguished it from the other group of psychoses he had identified — the manic-depressive psychoses — which did not lead to deterioration).

Bleuler focused on the schizophrenic process itself, hypothesising that the central feature of the disorder was a loosening of the associations or linkages that normally structure thought and give it its direction. As these linkages break up, other interrelated mental processes (such as mood and volition) are also affected and also give rise to symptoms. The end result is a fragmentation or splitting away from each other of those mental processes that normally work together in a harmonious and unified way.

Bleuler went on to reorganise the symptoms found in schizophrenia into a hierarchical system of two groups — those that he considered to be essential for the diagnosis (the primary symptoms) and those that could occur in schizophrenia but were not essential for the diagnosis (the secondary symptoms). His primary symptoms were all derived from the loosening of associations that he considered to be at the core of the schizophrenic process. They were:

1 disturbances of association (ie formal thought disorder);

2 mood disturbances (which included both a flattening of mood and an inappropriateness or incongruity of mood);

3 autism (which included both autistic thinking and the behaviour that could result from it);

4 extreme ambivalence.

The symptoms that Kraepelin had considered to be typical schizophrenic symptoms were relegated to the status of secondary symptoms. They included, inter alia:

1   hallucinations;
2   delusions;
3   certain catatonic symptoms;
4   disorders of person.

Kraepelin and Bleuler both had their supporters and their critics.[9] Kraepelin himself was critical of Bleuler's classification. He described Bleuler's division of symptoms into primary and secondary as "purely contrived" and rejected the underlying theory.[10] Nonetheless it was Bleuler's views on schizophrenia that gained the wider acceptance — at least until the 1950s when Kurt Schneider's work on first and second rank symptoms started to exert its influence.

A major problem with Bleuler's classification was the non-specificity of his primary symptoms. They could be found in other psychiatric conditions, in certain physical illnesses and even, at times, in normal people. A second major problem with Bleuler's work on schizophrenia, and one that had significant forensic consequences, especially in Switzerland, came from his concept of latent schizophrenia. According to Bleuler, there were a number of nonspecific symptoms such as:

> personality anomalies, indifference, anergia, querulousness, obstinacy, moodiness, and what Goethe could describe only with the English 'whimsicality', hypochondriasis etc [which] need not be symptoms of a mental disease; but only too often . . . are the only visible signs of schizophrenia.[11]

So as well as the primary and secondary symptoms he had described, there was a group of quite nonspecific symptoms which he thought indicated a diagnosis of latent schizophrenia and he became convinced that this was the most frequent form of schizophrenia. Wyrsh, a student of Bleuler, describes the consequences of this:

> Around 1920 and even during the subsequent decade, we in Switzerland had a rather wide concept of schizophrenia, much wider than Kraepelin in Germany . . . [We] believed we could glean the diagnosis before manifest unequivocal psychic symptoms were there. . .

> When certain delinquents in our large cities — mostly youths around 20 years, usually with minor but repeated thefts, break-ins, frauds — stood arraigned in court, and were referred for assessment to our university clinics, the assessor often concluded that there was a latent schizophrenia, and that the accused was mentally incompetent. Consequently, he was committed to the mental hospital in his home Canton.[12]

Wyrsh also notes that once the treating psychiatrist became better acquainted with the youth the diagnosis would usually be changed to "personality disorder".

Like Bleuler, Schneider also divided schizophrenic symptoms into two groups, which he called first and second rank symptoms, but they were quite different to Bleuler's primary and secondary symptoms. Schneider's first rank symptoms were:

1   audible thoughts (ie hallucinatory voices speaking the patient's thoughts aloud);

2   voices arguing, usually with the patient as the subject of the argument;

3   voices commenting on one's actions;

4   influences playing on the body (somatic passivity), experienced as both bodily change and external control;

5   thought withdrawal with the patient's thoughts being taken from their mind by some external force;

6   thought insertion;

7   diffusion or broadcasting of thoughts;

8   "made" feelings, with the patient experiencing feelings being imposed by an external source;

9   "made" impulses or drives;

10 "made" volitional acts with the patient feeling like an automaton, forced to carry out acts that are not of his or her own volition;

11 delusional perceptions (ie a delusion which arises from an otherwise normal perception).[13]

According to Schneider the presence of a first rank symptom in a psychosis meant that a decisive clinical diagnosis of schizophrenia could be made. Unlike Bleuler's primary symptoms, however, Schneider's first rank symptoms were not necessary for the diagnosis, which could also be made on the basis of second rank symptoms and behavioural abnormalities.

Schneider explained the significance of first rank symptoms for the diagnosis of schizophrenia as follows:

> When we say . . . that thought withdrawal is a 1st rank symptom this means: if this symptom is present in a psychosis in the absence of an organic pathology we call it schizophrenia, as opposed to a cyclothymic psychosis, a personality abnormality or a psychogenic reaction.[14]

Schneider's first rank symptoms were basically specific types of delusions and hallucinations. What they described was something completely different to what Bleuler had described and there was a great deal of controversy about whether or not the syndrome that Schneider had described was schizophrenia at all. In 1978, for example, in the 52nd Maudsley Lecture, Kety stated:

> Schneider established a new syndrome with features that are more easily perceived and described [than Bleuler's], and which therefore show a higher degree of inter-rater reliability. . . That syndrome may be more prevalent, have a more favourable

outcome, and be more responsive to a wide variety of treatments, but it is not schizophrenia.[15]

Both classifications, however, were major determinants of subsequent developments as will be seen in the discussion of the DSM and ICD classifications below. First, let us compare the DSM–III (1980) with the DSM–III–R (1987). According to the DSM–III, the diagnostic criteria for a schizophrenic disorder are:

A   At least one of the following during a phase of the illness:

(1)   bizarre delusions (content is patently absurd and has no possible basis in fact), such as delusions of being controlled, thought broadcasting, thought insertion or thought withdrawal;

(2)   somatic, grandiose, religious, nihilistic, or other delusions without persecutory or jealous content;

(3)   delusions with persecutory or jealous content if accompanied by hallucinations of any type;

(4)   auditory hallucinations in which either a voice keeps up a running commentary on the individual's behaviour or thoughts, or two or more voices converse with each other;

(5)   auditory hallucinations on several occasions with content of more than one or two words, having no apparent relation to depression or elation;

(6)   incoherence, marked loosening of associations, markedly illogical thinking, or marked poverty of content of speech if associated with at least one of the following:

(a)   blunted, flat, or inappropriate affect,

(b)   delusions or hallucinations,

(c)   catatonic or other grossly disorganized behaviour;

B   Deterioration from a previous level of functioning in such areas as work, social relations, and self-care.

C   Duration: Continuous signs of the illness for at least six months at some time during the person's life, with some signs of the illness at present.[16]

According to the revised version of the DSM–III (the DSM–III–R) published seven years later, the diagnostic criteria for the same disorder are:

A   Presence of characteristic psychotic symptoms in the active phase: either (1), (2), or (3) for at least one week (unless the symptoms are successfully treated):

(1)   two of the following:

(a)   delusions,

(b)   prominent hallucinations (throughout the day for several days or several times a week for several weeks, each hallucinatory experience not being limited to a few brief moments),

(c)   incoherence or marked loosening of associations,

(d)   catatonic behaviour,

(e)   flat or grossly inappropriate affect;

31

(2) bizarre delusions (ie, involving a phenomenon that the person's culture would regard as totally implausible, eg, thought broadcasting, being controlled by a dead person);

(3) prominent hallucinations (as defined in (1)(b) above) of a voice with content having no apparent relation to depression or elation, or a voice keeping up a running commentary on the person's behaviour or thoughts, or two or more voices conversing with each other.

B During the course of the disturbance, functioning in such areas as work, social relations, and self-care is markedly below the highest level achieved before onset of the disturbance (or, when the onset is in childhood or adolescence, failure to achieve expected level of social development).

. . .

D Continuous signs of the disturbance for at least six months.[17]

Both definitions include a selection of Bleuler's primary and secondary symptoms and Schneider's first rank symptoms but the requirements for diagnosing the condition are different. Also both definitions require the illness to be present for at least six months before the diagnosis can be made. Until the six-month period has expired, the condition is diagnosed as a schizophreniform disorder.

The ICD–10 uses a different approach again. After first noting that: "no strictly pathognomonic symptoms can be identified" it goes on to say that "for practical purposes it is useful to divide the . . . symptoms into groups that have special importance for the diagnosis and often occur together, such as":

(a) thought echo, thought insertion or withdrawal, and thought broadcasting;

(b) delusions of control, influence or passivity, clearly referred to body or limb movements or specific thoughts, actions or sensations; delusional perception;

(c) hallucinatory voices giving a running commentary on the patient's behaviour, or discussing the patient among themselves, or other types of hallucinatory voices coming from some part of the body;

(d) persistent delusions of other kinds that are culturally inappropriate and completely impossible, such as religious or political identity, or superhuman powers and abilities (for example being able to control the weather, or being in communication with aliens from another world);

(e) persistent hallucinations in any modality, when accompanied either by fleeting or half-formed delusions without clear affective content, or by persistent over-valued ideas, or when occurring every day for weeks or months on end;

(f) breaks or interpolations in the train of thought, resulting in incoherence or irrelevant speech, or neologisms;

(g) catatonic behaviour, such as excitement, posturing, or waxy flexibility, negativism, mutism, and stupor;

(h) "negative" symptoms such as marked apathy, paucity of speech, and blunting or incongruity of emotional responses, usually resulting in social withdrawal and lowering of social performance; it must be clear that these are not due to depression or to neuroleptic medication;[18]

32

(i) a significant and consistent change in the overall quality of some aspects of personal behaviour, manifest as loss of interest, aimlessness, idleness, a self-absorbed attitude, and social withdrawal.[19]

According to the diagnostic guidelines that follow:

The normal requirement for a diagnosis of schizophrenia is that a minimum of one very clear symptom (and usually two or more if less clear-cut) belonging to any one of the groups listed as (a) to (d) above, or symptoms from at least two of the groups referred to as (e) to (h), should have been clearly present for most of the time during a period of 1 month or more.[20]

The ICD–10 is obviously quite different to the DSM–III–R with regard to both the symptoms that must be present for the diagnosis to be made, the time interval that must elapse before the diagnosis can be made (one month as opposed to six months), and the continuous time period (ie the active phase) within that month or six months that the "very clear symptom(s)" or less clear symptoms (in the case of the ICD-10) and the "characteristic psychotic symptoms" (in the case of the DSM-III-R) have to be present to confirm the diagnosis - "most of the time" (ICD-10) as opposed to one week (DSM-III-R).

The DSM-IV, which came out two years after the ICD-10, changed the characteristic symptoms in Criterion A by simplifying their presentation and adding additional negative symptoms (alogia and avolition). It also made some minor changes to the wording of Criterion B. More importantly, it altered the required duration of the active-phase symptoms from one week (DSM-III-R) to one month "to reduce false-positive diagnoses and to increase compatibility with ICD-10 Diagnostic Criteria for Research".[21]

The DSM-IV classification of Criterion A is as follows:

Characteristic symptoms: Two (or more) of the following, each present for a significant portion of time during a one-month period (or less if successfully treated):

(1) delusions;

(2) hallucinations;

(3) disorganized speech (eg frequent derailment or incoherence);

(4) grossly disorganized or catatonic behaviour;

(5) negative symptoms (ie affective flattening, alogia, or avolition).

Note: Only one Criterion A symptom is required if delusions are bizarre or hallucinations consist of a voice keeping up a running commentary on the person's behaviour or thoughts, or two or more voices conversing with each other.[22]

And Bleuler, Schneider, the ICD and DSM aside, there is still the problem of the variations that occur in different textbooks; international differences of opinion on the subject; the experimental classifications that have been devised for particular purposes; and the idiosyncrasies of individual psychiatrists who may have their own ideas about what schizophrenia means.

In a study carried out in 1983, for example, 301 American psychiatrists were asked to describe the clinical findings that would lead them to a diagnosis of schizophrenia.[23] The tetrad of impaired thought or language, delusions, hallucinations, and affect (mood) disturbances headed the list but they were the only four responses that reached a 50 per cent accordance level. Agreement on the combination of signs and symptoms that constitute schizophrenia was very low. The complete list is significantly different to either the DSM–III–R or the ICD–10.

Symptom Categories	Percent
Impaired thought or language	75.4
Delusions	75.1
Hallucinations	73.4
Affect disturbance	66.8
Other	47.2
Interpersonal difficulties	42.2
Absence of organicity	34.9
Impaired reality testing	27.2
Bizarre behaviour	22.3
Absence of affective disorder	19.9
Duration of symptoms	17.3
Family history	16.3
Autism	15.3
Poor rapport with examiner	14.0
Suspiciousness	13.3
Deterioration in course	13.3
Ideas of reference	12.0
Age of onset	10.6
Ambivalence	10.3
Concrete thinking	9.0
Premorbid personality	6.6
Perceptual disturbance	5.3
Depersonalization	4.0

A minimum of 12 respondents mentioned at least one of these categories. What is particularly interesting, however, is a later list in the study which shows the symptoms listed by only 1–9 respondents. These are the symptoms listed as "Other" in the list above. Some of these are quite idiosyncratic. The following are the symptoms listed under four of the eight subcategories in the list:

Behaviour
> Crime without cause, sociopathy, violence
> Frequent drug abuse, illicit drug use
> Result of drug experimentation
> Poor impulse control
> Poor eye contact
> Hypervigilance
> Indecisiveness
> Lack of stamina

Physical
> Physical oddities
> Weight problems

Criteria of no help
> Bleulerian criteria
> Schneiderian criteria
> Blunted affect
> Loose associations
> Delusions, hallucinations

Unclassifiable
> "Smell of schizophrenia"
> Response to medications
> Patient "doesn't add up"
> Patient "walks in backwards"

Given the diversity of opinion as to what constitutes schizophrenia among classifications over time, between contemporary classifications, and among individual psychiatrists, one might well be justified in concluding that the question posed in one of the quotations at the beginning of this section, "What is meant by the term 'schizophrenia'?", is unanswerable in precise terms, which would raise questions about the use of the term in evidence. Before coming to any conclusions about this, however, it is necessary to consider briefly some of the various subclassifications of schizophrenia that are available.

Subclassifications of schizophrenia

Subclassifications of schizophrenia have been a feature of the nosology of schizophrenia since the time of Kraepelin. In their 1950 textbook on psychiatry, Henderson and Gillespie, writing at a time when the ideas of Kraepelin and Bleuler still predominated, identified some of the nosological dilemmas that existed at that time:

> Kraepelin differentiated three principal types, which he termed hebephrenic, katatonic and paranoid. Later he added a fourth variety, termed simplex. In the last edition of his text book he has added numerous other forms, for example, simple

depressive dementia praecox, delusional dementia praecox, circular dementia praecox, agitated dementia praecox and so on. No useful purpose is served by forming so many sub-groups. The main groups are fairly distinctive, but even these are not clear cut, and, *if we wished, we could form almost as many groups as there were individuals.* We prefer to use the term schizophrenia rather than dementia praecox and we suggest that it is preferable to group paranoid forms with paranoic and paranoid reaction types rather than schizophrenia. In this discussion, therefore, we limit the grouping of the schizophrenic states to the simple, the hebephrenic and katatonic forms, but we would emphasise that these differentiations are made merely for ease in classification rather than because of any fundamental difference.[24]

The DSM–I, published two years later, listed nine subtypes of schizophrenia:

1   Schizophrenia reaction, simple type
2   Schizophrenic reaction, hebephrenic type
3   Schizophrenic reaction, catatonic type
4   Schizophrenic reaction, paranoid type
5   Schizophrenic reaction, acute undifferentiated type
6   Schizophrenic reaction, chronic undifferentiated type
7   Schizophrenic reaction, schizo-affective type
8   Schizophrenic reaction, childhood type
9   Schizophrenic reaction, residual type[25]

The ICD–9 (1975) listed ten subtypes, including an "unspecified" subtype which it stated was "to be used only as a last resort":

1   Simple type
2   Hebephrenic type
3   Catatonic type
4   Paranoid type
5   Acute schizophrenic episode
6   Latent schizophrenia
7   Residual schizophrenia
8   Schizoaffective type
9   Other
10 Unspecified[26]

The DSM–III (1980), the DSM–III–R (1987) and the DSM-IV (1994) all list the same five subtypes although there are slight variations in their descriptions of the diagnostic criteria:

1   Disorganized type
2   Catatonic type
3   Paranoid type
4   Residual type

36

5   Undifferentiated type[27]

The ICD–10 (1992) lists nine subtypes:

1   Paranoid schizophrenia
2   Hebephrenic schizophrenia
3   Catatonic schizophrenia
4   Undifferentiated schizophrenia
5   Post-schizophrenic depression
6   Residual schizophrenia
7   Simple schizophrenia
8   Other schizophrenia
9   Schizophrenia, unspecified[28]

It is interesting to trace the vicissitudes of the subtype of schizophrenia known as "simple schizophrenia" as it illustrates clearly the type of decision-making that goes into determining whether or not a group of symptoms should be classified as a psychiatric disorder or not, especially symptoms that are "on the boundary between normality and pathology".[29] Bleuler, elaborating on the earlier work of Diem included simple schizophrenia in his classification. It was also included as a subtype in the DSM–I (Schizophrenic reaction, simple type) and DSM–II, where it was defined as:

> [A] psychosis characterised chiefly by a slow and insidious reduction of external attachments and interests and by apathy and indifference leading to impoverishment of interpersonal relations, mental deterioration, and adjustment on a lower level of functioning.[30]

It was deliberately excluded from the DSM–III and subsequently from the DSM–III–R. The authors explain why:

> The approach taken here excludes illnesses without overt psychotic features, which have been referred to as Latent, Borderline and Simple Schizophrenia. Such cases are likely to be diagnosed in this manual as having a Personality Disorder such as Schizotypal Personality Disorder.[31]

The authors of the ICD–10, however, deliberately decided to include it in their classification, stating:

> This category has been retained because of its continued use in some countries, and because of the uncertainty about its nature and its relationships to schizoid personality disorder and schizotypal disorder, which will require additional information for resolution.[32]

The ICD–10 defines simple schizophrenia as:

> An uncommon disorder in which there is an insidious but progressive development of oddities of conduct, inability to meet the demands of society, and decline in total performance. . . The characteristic 'negative' features of residual schizophrenia (eg blunting of affect, loss of volition) develop without being preceded by any overt

psychotic symptoms. With increasing social impoverishment, vagrancy may ensue and the individual may then become self-absorbed, idle and aimless.[33]

The ICD–10 goes on to state, however, that "Simple schizophrenia is a difficult diagnosis to make,"[34] a point that Black and Bofffeli take up in a review article where they summarise the main deficiencies of the concept as diagnostic imprecision, poor reliability and doubtful descriptive validity.[35]

The authors of the DSM-IV, obviously influenced by the fact that the ICD-10 had persisted with the diagnosis of simple schizophrenia, brought it back into their classification in a section called "Criteria Sets and Axes Provided for Further Study". They named it "simple deteriorative disorder (simple schizophrenia)", described its research criteria as:

Progressive development over a period of at least a year of all of the following:

(1) marked decline in occupational or academic functioning

(2) gradual appearance and deepening of negative symptoms such as affective flattening, alogia and avolition

(3) poor interpersonal rapport, social isolation, or social withdrawal[36]

and warned that "negative symptoms are difficult to evaluate because they occur on a continuum with normality, are nonspecific, and may be due to a variety of other factors."[37]

Simple schizophrenia aside, it is clear that there is a closer, but far from perfect correlation between the descriptions of the major subtypes in the DSM–III–R and the ICD–10 than there is between their general descriptions of schizophrenia. This is of little help in establishing a diagnosis, however, as the diagnosis of a subtype cannot be made unless the broader criteria for the umbrella term have already been met. The usefulness of the classic subtypes of schizophrenia has been questioned by the World Health Organization itself.[38] So if a diagnostic subcategory of schizophrenia is to be used in evidence in court, like schizophrenia itself it also requires precise definition. "Paranoid schizophrenia", for example, would suggest the ICD–10 classification but it might equally well refer to a textbook description, an idiosyncratic interpretation, or the DSM–IV classification.

But even when a precise definition is given, there is a further definitional problem still — the meaning of the terms used for individual signs and symptoms. And beyond that again there is the question of the subjective significance of those signs and symptoms for the individual experiencing them and, as pointed out in Chapter 1, the level of impairment or disability they produce.

Before leaving subtypes it is important to note that just because a person is given a subtype label on one occasion, it does not mean that this is their diagnosis for the duration of their illness. The particular set of signs and symptoms with which a person presents on one occasion may be different to the signs and symptoms with which they present on another occasion.

Schizophrenia — signs and symptoms

The definitions of individual signs and symptoms are more precise than the definitions of schizophrenia and its subtypes and there are fewer differences of opinion about what the terms mean, but this does not preclude the need to define them precisely when using them.

The definition of some terms, for example those used to describe hallucinations and the various forms of catatonic behaviour (excitement, waxy flexibility, mutism and stupor), pose few problems as most textbooks describe them in similar and consistent ways.

The term "delusion", however, is not so clear-cut. One might assume that because delusions have been at the very heart of the development of the criminal law in relation to mental illness for several centuries, that there would be little room for argument about what a delusion is. Unfortunately this is not so. As Ellard points out, "Delusion is more difficult to define than you might think".[39] First, there is sometimes no clear point at which delusions end and overvalued ideas begin and identifying the difference between them may be more a matter of a value judgement than the application of an objective criterion. Secondly, there are phenomenological problems in defining delusions. Spitzer,[40] for example, concerned about inconsistencies in the DSM–III–R definition, has argued for a new definition "that distinguishes between disorders of experience (which are not necessarily delusional) and delusions about external reality which because they can be more easily measured, may be considered delusional".[41] Thirdly, even textbook definitions, especially brief definitions, can be misleading. To say, for example, that a delusion is a "false, fixed belief" is not incorrect but it is incomplete. The definition in *Sainsbury's Key to Psychiatry*:

> A delusion is a belief which is
>
> (a) not true to fact;
>
> (b) cannot be corrected by an appeal to the reason of the person entertaining it;
>
> (c) is out of harmony with the individual's educational and cultural background,[42]

is a good definition but the phrase "not true to fact" needs qualifying as the truth or falsity of the end belief does not determine whether the belief is delusional. If a man believed that his wife was being unfaithful to him, and she was being unfaithful to him, it could still be a delusion. It is the reason a person gives for holding the belief; that is, the thought processes that lead to the belief, that make it delusional. It would probably be more correct to speak of delusional thinking than delusions per se.

Fourthly, even in experimental situations where structured definitions have been used, the interrater reliability amongst psychiatrists has been low.[43]

A third group of signs and symptoms can be difficult to evaluate at times, especially when they are present in their milder forms. These are the mood disturbances and the disorders of thought form that have been described in schizophrenia. The mood disturbances include a diminution in the intensity of emotional responses (flatness of mood), and an incongruity or inappropriateness of mood. As the range of normal moods varies quite considerably from person to person, it is often difficult to determine where normality ends and abnormality begins. And as well as individual differences, there are also cultural differences that must be taken into account. As Lehmann points out:

> Inexperienced observers should be extremely hesitant to make judgements in the highly subjective area of normal emotional depth. What is normal emotional expression in an Anglo-Saxon culture, for example, may suggest a schizoid reduction of emotional response in a Mediterranean culture.[44]

There is some doubt about whether emotional blunting is really a valid criterion for diagnosing schizophrenia at all.[45]

Disorders of thought form (or formal thought disorder) are disorders in the "organization, control and processing of thought",[46] that is, they are disorders of the way a person thinks. The disorders in association which are considered to underlie formal thought disorder were believed by Bleuler to be the basic symptom of schizophrenia from which all others resulted. The DSM–III–R defines formal thought disorder as follows:

> The most common example of this is loosening of associations, in which ideas shift from one subject to another, completely unrelated or only obliquely related subject, without the speaker's displaying any awareness that the topics are unconnected. Statements that lack a meaningful relationship may be juxtaposed, or the person may shift idiosyncratically from one frame of reference to another. When loosening of associations is severe, the person may become incoherent, that is, his or her speech may become incomprehensible. There may be poverty of content of speech, in which speech is adequate in amount, but conveys little information because it is vague, overly abstract, or overly concrete, repetitive, or stereotyped. The listener can recognise this disturbance by noting that little if any information has been conveyed although the person has spoken at some length. Less common disturbances include neologisms, perseveration, clanging and blocking.[47]

The DSM-IV is more cautious. It states:

> Because of the difficulty inherent in developing an objective definition of "thought disorder", and because in a clinical setting inferences about thought are based primarily on the individual's speech, the concept of disorganized speech has been emphasized in the definition for Schizophrenia used in this manual. The speech of individuals with Schizophrenia may be disorganized in a variety of ways. The person may "slip off the track" from one topic to another ("derailment" or "loose associations"); answers to questions may be obliquely related or completely unrelated ("tangentiality"); and, rarely, speech may be so severely disorganized that it is nearly incomprehensible and resembles receptive aphasia in its linguistic

disorganization ("incoherence" or "word salad"). Because mildly disorganized speech is common and nonspecific, the symptom must be severe enough to substantially impair effective communication.[48]

The problems of devising some way of measuring thought disorder will be obvious from the definition. Just as in the case of mood disturbances, the point at which normality is considered to end and abnormality to begin is often very much a matter of a value judgement. Such scales as have been devised, such as the TLC,[49] are little used in Australia in ordinary clinical practice. And as indicated in the above extract from the DSM-IV there is also the problem of distinguishing thought disorder from speech disorder.[50]

Even if satisfactory scales could be devised, however, one fundamental problem remains, and it is a problem that is common to all the signs and symptoms that are commonly associated with schizophrenia. They all occur in other conditions. Thought disorder, for example, occurs in other psychiatric disorders, in organic conditions and in normal people. Bleuler himself noted that "normal persons show a number of schizophrenic symptoms when they are emotionally preoccupied, particularly inattentive, or when their attention is concentrated on a single subject". The writings of some modern authors (including some psychiatrists) are replete with examples of what, in another context, would be called formal thought disorder.

Conclusion

As there is no general agreement upon how to define schizophrenia and as such definitions as do exist differ significantly from one another, the use, in evidence, of the general term "schizophrenia" or the use of terms indicating one of its subtypes, such as "paranoid schizophrenia", should be accompanied by an exact definition of what the person using the term means by it and a clear indication of where the definition comes from. A description of specific signs and symptoms should accompany the definition and where there is any doubt about their meaning, definitions should accompany them as well. Finally, there should be a clear description of the subjective significance of the signs and symptoms to the individual who is experiencing them and the degree of disability or impairment they produce.

Since the time of Kraepelin, schizophrenia has generally been considered to be a single homogeneous entity manifesting itself in a variety of ways. It may eventually turn out to be something quite different.[51] The "group of schizophrenias" that Bleuler referred to in his original monograph may be just that. Some may even end up being separated off as separate conditions.[52] In the meantime, if the term is to be used at all it should be used with caution and heavily qualified.

1   Mortimer, A, "Phenomenology. Its Place in Schizophrenia Research" (1992) 161 *Brit J Psychiat* 293.

2   See Zilboorg, G, *A History of Medical Psychology* (1967).

3   See Ellard, J, "Schizophrenia: here today, gone tomorrow" (1985) 28/1 *Mod Med Austr* 9; Ellard, J, "Did Schizophrenia Exist Before the Eighteenth Century" (1987) 21 *ANZ J Psychiat* 306; Hare, E, "Schizophrenia as a Recent Disease" (1988) 153 *Brit J Psychiat* 521; Carpenter, P, "Descriptions of Schizophrenia in the Psychiatry of Georgian Britain: John Haslam and James Tilly Matthews" (1989) 30/4 *Compr Psychiat* 332; Der, G, Gupta, S and Murray, R, "Is schizophrenia disappearing?" (1990) 335 *Lancet* 513, Harrison, G and Mason, P, "Schizophrenia - Falling Incidence and Better Outcome?" (1993) 163 *Brit J Psych* 535.

4   Weiner, H, "Schizophrenia: Etiology" in Freedman, A, Kaplan, H and Sadock, B, *Comprehensive Textbook of Psychiatry — II* (1975) p 866.

5   World Health Organization, *The ICD–10 Classification of Mental and Behavioural Disorders* (1992) p 87.

6   Hoenig, J, "Schneider's First Rank Symptoms and the Tabulators" (1984) 25/1 *Compr Psychiat* 77.

7   Hoenig, J, "The Concept of Schizophrenia. Kraepelin – Bleuler – Schneider" (1983) 142 *Brit J Psychiat* 548. See also Jablensky, A, Hugler, H, von Cranach, M and Kalinov, K, "Kraepelin revisited: a reassessment and statistical analysis of dementia praecox and manic-depressive insanity in 1908" (1993) 23 *Psychological Medicine* 843.

8   Bleuler's monograph "Dementia Praecox or the Group of Schizophrenias" was published as Volume II of Aschaffenburg's *Handbook of Psychiatry*.

9   Zilboorg, above n 2 p 457, notes that when Kraepelin presented a paper on his theories to the Twenty-ninth Congress of Southwestern German Psychiatry on November 27, 1898, only one person present, Aschaffenburg, approved its contents. The paper was entitled "The Diagnosis and Prognosis of Dementia Praecox". Pappenheim, Meyer, Korsakov and Serbski all subsequently raised objections to the classification. Serbski objected especially to Kraepelin's concept of personality deterioration pointing out that Kraepelin himself had admitted that 13 per cent of dementia praecox patients seemed to recover without defect.

10   Hoenig, above n 7 p 550.

11   Ibid p 551.

12   Id.

13   Kluft, R, "First-Rank Symptoms as a Diagnostic Clue to Multiple Personality Disorder" (1987) 144/3 *Amer J Psychiat* 293.

14   Hoenig, above n 7 p 554.

15   Ibid p 547.

16   American Psychiatric Association, *Diagnostic and Statistical Manual of Mental Disorders* (3rd ed; 1980) p 188.

17   American Psychiatric Association, *Diagnostic and Statistical Manual of Mental Disorders* (3rd ed, rev; 1987) p 194.

18   The distinction between positive symptoms (denoting the presence of abnormal functioning, for example delusions and hallucinations) and negative symptoms (denoting the absence of normal functioning, for example apathy and emotional blunting) was first noted by Kraepelin. Their classification, etiology, significance and assessment remains a matter of debate. See Leach, A, "Negative symptoms" (1991) 4 *Curr Op Psychiat* 18.

19   World Health Organization, above n 5 p 87.

20   Ibid p 88.

21   American Psychiatric Association, *Diagnostic and Statistical Manual of Mental Disorders* (4th ed; 1994) p 779.

22   Ibid p 285.

23   Lipkowitz, M and Idupuganti, S, "Diagnosing Schizophrenia in 1980: A Survey of US Psychiatrists" (1983) 140/1 *Amer J Psychiat* 52.

24   Henderson, D and Gillespie, R, *A Textbook of Psychiatry for Students and Practitioners* (1950) p 305. Emphasis added.

25   American Psychiatric Association, *Diagnostic and Statistical Manual. Mental Disorders* (1952) p 26.

26   World Health Organization, *Manual of the International Statistical Classification of Diseases, Injuries and Causes of Death* (1977) p 183.

27   American Psychiatric Association, above n 16 p 190; above n 17 p 196.

28   Above n 5 p 89.

29   American Psychiatric Association, above n 21 p xx1.

30   American Psychiatric Association, *Diagnostic and Statistical Manual of Mental Disorders* (2nd ed; 1968), p 33.

31   American Psychiatric Association, above n 17 p 181. More detailed accounts of the reasons for excluding simple schizophrenia from the classification of schizophrenic subtypes at this time can be found in Spitzer, R, Andreasen, N and Endicott, J et al, "Proposed classification of schizophrenia in DSM–III" in Wynne, L, Cromwell, R and Matthysse, S (eds), *The Nature of Schizophrenia: New Approaches to Research and Treatment* (1978) p 670; and Spitzer, R, Andreasen, N and Endicott, J, "Schizophrenia and other psychotic disorders in DSM–III" (1978) 4 *Schizophr B* p 489.

32   Above n 5 p 12.

33   Ibid p 95.

34   Id.

35   Black D and Boffeli, T, "Simple Schizophrenia: Revisited" (1990) 31/4 *Compr Psychiat* 345.

36   American Psychiatric Association, above n 21 p 714.

37   Ibid p 277.

38   World Health Organization, *An International Follow-up Study of Schizophrenia* (1979).

39   Ellard, J, "The Madness of Mental Health Acts" (1990) 24 *ANZ J Psychiat* 170.

40   Spitzer, M, "On Defining Delusions" (1990) 31 *Compr Psychiat* 377. Reviewed in Altman, E and Jobe, T, "Phenomenology of Psychosis" (1992) 5 *Curr Op Psychiat* 34.

41   Altman and Jobe, above n 40 p 34.

42   Sainsbury, M and Lambeth, L, *Sainsbury's Key to Psychiatry* (1988) p 77.

43   Flaum, M, Arnot, S and Andreasen, N, "The Reality of 'Bizarre' Delusions" (1991) 32 *Compr Psychiat* 59. Because the DSM–III–R refers specifically to bizarre delusions, Flaum et al gave a group of psychiatrists (ranging from experts to residents) forty delusions and asked them to divide them into bizarre and non-bizarre delusions, using structured definitions. Interrater reliability was low. Reviewed in Altman and Jobe, above n 40 p 37.

44   Lehmann, H, "Schizophrenia: Clinical Features" in Freedman et al, above n 4 p 900.

45   Boeringa, J and Castellani, S, "Reliability and Validity of Emotional Blunting as a Criterion for Diagnosis of Schizophrenia" (1982) 139/9 *Amer J Psychiat* 1131.

46   Holzman, P, "Thought Disorder in Schizophrenia: Editor's Introduction" (1986) 12/3 *Schizophr B* 342.

47   Above n 17 p 188.

48   American Psychiatric Association, above n 21 p 276.

49   Andreasen, N, "Scale for the Assessment of Thought, Language, and Communication" (1986) 12/3 *Schizophr B* 473.

50   See Chaika, E, "Thought Disorder or Speech Disorder in Schizophrenia" (1982) 8/4 *Schizophr B* 587; Lanin-Kettering, I and Harrow, M, "'The Thought Behind the Words' A View of Schizophrenic Speech and Thinking Disorders" (1985) 11/1 *Schizophr B* 1.

51   Hays, P, "The Nosological Status of Schizophrenia" (1984) I *Lancet* 1342.

52   See, for example, Magrinat, G, Danziger, J, Lorenzo, I and Flemenbaum, A, "A Reassessment of Catatonia" (1983) 24/3 *Compr Psychiat* 218.

4

DEPRESSIVE DISORDERS

All psychiatric classifications are at their weakest when trying to cope with affective disorders, mainly because we have no externally valid methods of identifying boundaries between the current concepts of the various affective symptoms. Noting the number and severity of symptoms is all that we can do for the moment.[1]

Introduction

The term "depression" has both commonplace and technical meanings. It is used in everyday speech somewhat loosely to describe a variety of normal feelings such as sadness, unhappiness, despair, disappointment, grief and alienation. Technically, it is reserved for abnormal or pathological states and can be used in three ways: to describe either a mood, a symptom or a syndrome.

When it is used to describe a mood it means something more than just normal sadness or unhappiness although there is no clear cut-off point between the two. Hamilton uses the following analogy to illustrate the problem:

> In the spectrum we can distinguish between green and blue, but there is a point between them where it cannot be said that the colour is definitely either one or the other. That does not signify that there is no real difference between the two colours.[2]

Hamilton suggests that the point at which normality shades over into abnormality depends upon: (1) how unrelated or out of proportion the mood appears to be to external events, and (2) the degree to which it affects other aspects of the personality, such as thinking, judgement and behaviour. The difference between normality and abnormality is also an existential one. As Hamilton points out:

> Some patients, who are sufficiently fluent and capable of expressing themselves, will say that the abnormal mood is clearly distinguishable from dejection, unhappiness and misery. In what way this is so, they cannot explain in a manner which can be understood, because our comprehension of the moods and feelings of others depends on our ability to recognise the similarity between our own experience and what they are indicating by words and behaviour.[3]

A pathologically depressed mood is a characteristic symptom of the depressive disorders but it is not restricted to them as it can also occur as a symptom in a range of physical illnesses, such as influenza, and in other psychiatric disorders, such as schizophrenia. The ICD–10, for example, has a specific category of post-schizophrenic depression.

This chapter is concerned mainly with the depressive disorders; that is, with the specific psychiatric syndromes characterised by the presence of a pathologically depressed mood.

Descriptions of depressive disorders, both literary and clinical, date back to antiquity. One of the earliest can be found in Homer's *Iliad* in the ninth century BC. As Zilboorg points out, "the Homeric tradition was theurgic: man becomes mentally ill because the gods take his mind away".[4] One of Homer's characters, Bellerophon, offends the gods and for this he is condemned to wander "evermore alone through his Aleian field" and to feed "upon the core of his sad bosome, flying all the loth'd consorts of men".[5]

Hippocrates, in the fourth century BC, included melancholia (states of abnormal depression) in his classification of psychiatric disorders.[6] He described it as a "difficult disease" which would prove fatal unless treated adequately and properly.[7]

Over the ensuing centuries many authors[8] and scientists have added to our knowledge of the depressive disorders but, as Hamilton points out, in spite of this, no classification "has been really satisfactory".[9] Some idea of the nature of the problem can be gleaned from the plethora of labels used to describe depressive disorders in the DSM and ICD classifications.

DSM–I[10]

Under the general heading of Psychotic Disorders, the DSM–I (1952) described three different types of depressive disorders — manic-depressive reaction (with three subtypes: manic, depressed and other); psychotic depressive reaction (in which there was evidence of gross misinterpretation of reality but which was caused by environmental factors); and involutional psychotic reaction, "characterized most commonly by depression occurring in the involutional period . . . and usually in individuals of compulsive personality type. . . Some cases are characterized chiefly by depression and others chiefly by paranoid ideas".[11]

Under the general heading of Psychoneurotic Disorders it listed a depressive reaction which, like the psychotic depressive reaction, was precipitated by environmental factors.

ICD–9[12]

Under the general heading of *Affective psychoses*, the ICD–9 (1977) described a manic-depressive psychosis with eight subtypes, one of which, the manic-depressive psychosis, depressed type, was clinically identical with depressive psychosis, endogenous depression, involutional melancholia, monopolar depression and psychotic depression.

Under the general heading of *Other nonorganic psychoses*, it described a depressive type with symptoms similar to those of a manic-depressive psychosis, depressed type, but "apparently provoked by saddening stress".[13] Other names for this were reactive depressive psychosis and psychogenic depressive psychosis.

Under the general heading of *neurotic disorders* it described a neurotic depression "characterized by disproportionate depression which has usually recognisably ensued on a distressing experience".[14] Alternative names for the neurotic depression were anxiety depression, depressive reaction, neurotic depressive state and reactive depression.

Under the general heading of *Adjustment reaction* it described a brief depressive reaction "in which the depressive symptoms are usually closely related in time and content to some stressful event";[15] and a prolonged depressive reaction "usually developing in association with prolonged exposure to a stressful situation".[16]

Finally, there was a classification known as depressive disorder, not elsewhere classified, which was to be used for "states of depression, usually of moderate but occasionally of marked intensity, which have no specifically manic-depressive or other psychotic depressive features and which do not appear to be associated with stressful events or other features specified under neurotic depression".[17]

ICD–10[18]

In the ICD–10 (1992), depressive disorders are grouped under the general heading of Mood (affective) disorders with the following categories:

1 Bipolar affective disorder, with three manic subtypes, three depressive subtypes and four other subtypes. The three depressive subtypes are Bipolar affective disorder, current episode mild or moderate depression (with or without somatic symptoms); Bipolar affective disorder, current episode severe depression without psychotic symptoms; and Bipolar affective disorder, current episode severe depression with psychotic symptoms.

2 Depressive episode, with six subtypes — Mild depressive episode (with or without somatic symptoms); Moderate depressive episode (with or without somatic symptoms); Severe depressive episode without psychotic symptoms; Severe depressive episode with psychotic symptoms; Other depressive disorders; and Depressive episode, unspecified.

3 Recurrent depressive disorder, with six subtypes identical with those in (2), except that they are recurrent instead of single episode.

4 Persistent mood (affective) disorders, under which four disorders are listed — Cyclothymia; Dysthymia; Other persistent mood (affective) disorders; and Persistent mood (affective) disorder, unspecified.

5   Other mood (affective) disorders.

6   Unspecified mood (affective) disorder, which is "to be used only as a last resort, when no other term can be applied".[19]

There are also two subcategories under the general heading of Neurotic, stress-related and somatoform disorders called, Other anxiety disorders and Reaction to severe stress, and adjustment disorders. In the first there is a disorder called "Mixed anxiety and depressive disorder". In the second there is a disorder called "Mixed anxiety and depressive reaction".

The DSM–IV and ICD–10 also have classifications for schizo-affective disorders, which the ICD–10 defines as "episodic disorders in which both affective and schizophrenic symptoms are prominent within the same period of illness, preferably simultaneously, but at least within a few days of each other".[20]

Finally, the ICD–10 has a category under the general heading of Schizophrenia, schizotypal and delusional disorders, of post-schizophrenic depression which is a "depressive disorder, which may be prolonged, arising in the aftermath of a schizophrenic illness".[21]

DSM-IV

In the DSM-IV depressive disorders are grouped under the general heading of Mood Disorders, with the following categories:

Mood Episodes

Major Depressive Episode ("at least two weeks of depressed mood or loss of interest accompanied by at least four additional symptoms of depression")[22]

Manic Episode

Mixed Episode ("a period of time (lasting at least a week) in which the criteria are met for a Manic Episode and for a Major Depressive Episode nearly every day")[23]

Hypomanic Episode

Depressive Disorder

Major Depressive Disorder ("one or more Major Depressive Episodes")[24]

Dysthymic Disorder ("at least two years of depressed mood for more days than not, accompanied by additional depressive symptoms that do not meet criteria for a Major Depressive Episode")[25]

Depressive Disorder Not Otherwise Specified

Bipolar Disorders

Bipolar I Disorder ("one or more Manic or Mixed Episodes, usually accompanied by Major Depressive Episodes")[26]

Bipolar II Disorder ("one or more Major Depressive Episodes accompanied by at least one Hypomanic Episode")[27]

Cyclothymic Disorder ("at least two years of numerous periods of hypomanic symptoms that do not meet criteria for a Manic Episode and numerous periods of depressive symptoms that do not meet criteria for a Major Depressive Episode")[28]

Bipolar Disorder Not Otherwise Specified

Other Mood Disorders

Mood Disorder Due to a General Medical Condition

Substance-Induced Mood Disorder

Mood Disorder Not Otherwise Specified

In addition to the above categories the DSM-IV also lists "Specifiers describing the most recent mood episode" and "Specifiers describing course of recurrent episodes".[29]

Unitary and binary approaches to classification

The easiest way to sift through the welter of diagnostic categories and labels is to trace the development of the nosology of depressive disorders. Before the 1970s, there were two main approaches to classification — the unitary and the binary.[30]

In the first, depression is viewed as a unitary concept, varying from mild to severe along a continuum. At the mild end of the spectrum the symptoms are less severe. They include a depressed mood, feelings of hopelessness, worthlessness and guilt, low self-esteem, altered appetite, sleep disturbance, low energy, fatigue, poor concentration, a diminished capacity for enjoyment, and loss of interest. At the severe end of the spectrum, the symptoms are more severe and there are, in addition, (a) certain symptoms that are more pronounced at that end of the spectrum, such as suicidal thoughts and suicidal attempts, and (b) certain symptoms that only occur at that end of the spectrum such as delusions and psychomotor retardation.

In the second approach, a binary concept is employed. According to this approach there are at least two types of depressive disorder which differ in their symptoms, etiology and outcome.

The first type of depressive disorder has a number of labels in which the terms "neurotic", "exogenous" and "reactive" occur in various combinations, for example "neurotic depression", "neurotic depressive reaction", "exogenous depressive reaction", "depressive reaction", "reactive depression". This type of depressive disorder was thought to be caused mainly by stress factors, especially those associated with some current situation, such as a significant loss.

The second type of depressive disorder also has a number of different names, such as "psychotic depressive reaction", "endogenous depressive reaction", and "depressive psychosis". Its cause or causes were uncertain but they were thought to be multifactorial. Psychodynamic, behavioural, sociological, existential and biological factors have all been suggested as possible contributors, although biological factors have generally been considered to have more weight than the others.[31]

Some of the differences between these two types of depression are set out in the following table from Maddison, Day and Leabeater's 1965 textbook on psychiatric nursing.[32] Similar tables can be found in a number of textbooks of that era and, indeed, in textbooks up to the 1980s.[33] The Royal Australian and New Zealand College of Psychiatrists utilised the binary concept in a Quality Assurance Project in 1982.[34]

	Psychotic depression	Neurotic depression
1.	Environmental changes have little or no effect on depression	Mood may lift in cheerful company
3.	Sleep disturbance always severe. Early morning waking characteristic (delayed insomnia)	Sleep disturbance may or may not be present, if so there is difficulty getting off to sleep (initial insomnia)
3.	Retardation of thought and action is common	No retardation in physiological sense but may complain of fatigue
4.	Speech slowed as part of process of retardation	Usually talkative, keen to discuss symptoms and frequently complains a lot
5.	Physical symptoms are marked. They include anorexia, weight loss, impotence, amenorrhoea, and commonly constipation	Anorexia and weight loss less marked and may even be absent. Impotence, amenorrhoea and constipation are not associated physiological symptoms
6.	Delusions are commonly present	Delusions never present
7.	Patient tends to blame himself for his state	Patient usually blames others or his environment for his state

Some textbooks added diurnal variation to the above table, the depression being worse in the mornings in a psychotic depression and worse in the afternoons in a neurotic depression.

Although Bright had proposed a binary classification for depressive disorders in the sixteenth century,[35] the unitary approach was the predominant one through to the late nineteenth century when Kraepelin introduced his new classification of mental disorders. In it he divided depressive disorders into two main types — those which had an organic cause (a claim for which he had little evidence at the time) and those which were reactions to life events. This binary concept took over from the unitary one and, despite some serious challenges from the unitary camp in the late 1920s and 1930s,[36] it was well established by the 1950s and 1960s. By the 1970s, however, it was apparent that the binary concept, whether it was conceptualised on a neurotic-psychotic dimension or a reactive-endogenous dimension, was not sustainable on either clinical or experimental grounds. As Nemiah pointed out in 1976: "most patients fall into a middle ground where the criteria are mixed and lines of differentiation are blurred into nonexistence".[37]

The problem with the binary concept is that it is far too simplistic and confuses several separate issues. It tends to equate "neurotic" with "reactive" and "mild", and "psychotic" with "endogenous" and "severe". This is a mistake. These terms actually represent three quite separate pairs of factors. The neurotic-psychotic dichotomy (or continuum, depending upon how you look at it), refers to the nature of the symptoms present. "Psychotic" here means the presence of such symptoms as delusions, hallucinations, severe psychomotor retardation and somatic symptoms. The second dichotomy is the reactive-endogenous one. "Reactive" (or exogenous) means that there are identifiable environmental events, such as a severe loss, which can be demonstrated to play some part in the etiology of the disorder. "Endogenous" means that the causes are internal ones, either unconscious psychodynamic factors or organic factors or both. Psychotic symptoms can occur in response to environmental stress just as neurotic ones can. The descriptions of psychotic depression in the DSM–I and of other nonorganic psychoses-depressive type in the ICD–9, as well as everyday clinical experience, make this quite clear. The mild to severe continuum can apply to both reactive and endogenous depression and to neurotic and psychotic depression.

The current situation

If one could attempt to summarise where current thinking is on the subject of depressive disorders, it would be fair to say that most Australian psychiatrists would probably agree upon the following two points:

Major Depressive Episode

There is a definable psychiatric syndrome with some or all of the features described in the DSM–IV as a *"Major Depressive Episode"* (which is identical to a "Major Depressive Disorder, Single Episode"), and in the ICD–10 as a "Depressive episode". Although the two definitions are different in a number of ways, they describe a similar group of symptoms. A Major Depressive Episode is described in the DSM–IV as follows:

> Five (or more) of the following symptoms have been present during the same 2 week period and represent a change from previous functioning; at least one of the symptoms is either (1) depressed mood or (2) loss of interest or pleasure.

51

(1) depressed mood most of the day, nearly every day, as indicated by either subjective report (eg feels sad or empty) or observation made by others (eg appears tearful). Note: In children and adolescents can be irritable mood.

(2) markedly diminished interest or pleasure in all, or almost all, activities most of the day, nearly every day (as indicated by either subjective account or observation made by others)

(3) significant weight loss when not dieting or weight gain (eg, a change of more than 5 per cent of body weight in a month), or decrease or increase in appetite nearly every day. Note: In children, consider failure to make expected weight gains.

(4) insomnia or hypersomnia nearly every day

(5) psychomotor agitation or retardation nearly every day (observable by others, not merely subjective feelings of restlessness or being slowed down)

(6) fatigue or loss of energy nearly every day

(7) feelings of worthlessness or excessive or inappropriate guilt (which may be delusional) nearly every day (not merely self-reproach or guilt about being sick)

(8) diminished ability to think or concentrate, or indecisiveness, nearly every day (either by subjective account or as observed by others)

(9) recurrent thoughts of death (not just fear of dying), recurrent suicidal ideation without a specific plan, or a suicide attempt or a specific plan for committing suicide[38]

Apart from the symptoms themselves, a further criterion for a major depressive episode is that "the symptoms cause clinically significant distress or impairment in social, occupational or other important areas of functioning".[39]

A major depressive episode may be of varying degrees of severity — mild, moderate or severe. Assessment of the degree of severity is done on the basis of "the number of criteria symptoms, the severity of the symptoms, and the degree of functional disability and distress".[40] The degrees of severity are defined as follows:

Mild:	Few, if any, symptoms in excess of those required to make the diagnosis and symptoms result in only minor impairment in occupational functioning or in usual social activities or relationships with others.
Moderate:	Symptoms of functional impairment between "mild" and "severe".
Severe Without Psychotic Features:	Several symptoms in excess of those required to make the diagnosis, and symptoms markedly interfere with occupational functioning or with usual social activities or relationships with others.
Severe With Psychotic Features:	Delusions or hallucinations.[41]

When delusions and hallucinations are present they may be mood-congruent or mood-incongruent. The content of mood-congruent delusions and hallucinations "is entirely consistent with the typical depressive themes of personal inadequacy, guilt, disease, death, nihilism or deserved punishment".[42] The content of mood-incongruent delusions and hallucinations has other themes such as "persecutory delusions (not directly related to depressive themes), thought insertion, thought broadcasting, and delusions of control".[43]

The DSM-IV criteria for Melancholic Features Specifier are interesting as they contain most of the symptoms that were originally used as diagnostic criteria for a psychotic depressive reaction. They are:

A. Either of the following, occurring during the most severe period of the current episode:

(1) loss of pleasure in all, or almost all, activities

(2) lack of reactivity to usually pleasurable stimuli (does not feel much better, even temporarily, when something good happens)

B. Three (or more) of the following:

(1) distinct quality of depressed mood (ie the depressed mood is experienced as distinctly different from the kind of feeling experienced after the death of a loved one)

(2) depression regularly worse in the morning

(3) early morning awakening (at least two hours before usual time of awakening)

(4) marked psychomotor retardation or agitation

(5) significant anorexia or weight loss

(6) excessive or inappropriate guilt.[44]

The ICD-10 (see below) describes a similar (though not identical) group of symptoms as "somatic" symptoms and questions whether they need to be separately identified or not. The IDC-10 states:

It is acknowledged that . . . [they] could also have been called "melancholic", "vital", "biological", or "endogenomorphic", and that the scientific status of the syndrome is in any case somewhat questionable. It is to be hoped that the result of its inclusion here will be widespread critical appraisal of the usefulness of its separate identification.[45]

In the ICD–10 a Depressive episode is defined as follows:

[The] individual usually suffers from depressed mood, loss of interest and enjoyment, and reduced energy leading to increased fatiguability and diminished activity. Marked tiredness after only slight effort is common. Other common symptoms are: (a) reduced concentration and attention; (b) reduced self-esteem and confidence; (c) ideas of guilt and unworthiness (even in a mild type of episode); (d) bleak and pessimistic views of the future; (e) ideas or acts of self-harm or suicide; (f) disturbed sleep; (g) diminished appetite.

The lowered mood varies little from day to day, and is often unresponsive to circumstances, yet may show a characteristic diurnal variation as the day goes on... . In some cases, anxiety, distress, and motor agitation may be more prominent at times than the depression, and the mood change may also be masked by added features such as irritability, excessive consumption of alcohol, histrionic behaviour, and exacerbation of pre-existing phobic or obsessional symptoms, or by hypochondriacal preoccupations. For depressive episodes of all three grades of severity, a duration of at least 2 weeks is usually required for diagnosis, but shorter periods may be reasonable if symptoms are unusually severe and of rapid onset.

Some of the above symptoms may be marked and develop characteristic features that are widely regarded as having special clinical significance. The most typical examples of these "somatic" symptoms are: loss of interest or pleasure in activities that are normally enjoyable; lack of emotional reactivity to normally pleasurable surroundings and events; waking in the morning 2 hours or more before the usual time; depression worse in the morning; objective evidence of definite psychomotor retardation or agitation (remarked on or reported by other people); marked loss of appetite; weight loss (often defined as 5 per cent or more of body weight in the past month); marked loss of libido. Usually, this somatic syndrome is not regarded as present unless about four of these symptoms are definitely present.[46]

Like the DSM–IV, the ICD–10 also distinguishes three grades of severity — mild, moderate and severe but they differ in detail to the grades of severity described in the DSM-IV.

Bipolar Disorder

There is a disorder known variously as a bipolar disorder (DSM–IV),[47] a bipolar affective disorder (ICD–10), or a manic-depressive illness, psychosis or reaction. The disorder is characterised by the presence of various combinations of hypomanic or manic episodes[48] and depressive episodes alternating over time. The depressive episodes are clinically identical with either a major depressive episode (DSM–IV) or a depressive episode (ICD–10). Bipolar disorders were first described by Aretaeus of Cappadocia in the first century AD.[49]

There is also a chronic condition known as cyclothymia (or cyclothymic disorder) which is characterised by the presence of various combinations of mild mood disturbances (both elated and depressed moods) alternating over a long period of time, usually a lifetime. Cyclothymia is usually classified as a personality disorder.

As already noted, there would probably be a reasonable level of agreement among Australian psychiatrists about the above two groups of conditions. This would not be the case with the following two.

1. Dysthymic Disorder

The DSM–III–R called this dysthymia and referred to it as a depressive neurosis. From the description in the DSM–III–R and the DSM-IV it appears to be closer to what has been described as a depressive personality. The uncertainty about the existence of this disorder as a separate entity can be demonstrated by following its course in the literature. Bleuler, in his 1924 textbook, described a condition called constitutional ill-temper or depressive disposition ("melancholic mood") which had the following features: "a protracted dark emotional coloration of all life experiences, difficulty in making resolutions; lack of self-confidence".[50] It is not mentioned in Henderson and Gillespie's 1950 textbook.[51] Noyes and Kolb, in their 1958 textbook, describe a melancholic personality but it is not clear whether they see it as a separate personality type or as one pole of a cyclothymic personality.[52] In Meyer-Gross, Slater and Roth's 1960 textbook there is a condition called The Constitutional Depressive, which is described as follows:

> This temperament frequently passes unrecognized because the constitutional depressive is quiet, reserved, and likes to remain in the background. He takes everything as a heavy burden and is always inclined to see the sad side of any event. He is pessimistic, easily moved to tears or to prolonged brooding and lacks self-confidence. He is . . . not always sad, but he responds more easily to depressing events. . . While most of these persons lack somewhat in energy and drive, yet they are efficient within restricted fields, for example as Civil servants or scientists.[53]

It is not mentioned in the DSM–I or the ICD–9. In 1980, Arieti and Bemporad, in their analysis of premorbid types of depressive personality, based on a longitudinal study of 40 depressed patients over two decades, described:

> a form of chronic character structure or personality . . . [in which] depression appears to be a constant mode of feeling lurking in the background during everyday life. . . [Such individuals] suffer from a chronic, mild sense of futility and hopelessness, which results from a lack of involvement in everyday activities. There is also a sense of emptiness because they do not develop deep relationships for fear of being exploited or rejected.[54]

In the DSM–III and the ICD–10 it reappears as Dysthymia, becomes Dysthymic Disorder in the DSM-IV and is described in the latter as follows:

> The essential feature of Dysthymic Disorder is a chronically depressed mood that occurs for most of the day more days than not for at least two years. Individuals with Dysthymic Disorder describe their mood as sad or "down in the dumps". In children, the mood may be irritable rather than depressed, and the required minimum duration is only 1 year. During periods of depressed mood, at least two of the following additional symptoms are present: poor appetite or overeating, insomnia or hypersomnia, low energy or fatigue, low self-esteem, poor concentration or difficulty making decisions, and feelings of hopelessness. Individuals may note the prominent presence of low interest and self-criticism, often seeing themselves as uninteresting or incapable.[55]

The ICD–10 definition is slightly different but describes much the same condition. According to the ICD–10: "Sufferers usually have periods of days or weeks when they describe themselves as well, but most of the time (often for months at a time) they feel tired and depressed; everything is an effort and nothing is enjoyed".[56]

Whether it should be considered a psychiatric disorder or simply part of the human condition is arguable.

2. Neurotic Depressive Reaction

There is no doubt that, in response to stress, especially loss, people can develop depressive disorders ranging from a major depressive episode to an adjustment disorder with depressed mood. The question is whether there is such an entity as the neurotic depressive reaction described above in the discussion on the binary approach to classification. Some psychiatrists still see it as a useful category and support its continued use. Others feel that the symptoms are simply part of a larger neurotic picture and that there is no justification for treating it as a separate psychiatric entity at all. The case for the latter view has been put quite forcibly by Parker et al:

> According to Kiloh et al, 'so-called neurotic depression is a diffuse entity encompassing some of the ways in which the patient utilises his defence mechanisms to cope with his own neuroticism and current environmental stress'. We go further, however, by arguing that there is no neurotic depressive 'entity' — be it circumscribed or diffuse, and that what has been so described is a residual collection of disorders, equally diffuse in terms of likely aetiological factors and clinical patterns. We suggest that a pseudo-entity was created and reified by the interpretation of early factor analytic studies, and that it lacks any consistent clinical features, which has frustrated attempts to make a positive diagnosis and precluded identification of aetiological risk factors and treatment responses.[57]

Conclusion

In spite of the fact that depressive disorders have been described and studied for nearly three millennia, their classification is far from settled. According to Mollica:

> The disease concept called mood disorder is a convention; the clinical criteria for defining it are artificial. . . There are no final arbitrators of the validity of the classification system for mood disorders that can serve as a final and independent test.[58]

As the authors of the ICD-10 point out:

> It seem likely that psychiatrists will continue to disagree about the classification of disorders of mood until methods of dividing the clinical syndromes are developed that rely at least in part upon physiological or biochemical measurement, rather than being limited as at present to clinical descriptions of emotions and behaviour. As long as this limitation persists, one of the major choices lies between a comparatively simple classification with only a few degrees of severity, and one with greater details and more subdivisions.[59]

While there are some points of agreement between the major classifications (the DSM–IV and the ICD–10) there are many differences as well. There is also disagreement among psychiatrists as to how depressive disorders are to be categorised, labelled and defined. Given this, and given the fact that people with depressive disorders do not present regularly with one of the classic textbook or ICD or DSM descriptions, what is important, from a forensic point of view, is not the diagnostic label but an accurate description of the depth of the depression, its associated signs and symptoms, and the effect that they are having on the person's thinking and behaviour.

What is needed is a full and detailed description of how the depressed person is responding to and reacting to the symptoms described and of the nature and extent of the social and occupational impairment and the disability that the symptoms are causing.

It is only when the court is in possession of the fullest possible description of the defendant's depressive disorder, along the lines suggested above, that it will be in a position to consider the relationship, if any, between the depression and the criminal activity of which the defendant is accused.

NOTES

1   Cooper, J, "On the Publication of the Diagnostic and Statistical Manual of Mental Disorders: Fourth Edition (DSM-IV)" (1995) 166 *Brit J Psychiat* 6.

2   Hamilton, M, "Frequency of Symptoms in Melancholia (Depressive Illness)" (1989) 154 *Brit J Psychiat* 201.

3   Id.

4   Zilboorg, G, *A History of Medical Psychology* (1967) p 37.

5   Starobinski, J, *History of the Treatment of Melancholy from the Earliest Times to 1900* (1962) p 11.

6   Hippocrates' classification of mental diseases also included epilepsy, mania and paranoia, although the latter term meant something quite different to what it means today. Melancholia literally means 'black bile'. Black bile, blood, yellow bile and phlegm were considered to be the four natural humours of the body. While they were in balance, a person stayed healthy. An excess of black bile led to depression. See Starobinski, above n 5 p 12.

7   Ibid p 15.

8   Chaucer, in the fourteenth century, in *The Book of the Duchess*, gave the following description of a case of melancholia which some think is an autobiographical account of his own depression: 'For sorrowful imagination is always wholly in my mind. . . This melancholy and dread I have for dying, default of sleep and heaviness have slain my spirit of quickness that I have lost all happiness'. Mora, G, "Historical and Theoretical Trends in Psychiatry" in Freedman, A, Kaplan, H and Sadock, B (eds), *Comprehensive Textbook of Psychiatry–II* (1975) p 24.

In 1621, Robert Burton, an English divine, produced *The Anatomy of Melancholy*, a book that was so popular that it went through five editions in Burton's own lifetime and three more in the following century. He wrote the book, in which nearly a thousand authors are cited, not only to 'helpe others out of a fellow feeling' but to rid himself of its symptoms: 'I write of Melancholy, by being busie to avoid Melancholy . . . to exercise my selfe . . . to ease my mind.' Hunter, R and Macalpine, I, *Three Hundred Years of Psychiatry* (1963) p 94.

9   Hamilton, M, "Mood Disorders: Clinical Features" in Kaplan, H and Sadock, B, (eds) *Comprehensive Textbook of Psychiatry* (5th ed; 1989) p 893.

10   American Psychiatric Association, *Diagnostic and Statistical Manual — Mental Disorders* (1952).

11   Ibid p 24.

12   World Health Organization, *International Classification of Diseases* (vol 1; 1977).

13   Ibid p 188.

14   Ibid p 192.

15   Ibid p 205.

16   Id.

17   Ibid p 207.

18   World Health Organization, *The ICD–10 Classification of Mental and Behavioural Disorders* (1992).

19   Ibid p 131.

20   Ibid p 105.

21   Ibid p 93.

22   American Psychiatric Association, *Diagnostic and Statistical Manual of Mental Disorders* (4th ed, 1994) p 317.

23   Ibid p 333.

24   Ibid p 317.

25   Id.

26   Id.

27   Ibid p 318.

28   Id.

29   Ibid p 319.

30   Nemiah, J, "Depressive Neurosis" in Freedman, Kaplan and Sadock, above n 8 p 1255.

31   Akiskal, H and McKinney, W, "Overview of recent research in depression. Integration of ten conceptual models into a comprehensive clinical frame" (1975) 32 *Archiv Gen Psychiat* 285.

32   Maddison, D, Day, P and Leabeater, B, *Psychiatric Nursing* (1965) p 238.

33   See, for example, Sainsbury, M and Lambeth, L, *Sainsbury's Key to Psychiatry* (1988) p 277.

34   Royal Australian and New Zealand College of Psychiatrists, "A Treatment Outline For Depressive Disorders" (1983) 17 *ANZ J Psychiat* 129.

35   In 1586, Timothy Bright, a physician to St Bartholomew's Hospital in London, wrote *A Treatise of Melancholie*.

> Bright distinguished two kinds of melancholy: the first where the 'perill is not of body' but 'proceedeth from the mindes apprehension' requiring 'cure of the minde', that is, psychotherapy. The second 'being not moved by any adversity present or imminent' in which the melancholy humour 'deluding the organicall actions, abuseth the minde' needed physical treatment, since 'no counsel of philosophy, nor precept of wise men were comparable to calme these raging passions, unto the purging potions of Physitians.' (Hunter and Macalpine, above n 8 p 36.)

36   Nemiah, above n 30 p 1255.

37   Ibid p 1256.

38   American Psychiatric Association, above n 22 p 327.

39   Id.

40   Ibid p 376.

41   Ibid pp 377-378.

42   Ibid p 378.

43   Id.

44   Ibid p 384.

45   World Health Organisation, above n18 p 112.

46   Above n 18 p 119.

47   For a person to be diagnosed as having a bipolar disorder, at least one episode of hypomania or mania and one of major depression must have occurred. Unipolar affective disorders are episodes, either single or recurrent, of hypomania or mania, or major depression, by themselves.

48   Mania is at the opposite end of the mood spectrum to depression. The ICD–10 describes three grades — hypomania, mania without psychotic symptoms and mania with psychotic symptoms. Mania without psychotic symptoms is described as follows:

> Mood is elevated out of keeping with the individual's circumstances and may vary from carefree joviality to almost uncontrollable excitement. Elation is accompanied by increased energy, resulting in overactivity, pressure of speech, and a decreased need for sleep. Normal social inhibitions are lost, attention cannot be sustained, and there is often marked distractability. Self-esteem is inflated, and grandiose or over-optimistic ideas are freely expressed... The individual may embark on extravagant and impractical schemes, spend money recklessly, or become aggressive, amorous, or facetious in inappropriate circumstances. In some manic episodes the mood is irritable and suspicious rather than elated (World Health Organization, above n 18 p 114).

49   Aretaeus saw that mania and melancholia could occur separately or in combination, thus anticipating the theory of unipolar and bipolar illness by almost two millennia. See Zilboorg, above n 4 p 74.

50   Bleuler, E, *Textbook of Psychiatry* (1924) p 485.

51   Henderson, D and Gillespie, R, *A Text-Book of Psychiatry for Students and Practitioners* (1950).

52   Noyes, A and Kolb, L, *Modern Clinical Psychiatry* (1958) p 36.

53   Mayer-Gross, W, Slater, E and Roth, M, *Clinical Psychiatry* (1960) p 206.

54   Arieti, S and Bemporad, J, "The Psychological Organization of Depression" (1980) 137 *Amer J Psychiat* 1362.

55   American Psychiatric Association above n 22 p 345.

56   World Health Organisation, above n 18 p 130.

57   Parker, G, Hall, W, Boyce, P, Hadzi-Pavlovic, D, Mitchell, P, Wilhelm, K Brodaty, H, Hickie, I and Eyers, K, "Depression Sub-Typing: Unitary, Binary or Arbitrary?" (1991) 25 *ANZ J Psychiatry* 64.

58   Mollica, R, "Mood Disorders: Epidemology" in Kaplan and Sadock, above n 9 p 860.

59   World Health Organisation, above n 18 p 13.

5

PSYCHOPATHY

The terms "psychopathy", or "psychopathic disorder", and "psychopath" are no longer used as frequently as they once were in psychiatry, although they are still common in everyday speech. "Psychopath" has been replaced in psychiatric textbooks and psychiatric classifications with such terms as "sociopath" (which can also be used in a broader sense to include such categories as alcohol and drug dependency and psychosexual disorders), "antisocial personality disorder" (DSM–IV) and "dissocial personality disorder" (ICD–10). What these terms mean and whether certain types of antisocial behaviour should be considered manifestations of a specific underlying personality disorder in some people, are the subjects of this chapter. In spite of the fact that the ICD-10 and the DSM-IV no longer use the term, "psychopathy" and its derivatives will be used in this chapter instead of "antisocial personality disorder" for reasons that will become clearer later.

EARLY DEVELOPMENT OF THE CONCEPT

The first recorded case of what appears to have been a psychopathic personality was described by Pinel in 1806. He used the term "manie sans delire" (mania without delirium) to describe the behaviour of a French peasant who had thrown a woman down a well in a fit of rage after the woman had abused him.[1]

In 1835, Prichard, an English psychiatrist, who was the first practising psychiatrist to be appointed a Commissioner in Lunacy, described a new group of mental disorders which he named "moral insanity".[2] The term was fairly broad at this stage and included a number of psychiatric syndromes other than what later became known as psychopathy. Prichard described moral insanity as:

> consisting in a morbid perversion of the feelings, affections, and active powers, without any illusion on erroneous conviction impressed upon the understanding . . . the varieties of moral insanity are perhaps as numerous as the modifications of feeling or passion in the human mind.[3]

As Rappeport points out, although the term "moral insanity" suited some members of the medical fraternity in that it provided a useful explanation of what was basically criminal behaviour, it concerned other professionals, especially lawyers and clergymen, who felt that linking morality and insanity in this way suggested that because these people were insane they could not be held responsible for their actions. Because of this concern, Koch in 1888 renamed the condition "psychopathic inferiority" and then "constitutional psychopathic inferiority".[4] It continued, however, to cause controversy. Tuke, in his 1892 Dictionary of psychological medicine, stated that moral insanity was:

> a form of mental illness, in regard to which so much difference of opinion exists among mental physicians . . . [that it] calls for dispassionate consideration, and a mode of treatment altogether free from heated assertion and dogmatism. We have no doubt that . . . the divergence of sentiment among medical men . . . is due to the want of definition of the terms employed in discussing the question. Probably those who entertain different views on moral insanity would agree in their recognition of certain cases, as clinical facts, but would label them differently.[5]

This would be a reasonable comment on the situation today.

In 1922, Visher gave the first exclusive description of a psychopathic personality, a description that Rappeport described, over 50 years later, as "an almost modern picture": "Extreme impulsivity, lack of concentration, marked egotism, and abnormal projection. The most critical disability of the patients centred around a guiltless, uninhibited social nihilism".[6]

The textbooks of the time were having a lot more difficulty with the concept. Bleuler, for example, in his 1924 textbook, following Kraepelin, included in his chapter on the psychopathies a wide range of conditions including "nervosity; aberrations of the sexual impulse; abnormal irritability; instability; special impulses; the eccentric; liars and swindlers; and constitutional ethical aberrations".[7]

Throughout the next three decades, however, the definition of the psychopathic personality was gradually narrowed and refined in the direction of Visher's 1922 definition.

THE 1950s

In 1950, Henderson and Gillespie described "psychopathic states" as follows. Their language gives some indication of the frustration being experienced in the management of these conditions:

> They constitute a rebellious, individualistic group who fail to fit in to their social milieu, and whose emotional instability is largely determined by a state of psychological immaturity which prevents them from adapting to reality and profiting from experience. They may be adult in years, but emotionally they are so slow and backward and uncontrolled that they behave like dangerous children. They lack judgment, foresight and ordinary prudence. It is the sheer stupidity of their conduct which is so appalling. 'The judicial, deciding, selecting processes described as intelligence, and the energising, emotivating, driving powers called character' do not work in harmony. They are the misfits of society, the despair of parents, doctors, ministers, lawyers and social workers.[8]

Henderson and Gillespie subdivided psychopathic states into three types: (1) predominantly aggressive; (2) predominantly inadequate and passive; and (3) predominantly creative, the latter being "intense, individualistic people who carve out a way for themselves irrespective of the obstacles which bestrew their path".[9] Henderson and Gillespie cite Joan of Arc, Napoleon and Lawrence of Arabia as examples of the last category.

Textbooks of that period were always several years behind the times, however, and by 1952 the concept of the psychopathic personality was sufficiently well-established for it to be included in the DSM–I.

The DSM–I took an interesting approach to the topic. It described two types — an "Antisocial reaction" and a "Dyssocial reaction" and included them both under the broader heading of "Sociopathic Personality Disturbance" which also included "Sexual Deviation" and "Addiction". It defined people with Sociopathic Personality Disturbances as being "ill primarily in terms of society and of conformity with the prevailing cultural milieu, and not only in terms of personal discomfort and relations with other individuals".[10]

"Antisocial reaction" referred to:

> chronically antisocial individuals who are always in trouble, profiting neither from experience nor punishment, and maintaining no real loyalties to any person, group, or code. They are frequently callous and hedonistic, showing marked emotional immaturity, with lack of sense of responsibility, lack of judgement, and an ability to rationalize their behaviour so that it appears warranted, reasonable, and justified.[11]

"Dyssocial reaction" referred to:

> individuals who manifest disregard for the usual social codes, and often come in conflict with them, as the result of having lived all their lives in an abnormal moral environment. They may be capable of strong loyalties. These individuals typically do not show significant personality deviations other than those implied by adherence to the value or code of their own predatory, criminal, or other social group.[12]

If the underlying etiology is assumed to include a super-ego deficiency of some sort, the division into two types makes sense. The antisocial personality or antisocial reaction can be seen to be the result of large gaps in the super-ego due to a failure to incorporate any, or very few, moral and cultural standards into the personality at the time the super-ego was being formed. The dyssocial personality or dyssocial reaction could be the result of incorporating sub-cultural standards (such as criminal standards) into the super-ego. The distinction between the two types was dropped in subsequent editions of the DSM.

In spite of the inclusion of these two conditions in the DSM–I there was still considerable argument about the nature of the psychopathic personality and whether or not it constituted a separate clinical entity at all. In 1956 the McCords, supporting the existence of the psychopathic personality, described the specific features differentiating the psychopath "from other deviants" as "[the] psychopath's underdeveloped conscience and his inability to identify with others".[13]

THE 1960s

In 1964, Cleckley, in his book *The Mask of Insanity*, described the following list of symptoms as characteristic of the psychopathic personality:

1 Superficial charm and good intelligence.
2 Absence of delusions and other signs of irrational thinking.
3 Absence of "nervousness" or psychoneurotic manifestations.
4 Unreliability.
5 Untruthfulness and insincerity.
6 Lack of remorse or shame.
7 Inadequately motivated antisocial behaviour.
8 Poor judgment and failure to learn by experience.
9 Pathological egocentricity and incapacity for love.
10 General poverty in major affective reactions.
11 Specific loss of insight.
12 Unresponsiveness in general interpersonal relations.
13 Fantastic and uninviting behaviour with drink and sometimes without.
14 Suicide rarely carried out.
15 Sex life impersonal, trivial and poorly integrated.
16 Failure to follow any life plan.[14]

Cleckley believed that the psychopath was able "only to mimic well-socialised human reactions without feeling the underlying sentiment".[15]

As Roth points out, considerable criticism has been levelled at Cleckley's profile, on such grounds as lack of specificity, subjectivity and social bias.[16] Nonetheless his work, especially his clinical descriptions, was quite influential at the time and has remained influential due to the work of Hare.

A survey of psychiatrists in Canada in 1964 (the same year as Cleckley's book was published) showed that the features they considered most significant in diagnosing psychopathy were:

1 Does not profit from experience.
2 Lacks a sense of responsibility.
3 Unable to form meaningful relationships.
4 Lacks control over impulses.
5 Lacks moral sense.
6 Chronically or recurrently antisocial.
7 Punishment does not alter behaviour.

8   Emotionally immature.

9   Unable to experience guilt.

10   Self-centered.[17]

Craft, in 1966, emphasised the psychopath's inability to love and feel affection, as well as "a liability to act on impulse without forethought". He also speaks of aggression, lack of shame or remorse, an inability to learn from experience, and lack of motivation.[18]

So by the mid 1960s, there was some general agreement starting to emerge among psychiatrists as to the type of symptoms that would constitute a diagnosis of the psychopathic personality. This was encapsulated in the DSM–II in 1968 which described the "antisocial personality" as follows:

> This term is reserved for individuals who are basically unsocialized and whose behaviour pattern brings them repeatedly into conflict with society. They are incapable of significant loyalty to individuals, groups, or social values. They are grossly selfish, callous, irresponsible, impulsive and unable to feel guilt or to learn from experience and punishment. Frustration tolerance is low. They tend to blame others or offer plausible rationalisations for their behaviour. A mere history of repeated legal or social offences is not sufficient to justify this diagnosis.[19]

It is important to note that up to this point it was the personality factors that were considered to be the most important part of the definition. The antisocial behaviour was considered to be a consequence of the personality deficits.

THE 1970s

In 1977, the ICD–9 described a "Personality disorder with predominantly sociopathic or asocial manifestations":

> Personality disorder characterised by disregard for social obligations, lack of feeling for others, and impetuous violence or callous unconcern. There is gross disparity between behaviour and the prevailing social norms. Behaviour is not readily modifiable by experience, including punishment. People with this personality are often affectively cold and may be abnormally aggressive or irresponsible. Their tolerance to frustration is low; they blame others or offer plausible rationalisations for the behaviour which brings them into conflict with society.[20]

THE 1980s

In 1980, the DSM–III listed the diagnostic criteria for "Antisocial Personality Disorder" as follows:

A   Current age at least 18.

B   Onset before age 15 as indicated by a history of three or more of the following before that age:

1 truancy (positive if it amounted to at least five days per year for at least two years, not including the last year of school);

2 expulsion or suspension from school for misbehaviour;

3 delinquency (arrested or referred to juvenile court because of behaviour;

4 running away from home overnight at least twice while living in parental or parental surrogate home;

5 persistent lying;

6 repeated sexual intercourse in a casual relationship;

7 repeated drunkenness or substance abuse;

8 thefts;

9 vandalism;

10 school grades markedly below expectations in relation to estimated or known IQ (may have resulted in repeating a year);

11 chronic violations of rules at home and/or at school (other than truancy);

12 initiation of fights.

C   At least four of the following manifestations of the disorder since age 18:

1 inability to sustain consistent work behaviour, as indicated by any of the following: (a) too frequent job changes (e.g. three or more jobs in five years not accounted for by nature of job or economic or seasonal fluctuation), (b) significant unemployment (e.g. six months or more in five years when expected to work), (c) serious absenteeism from work (e.g., average three days or more of lateness or absence per month, (d) walking off several jobs without other jobs in sight (Note: similar behaviour in an academic setting during the last few years of school may substitute for this criterion in individuals who by reason of their age or circumstances have not had an opportunity to demonstrate occupational adjustment);

2 lack of ability to function as a responsible parent as evidenced by one or more of the following: (a) child's malnutrition, (b) child's illness resulting from lack of minimal hygiene standards, (c) failure to obtain medical care for a seriously ill child, (d) child's dependence on neighbours or nonresident relatives for food or shelter, (e) failure to arrange for a caretaker for a child under six when parent is away from home, (f) repeated squandering, on personal items, of money required for household necessities;

3 failure to accept social norms with respect to lawful behaviour, as indicated by any of the following: repeated thefts, illegal occupation (pimping, prostitution, fencing, selling drugs), multiple arrests, a felony conviction;

4 inability to maintain enduring attachment to a sexual partner as indicated by two or more divorces and/or separations (whether legally married or not), desertion of spouse, promiscuity (ten or more sexual partners within one year);

5 irritability and aggressiveness as indicated by repeated physical fights or assault (not required by one's job or to defend someone or oneself), including spouse or child beating;

6   failure to honor financial obligations, as indicated by repeated defaulting on debts, failure to provide child support, failure to support other dependents on a regular basis;

7   failure to plan ahead, or impulsivity, as indicated by traveling from place to place without a prearranged job or clear goal for the period of travel or clear idea about when the travel would terminate, or lack of a fixed address for a month or more;

8   disregard for the truth as indicated by repeated lying, use of aliases, "conning" others for personal profit;

9   recklessness, as indicated by driving while intoxicated or recurrent speeding.

D   A pattern of continuous antisocial behaviour in which the rights of others are violated, with no intervening period of at least five years without antisocial behaviour between age 15 and the present time (except when the individual was bedridden or confined in a hospital or penal institution).

E   Antisocial behaviour is not due to either Severe Mental Retardation, Schizophrenia or manic episodes.[21]

The DSM-III represented a dramatic shift in approach. The personality factors that were previously considered to be the core of the disorder were, to a large extent, disregarded and the description of the antisocial personality disorder became a list of antisocial behaviours beginning in childhood or early adolescence and continuing through into adulthood. This was in line with the atheoretical and descriptive approach adopted in the DSM-III but it resulted in a category that was no longer in accord with traditional thinking on the subject.

In 1981, Davies and Feldman surveyed 34 forensic specialists in England (all working in the Prison Service) and asked them to rate 22 alleged signs of psychopathy in order of importance. Only 15 of the signs were considered to be important. The signs were ranked as follows (rating 10 = very important; rating 0 = not at all important), as shown in the table on the following page.[22]

It should be noted that in Davies and Feldman's study:

three psychiatrists were unwilling to rate the signs, and three more were unhappy with the global term psychopathy, preferring to think in terms of aggressive psychopaths, inadequate psychopaths, etc. Of those unwilling to rate, two did not believe in the concept of psychopathy as a clinical entity. Another five psychiatrists volunteered that they were reluctant to use the label psychopath because of its damning connotation. Various signs additional to the list supplied were suggested, although only one, namely that the person would probably be under 30 years, was mentioned twice. In response to the item on intelligence, three respondents thought that psychopaths were less, rather than more intelligent than average.[23]

	Sign	Mean Rating
1	Not profiting from experience	8.25
2	Lacking control over impulses	8.22
3	Chronically or recurrently antisocial	8.16
4	Lacking a sense of responsibility	7.53
5	Behaviour unaffected by punishment	7.50
6	Inability to form meaningful relationships	7.28
7	Emotional immaturity	7.28
8	Inability to experience guilt	7.25
9	Lack of moral sense	6.75
10	Deficiency in goal-directed behaviour	6.31
11	Self-centred	6.25
12	Frequent law-breaking	5.81
13	Frequent lying	5.75
14	Is aggressive	5.63
15	Occupationally unstable	5.45
16	Irresponsible sexual behaviour	4.03
17	Excessive alcohol consumption	3.84
18	Shows pronounced swings in mood	3.13
19	Abnormal EEG	3.00
20	Hyperactivity	1.25
21	More intelligent than average	1.19
22	Homosexuality	1.13

In 1987, the DSM–III–R refined the definition in the DSM–III. Section A was the same in both. In Section C in the DSM–III–R the wording was rearranged but the topics covered were very similar. One paragraph was added: "10 lacks remorse (feels justified in having hurt, mistreated, or stolen from another)".[24]

This was a significant change as it brought back into the definition one of the personality traits that earlier definitions, such a Cleckley's, considered an essential part of the definition.

Section B was changed and the changes appear to reflect the increasing violence among American youth:

B   Evidence of Conduct Disorder with onset before age 15, as indicated by a history of three or more of the following:

1   was often truant;

2   ran away from home overnight at least twice while living in parental or parental surrogate home (or once without returning);

3   often initiated physical fights;

4   used a weapon in more than one fight;

5   forced someone into sexual activity with him or her;

6   was physically cruel to animals;

7   was physically cruel to other people;

8   deliberately destroyed others' property (other than by fire-setting);

9   deliberately engaged in fire-setting;

10 often lied (other than to avoid physical or sexual abuse);

11 has stolen without confrontation of a victim on more than one occasion (including forgery);

12 has stolen with confrontation of a victim (e.g., mugging, purse-snatching, extortion, armed robbery.[25]

This definition, like its predecessor, was criticised on a number of counts. As Roth points out:

> traits widely recognised as characteristic, such as general poverty of emotional reactions, do not figure among the criteria. Yet they might be of central importance, as in the case of the emotionless psychopath whose sadistic assaults or murders are carried out without compunction or mercy.

> Other omissions include specific loss of insight and pathological egocentricity and the incapacity for love that flows from it. There is no direct reference to the range of self-damaging and socially dangerous forms of conduct: they may be manifest in sexual life, the spending and acquisition of money, driving, binge eating, alcohol and drug usage, and suicidal and self-mutilating behaviour, in which impulsiveness may be manifest. But they are noted as criteria in borderline personality disorder.[26]

THE 1990s

In 1992 the ICD–10 gave the disorder a new name again, calling it a "Dissocial personality disorder". Unlike the DSM–III–R which described the corresponding condition of Antisocial Personality Disorder mainly in terms of its behavioural manifestations, the ICD–10 described the Dissocial personality disorder in terms of the underlying personality characteristics present:

> Personality disorder, usually coming to attention because of a gross disparity between behaviour and the prevailing social norms, and characterised by:

> (a)   callous unconcern for the feelings of others;

> (b)   gross and persistent attitude of irresponsibility and disregard for social norms, rules and obligations;

> (c)   incapacity to maintain enduring relationships, though having no difficulty in establishing them;

> (d)   very low tolerance to frustration and a low threshold for discharge of aggression, including violence;

> (e)   incapacity to experience guilt and to profit from experience, particularly punishment;

(f)   marked proneness to blame others, or to offer plausible rationalizations, for the behaviour that has brought the patient into conflict with society.

There may also be persistent irritability as an associated feature. Conduct disorder during childhood and adolescence, though not invariably present, may further support the diagnosis.[27]

In 1994 the DSM-IV shortened the list of items in the DSM-III-R by deleting two – irresponsible parenting and failure to sustain a monogamous relationship – (which may be a reflection on what is defined as normal behaviour in modern American society), and collapsing two other items – failure to maintain consistent work behaviour or honour financial obligations – into one item called "consistent irresponsibility".[28]

Since 1980, Hare has been working on a checklist of items that could be used as a research tool in the field of psychopathy. Unimpressed with the DSM-III approach of excluding personality traits, Hare went back to Cleckley's 16-item description, field-tested it on a series of prisoners, expanded it into a 22-item version (the Psychopathy Checklist), and then revised it to a 20-item version (the PCL-R)[29] with the following items:

1   Glibness/superficial charm
2   Grandiose sense of self-worth
3   Need for stimulation/proneness to boredom
4   Pathological lying
5   Cunning/manipulative
6   Lack of remorse or guilt
7   Shallow affect
8   Callous/lack of empathy
9   Parasitic lifestyle
10   Poor behavioural controls
11   Promiscuous sexual behaviour
12   Early behaviour problems
13   Lack of realistic, long-term goals
14   Impulsivity
15   Irresponsibility
16   Failure to accept responsibility for own actions
17   Many short-term marital relationships
18   Juvenile delinquency
19   Revocation of conditional release
20   Criminal versatility[30]

As Hart et al point out:

> The PCL-R meets statistical criteria for a homogeneous measure of a unidimensional construct, yet research indicates that two stable factors underly it. . . Factor 1 reflects interpersonal and affective characteristics, such as egocentricity, manipulativeness, callousness, and a lack of remorse. . . Factor 2 reflects those characteristics of psychopathy associated with an impulsive, antisocial and unstable lifestyle or social deviance.[31]

The PCL-R was originally devised for "clinical use only in adult male forensic populations (offenders and forensic psychiatric patients)" but it is being increasingly used, following validation studies,[32 33] with younger male offenders and female offenders. In 1993, in response to our request from Monahan for a shorter but still valid version of the PCL-R which could be used as a screening tool in civil settings as well as forensic settings, Hart, Hare and Forth devised the Screening Version of the PCL (PCL:SV), which contains the following twelve items:

Part 1

1 Superficial

2 Grandiose

3 Manipulative

4 Lacks remorse

5 Lacks empathy

6 Doesn't accept responsibility

Part 2

7 Impulsive

8 Poor behavior controls

9 Lacks goals

10 Irresponsible

11 Adolescent antisocial behavior

12 Adult antisocial behavior[34]

DISCUSSION

There are two major problems here – the terminology and the clinical status, as an independent syndrome, of whatever it is that is being described. With regard to the terminology it will be clear from the above that there are a number of different terms that are often used synonymously by clinicians even though it is clear that their defining criteria differ in a number of ways, the major differences being whether the emphasis is on personality traits (as in the ICD-10 description of a "Dissocial personality disorder"), or antisocial behaviours (as in the DSM-IV description of "Antisocial Personality Disorder" or whether equal emphasis is given to both (as in Hare's PCL-R). Hare believes that the terms "psychopathy" and "antisocial personality disorder" should not be used synonymously. He sees the former (as he defines it) as being a much broader concept than the latter (as the DCM-IV defines it), although many of the features of the latter correspond to the social deviance components (Factor 2) of the former.

The second problem, the independent status of psychopathy as a separate syndrome, is a major one and it is not just an academic problem. Ever since the case of Byrne[35] it has been a major issue for forensic psychiatry. And, as Parker points out in his discussion of the Garry David case in Victoria, it is an issue which can have profound legal, personal, social and even economic consequences.[36]

Blackburn looked at this issue in a paper entitled "On Moral Judgements and Personality Disorders: The Myth of Psychopathic Personality Revisited" in 1988. As he points out:

> The most frequent objection to the concept has been that such a category is a fiction. Vaillant (1975), for example, regards it as a misleading stereotype, while Karpman (1984) claimed that it is "a myth . . . a nonexistent entity". Similarly, Wulach (1983) suggests that the notion of a specifically antisocial personality exaggerates the difference between the deviant and the conforming, while minimising individual variations among the antisocial. Counterclaims that the term is clinically meaningful commonly rest on anecdote, but Cleckley's concept of psychopathic personality has inspired research that seems to validate it to some extent. . . However, research findings have not been sufficiently consistent to eradicate suspicions that the term remains a speculative construct.[37]

After a detailed analysis of the concept he concludes:

> The current concept of psychopathic or antisocial personality remains 'a mythical entity'. The taxonomic error of confounding different universes of discourse has resulted in a diagnostic category that embraces a variety of deviant personalities. Such a category is not a meaningful focus for theory and research, nor can it facilitate clinical communication and prediction. . . Such a concept is little more than a moral judgement masquerading as a clinical diagnosis. Given the lack of demonstrable scientific or clinical utility of the concept, it should be discarded.[38]

Roth, on the other hand, believes that the concept is acceptable and clinically relevant but that "in its present stage of development . . . [it] is fuzzy at the edges and in need of refinement".[39] According to Roth:

> There is a wide consensus among psychiatrists and related disciplines regarding the main features of the psychopathic personality. . . It comprises forms of egotism, immaturity, aggressiveness, low frustration tolerance and inability to learn from experience that places the individual at high risk of clashing with any community that depends upon co-operation and individual responsibility of its members for its continued existence. It has a characteristic sex distribution, age of onset, family history of similar symptoms and disorders and family constellations and influences that show a large measure of consistency in their course and outcome.[40]

This may sound persuasive but what Roth is saying in sophisticated psychological language could equally well be translated as: "Some male children and adolescents are self-centred, prone to violence and criminal behaviour and don't learn from experience. It runs in families: like father, like son".

Those who, like Roth, believe in the existence of the psychopathic personality disorder would probably agree that the following description by Finlay-Jones accurately sums up their clinical impressions:

> Psychopathic disorder is thought to be a developmental disorder. It begins in childhood with symptoms and signs sufficient to make a DSM–III diagnosis of Conduct Disorder, and continuing through young adulthood until waning among people over 40 years of age. The parts of psychic life which are thought not to develop normally during childhood include the conscience, the ability to empathize, and the gaining of control over impulses to act violently. The symptoms and signs among adults include antisocial aggressive acts and impaired social relationships sufficient to diagnose Antisocial Personality Disorder. Other signs include impulsive behaviour, lack of remorse, and a tendency to blame others. There appears to be no unanimity over whether people with psychopathic disorder are enraged when they act aggressively, although it is a fundamental point.
>
> The British legal definition of psychopathic disorder is looser than its medical description, depending only on the presence of 'abnormally aggressive or seriously irresponsible conduct'. Psychopathic disorder, like Antisocial Personality Disorder, is not a synonym for antisocial behaviour in adults, but is rather one of its differential diagnoses.[41]

Finlay-Jones goes on, however, to suggest that on the basis of research evidence:

> Psychopathic disorder may consist of at least two syndromes, including one of psychological impairments such as egocentricity and callousness, and the other of social handicaps such as criminality and poor parenting. These syndromes are likely to have different causes and consequences.[42]

Finally, it should be noted that part of the problem may lie in the use of the categorical system itself. The DSM-IV and the ICD-10 both use a categorical approach, that is they assume that personality traits fall into bundles that are so distinct that they can be given separate names. Yet it is clear that this is far from the case. In clinical practice it is not at all uncommon to find traits of several different "personality disorders" in the one person. As far as personality disorders are concerned, the categorical system is far from ideal. As Mack et al point out:

> [It] has many weaknesses, particularly because nature seems to abhor clear boundaries (particularly for . . . the personality disorders. . .). The limitations of the categorical model result in a high prevalence of boundary patients, the need for boundary categories, and an artifactually elevated rate of definitional co-morbidity. A possible solution would be to adopt a dimensional system of continuous variables.[43]

The DSM-IV itself suggests that an alternative, dimensional approach could be considered for personality disorders:

The diagnostic approach used in this manual represents the categorical perspective that Personality Disorders represent qualitatively distinct clinical syndromes. An alternative to the categorical approach is the dimensional perspective that Personality Disorders represent maladaptive variants of personality traits that merge inperceptibly into normality and into one another.[44]

It goes on to point out, however, that so far, no satisfactory dimensional models have been developed, although they remain under active investigation. Mack et al sum up the present situation succinctly: "It seems clear that categorical systems, despite their limitations, continue to have great utility in clinical and research practice, but that dimensional systems continue to have great appeal".[45]

CONCLUSION

It is obvious from the above that there is still a great deal of controversy about the concept of the psychopathic personality disorder. Some would argue that it "merely medicalizes bad behaviour in some circular fashion ('Why has this man done terrible things? Because he is a psychopath. How do we know he is a psychopath? Because he has done terrible things.')",[46] or, that it is "a device for attaching the scientific prestige associated with health with what are essentially judgements of value".[47]

Others would argue, like Roth does above, that there is sufficient evidence to support the belief that it is a personality disorder and that its inclusion in major psychiatric classifications is justified, even if it still needs refinement.

Others take a more cautious but optimistic approach somewhere between the two extremes. A Quality Assurance Project carried out under the aegis of the Royal Australian and New Zealand College of Psychiatrists in 1991, for example, stated:

> It is important to realise that making the diagnosis is no more than providing a name for a set of behaviours that have been noted to occur together. The issue of psychiatric interest is the possibility that consistent and specific abnormalities in personality traits such as aggression, impulsivity, guilt, loyalty and empathy co-occur in these persons. The behaviours that derive from these traits are seldom of psychiatric interest for there is, for example, unlikely to be a specific aetiology or treatment for vagrancy, felony or assault, whereas it is conceivable that the trait disturbances listed above may eventually be related to some enduring pattern of personality organisation, be that acquired on a genetic or environmental basis.[48]

There is no right or wrong answer to this problem at the present time. All that can be said, by way of conclusion, is that whether or not there is, in some people, an identifiable personality disorder (that is, an enduring and abnormal pattern of personality organisation) underlying and responsible for their antisocial behaviour, however this may be defined, is something that remains to be demonstrated. In the meantime, it would be a decided advantage to both psychiatry and the law if the clinical concept could be put to one side and excluded from legal debate until a great deal more research has been done. Legal argument is not going to advance our knowledge of the subject or help to reconcile the current opposing points of view one whit. Unfortunately, as the cases of Byrne and David both demonstrate, this does not appear to be an option at the present time.

NOTES

1   Freedman, A, Kaplan, H and Sadock, B, *Comprehensive Textbook of Psychiatry–II* (1975) p 1287.

2   Prichard, J, *A treatise on insanity and other disorders affecting the mind* (1835).

3   Above n 2, cited in Hunter, R and Macalpine, I, *Three Hundred Years of Psychiatry* (1963) p 839.

4   Rappeport, J, "Antisocial Behaviour" in Arieti, S, (ed) *American Handbook of Psychiatry* (1974) p 257.

5   Hunter and Macalpine, above n 3 p 838.

6   Rappeport, above n 4 p 257.

7   Bleuler, E, *Textbook of Psychiatry* (1924) p 569–592.

8   Henderson, D and Gillespie, R, *A Text-book of Psychiatry for Students and Practitioners* (1950) p 388.

9   Ibid p 403.

10   American Psychiatric Association, *Diagnostic and Statistical Manual — Mental Disorders* (1952) p 38.

11   Id.

12   Id.

13   Rappeport, above n 4 p 258.

14   Id.

15   Davies, W and Feldman, P, "The Diagnosis of Psychopathy by Forensic Specialists" (1981) 138 *Brit J Psychiat* 329.

16   Roth, M, "Psychopathic (sociopathic) personality" in Bluglass, R and Bowden, P, (eds) *Principles and Practice of Forensic Psychiatry* (1990) p 439.

17   Rappeport, above n 4 p 258.

18   Id.

19   American Psychiatric Association, *Diagnostic and Statistical Manual of Mental Disorders* (2nd ed: 1968) p 43.

20   World Health Organisation, *International Classification of Diseases* (vol 1; 1977) p 195–196.

21   American Psychiatric Association, *Diagnostic and Statistical Manual of Mental Disorders* (3rd ed; 1980) p 320–321.

22   Davies and Feldman, above n 15 p 330.

23   Id.

24   American Psychiatric Association, *Diagnostic and Statistical Manual of Mental Disorders* (3rd ed, rev; 1987) p 346.

25   Ibid p 344.

26   Roth, above n 16 p 439.

27   World Health Organisation, *The ICD–10 Classification of Mental and Behavioural Disorders* (1992) p 204.

28   American Psychiatric Association, *Diagnostic and Statistical Manual of Mental Disorders* (4th ed. 1994) p650.

29   Hare, R, *The Hare Psychopathy Checklist-Revised* (1991).

30   Dolan, B and Coid, J, *Psychopathic and Antisocial Personality Disorder* (1993) p19.

31   Hart, S, Hare, R and Forth, A, "Psychopathy as a Risk Marker for Violence: Development and Validation of a Screening Version of the Revised Psychopathy Checklist" in Monahan, J and Steadman, H, (eds), *Violence and Mental Disorder*, p 82.

32   Forth, A, Hart, S and Hare, R, "Assessment of psychopathy in male young offenders" (1990) 2 *Psychological Assessment* 342.

33   Strachan, C, *Assessment of psychopathy in female offenders* (1993).

34   Hart et al, above n 31, p 87.

35   Byrne was a sexual psychopath who strangled a girl and mutilated her body. It was claimed that he suffered "from violent and perverted desires which he found it difficult or impossible to control". This was accepted as evidence of an "abnormality of mind" for the qualified defence of diminished responsibility. Parker LJ, in *R v Byrne* (1960) 2 QB 396, said that "abnormality of mind" included, inter alia, the inability "to exercise will power to control acts in accordance with rational judgements". This has been heavily and justifiably criticised by lawyers and psychiatrists alike. As Barclay pointed out in a talk delivered to the Section of Forensic Psychiatry of the New South Wales Branch of the Royal Australian and New Zealand College of Psychiatrists in April, 1991:

> It is very questionable that psychiatry can distinguish between that impulse which cannot be resisted and that which is not resisted. It is one thing to be sympathetically concerned about the obsessive compulsive who cannot control his impulses to engage in repetitive hand washing or magical rituals which are self punishing to relieve his anxiety and quite another to believe that the sexual psychopath cannot resist his perverse sexual desires solely on the basis of his own assertions and the assertions of a psychiatrist who believes what the psychopath says.

36
> Garry David . . . spent most of his life in orphanages, Youth Training Centres and Prisons. . . In 1976 he was convicted of armed robbery, the following year for threatening to kill and the next year for discharging a firearm in public. Ten days after his release in 1980, he shot a policeman and a woman (who has been left a quadriplegic); neither had given him any provocation whatever. He was sentenced to fifteen years imprisonment and was due for release in February 1990, for he automatically received a remission of one third of his sentence for "good behaviour". While in prison he was exceptionally difficult to manage, repeatedly mutilating himself and swallowing a variety of dangerous objects — razor blades, glass and the like. There were at least eighty-four incidents, including partial amputation of his penis and interfering with the exposed urethra several times. (Parker, N, "The Garry David Case" (1991) 25 *ANZ J Psychiat* 371.)

Most of the psychiatrists who assessed him considered him to have an antisocial personality disorder. Concern over his imminent release led to several inquiries, appeals and reviews costing millions of dollars. Eventually the Victorian Parliament passed a special Act of Parliament to enable him to be detained.

37   Blackburn, R, "On Moral Judgements and Personality Disorders. The Myth of Psychopathic Personality Revisited" (1988) 153 *Brit J Psychiat* 505.

38   Ibid p 511.

39   Roth, above n 16 p 449.

40   Id.

41   Finlay-Jones, R, "Psychopathic disorder" (1991) 4 *Curr Op Psychiat* 850.

42   Id.

43   Mack, A, Forman, L, Brown, R and Frances, A, "A Brief History of Psychiatric Classification From the Ancients to DSM-IV" (1994) 17 *Psychiatric Clinics of North America* 521.

44   American Psychiatric Association, above n28 p 521.

45   Mack et al, above n43, p521.

46   The Quality Assurance Project, "Treatment Outlines for Antisocial Personality Disorder" (1991) 25 *ANZ J Psychiat* 542.

47   Wooton, B, cited in Roth, above n 16 p 449.

48   Above n 46 p 542.

6

POST-TRAUMATIC STRESS DISORDER

Post-traumatic stress disorder (PTSD) first appeared in the DSM in 1980 (DSM-III). Its relatively recent appearance in the official nomenclature has led some critics to question whether the symptoms are those of a genuine psychiatric disorder at all or simply part of the spectrum of cognitive, emotional and behavioural manifestations that constitute normal human response to stress.[1] Other critics accept the fact that the symptoms are those of a genuine psychiatric illness but, given the high co-morbidity of PTSD with other psychiatric syndromes[2] and the overlap of the symptoms of PTSD with those of other psychiatric syndromes, such as borderline personality disorder[3] and anxiety disorders,[4] question whether they constitute an independent psychiatric syndrome or not. A relevant factor here is the fact that the documented psychological effects of trauma are much wider that the group of symptoms listed in either the DSM or the ICD. As Taylor puts it:

> There is no evidence that traumatic events are associated exclusively with the cluster of symptoms defining PTSD, quite the contrary. There is equally no evidence that noxious events, even those generally accepted as outside the range of human experience, invariably lead to such a disorder.[5]

Furthermore, between the DSM-III and the DSM-IV, a number of changes occurred in both the definition of the type of trauma that is said to lead to PTSD and the diagnostic criteria for PTSD. The changes to the diagnostic criteria were mainly in the form of either expanded or contracted descriptions of some of the criteria or a re-organisation of the way the criteria are grouped and are of little overall significance.[6] The changes to the degree and type of trauma, however, are significant. The type of trauma was gradually tightened from "a psychologically traumatic event that is *generally* outside the range of usual human experience (DSM-III),[7] to "a psychologically distressing event that *is* outside the range of usual human experience" (DSM-III-R)[8] to "an extreme traumatic stressor" (DSM-IV).[9] The ICD-10 specifies the type of trauma as "a stressful event or situation (either short- or long-lasting) of an exceptionally threatening or catastrophic nature, which is likely to cause pervasive distress in almost anyone".[10] Against this, Kleinman notes, "Notably, on occasion an individual develops genuine (nonmalingered) symptoms of a PTSD after exposure to an event that does not fulfil the criteria of a stress sufficient to cause a PTSD".[11]

More importantly, the type of event that could lead to the degree of trauma necessary for PTSD to develop was also gradually changed and widened. In the DSM-III it included rape, assault, military combat, natural disasters (floods, earthquakes), accidental man-made disasters (car accidents with serious physical injury, aeroplane crashes, large fires), or deliberate man-made disasters (bombing, torture, death camps), that is events that directly threatened the individual's life or integrity. In the DSM-III-R this was considerably expanded to include events that threatened the life of significant others ("a serious threat or harm to one's children, spouse, or other close relatives or friends") as well as "sudden destruction of one's home or community" or "seeing another person who has recently been, or is being, seriously injured or killed as the result of an accident or physical violence. In some cases the trauma may be learning about a serious threat or harm to a close friend or relative, e.g. that one's child has been kidnapped, tortured, or killed".[12] In the DSM-IV it was expanded again. "Being diagnosed with a life-threatening illness" or "learning that one's child has a life-threatening disease" were added to the list[13] "Sudden destruction of one's home" was deleted from the list.

The DSM-IV groups the diagnostic criteria as follows:[14]

A. The person has been exposed to a traumatic event in which both of the following were present:

   (1) the person experienced, witnessed, or was confronted with an event or events that involved actual or threatened death or serious injury, or a threat to the physical integrity of self or others

   (2) the person's response involved fear, helplessness, or horror.

B. The traumatic event is persistently re-experienced in one (or more) of the following ways:

   (1) recurrent and intrusive distressing recollections of the event, including images, thoughts, or perceptions

   (2) recurrent distressing dreams of the event

   (3) acting or feeling as if the traumatic event were recurring (includes a sense of reliving the experience, illusions, hallucinations, and dissociative flashback episodes, including those that occur on awakening or when intoxicated)

   (4) intense psychological distress at exposure to internal or external cues that symbolize or resemble an aspect of the traumatic event

   (5) physiological reactivity on exposure to internal or external cues that symbolize or resemble an aspect of the traumatic event

C. Persistent avoidance of stimuli associated with the trauma and numbing of general responsiveness (not present before the trauma), as indicated by three (or more) of the following:

   (1) efforts to avoid thoughts, feelings, or conversations associated with the trauma

(2) efforts to avoid activities, places, or people that arouse recollections of the trauma

(3) inability to recall an important aspect of the trauma

(4) markedly diminished interest or participation in significant activities

(5) feeling of detachment or estrangement from others

(6) restricted range of affect (e.g., unable to have loving feelings)

(7) sense of a foreshortened future (e.g., does not expect to have a career, marriage, children, or a normal life span)

D. Persistent symptoms of increased arousal not present before the trauma), as indicated by two (or more) of the following:

(1) difficulty falling or staying asleep

(2) irritability or outbursts of anger

(3) difficulty concentrating

(4) hypervigilance

(5) exaggerated startle response

E. Duration of the disturbance (symptoms in Criteria B, C, and D) is more than one month.

F. The disturbance causes clinically significant distress or impairment in social, occupational, or other important areas of functioning.

The ICD-10 is not so specific. It simply describes the symptoms as follows, without attempting to group them:

> Typical symptoms include episodes of repeated reliving of the trauma in intrusive memories ("flashbacks") or dreams, occurring against the persisting background of a sense of "numbness" and emotional blunting, detachment from other people, unresponsiveness to surroundings, anhedonia, and avoidance of activities and situations reminiscent of the trauma. Commonly there is fear and avoidance of cues that remind the sufferer of the original trauma. Rarely, there may be dramatic, acute bursts of fear, panic or aggression, triggered by stimuli arousing a sudden recollection and/or re-enactment of the trauma or of the original reaction to it. There is usually a state of autonomic hyperarousal with hypervigilance, an enhanced startle reaction, and insomnia. Anxiety and depression are commonly associated with the above symptoms and signs, and suicidal ideation is not infrequent. Excessive use of alcohol or drugs may be a complicating factor.[15]

Comparing the two classifications, it is clear that although there is some considerable overlap of symptoms, they are far from identical. As the ICD-10 does not require a specific number of symptoms in particular combinations to be present it is much easier, for legal purposes, to fit a person into the ICD-10 definition that the DSM-IV definition (even allowing for the comment in the introduction to the DSM-IV that "The specific diagnostic criteria included in the DSM-IV are meant to serve as guidelines to be informed by clinical judgment and are not meant to be used in a cookbook fashion"[16]).

80

Although PTSD only came into the DSM in 1980, the symptoms have been recorded for several centuries. As Burges Watson et al point out:

> Samuel Pepys, following the Great Fire of London, satisfied the criteria for a diagnosis of PTSD . . . [and] Hotspur's wife (in Shakespeare's *Henry IV* Part II) describes symptoms in her husband which would satisfy the criteria for, at least, a provisional diagnosis of PTSD.[17]

If the symptoms have been known for centuries, why has it taken so long for the syndrome to be recognised and become part of the official nomenclature? This can best be understood by tracing psychiatric interest in the psychological effects of severe stress from World War One to the present. Van der Kolk et al, reviewing the history of psychiatric interest in the effects of trauma generally, suggest that:

> psychiatry has suffered periodically from marked amnesias in which well-established knowledge was forgotten abruptly and the psychological impact of man's inhumanity to man was ascribed to constitutional or intrapsychic factors alone. . . The psychiatric profession at times has embraced and been fascinated by trauma and, at other times, expressed stubborn disbelief about the relevance of patients' stories.[18]

There are two points here. First, the tendency of psychiatry to use existing and traditional models of human behaviour, however inappropriate and deficient they may be, to explain (and treat) behaviours which the models were not designed to explain in the first place.[19] Secondly, the tendency of psychiatry, like any other profession, to take an interest in issues that are current. In the absence of major stressful events affecting many people (and, until recently, wars and natural catastrophes provided the major source of research material and the major stimulus to research activity) psychiatric interest in the psychological effects of trauma waned. World War One saw an emergence of interest in the psychological effects (both acute and long term) of stress but between the wars there was little interest.[20] As van der Kolk et al point out, between the wars "little was published on trauma in the psychiatric literature" at all.[21]

World War Two saw a resurgence of interest but after the war interest again declined. It was during World War Two, however, that the combination of symptoms of what is now known as PTSD (the nature of the stressor, numbing and hyperarousal) was first described in detail.[22] It was not until the Vietnam War that interest in the subject emerged again and this time the sociopolitical environment was quite different. The anti-war movement and its aftermath meant that the veterans who suffered psychological damage as a result of the war were better organised, more vocal and had a much higher public profile. The outcome was the inclusion of PTSD in the DSM-III.[23] In the late 1970s also, research occurred which established links between the effects of the traumas of war and the effects of the traumas of civilian life ("rape trauma syndrome", "stress response syndrome"). This research was too late to be included in the DSM-III but it was incorporated

81

into the DSM-III-R.[24] This historical background goes some way towards explaining why the syndrome of PTSD was relatively late in entering the DSM.

Problems, however, remain, the major ones being the diagnostic criteria themselves, the ease with which they can be feigned and the difficulty relating them to the supposed stressor. With regard to the diagnostic criteria, Burges Watson comments that, "Currently, 'stress', 'trauma' and 'flashbacks' must be among the most sloppily used terms in contemporary discourse".[25] Hocking suggests that it may be impossible to determine degrees of stress because "the assessment of any degree of stress present in any situation is an expression of a personal rather than a medical opinion".[26] What one person reports to be an extremely stressful situation may be considered to be of little consequence by another. People experience events and interpret events differently.[27] With regard to the symptoms, Sparr and Atkinson note that they are "mostly subjective and nonspecific".[28] Few of the symptoms, with the possible exception of "physiological reactivity on exposure to internal or external cues that symbolize or resemble an aspect of the traumatic event" in Group B[29] or "exaggerated startle response" in Group D[30] can be tested objectively and neither of these symptoms is necessary for the diagnosis. So the diagnosis can be made entirely on what the patient tells the psychiatrist, which makes feigning the symptoms a relatively simple process. The psychiatrist can check some of the symptoms with friends and relatives but there is no guarantee that the friends and relatives will be entirely objective and truthful in what they report. In any case, as Raifman points out, "A psychiatrist is a doctor, not a lie detector. . . A good poker player probably knows better than a mental health professional whether or not a person is lying".[31] Kleinman notes that even the absence of anxiety or distress during the interview (which is sometimes considered to be evidence of malingering) may, in fact, be a symptom of the disorder. According to Kleinman, "The lack of overt distress . . . is an unreliable index of malingering as individuals suffering from PTSD may dissociate while telling their 'story' as a means of protecting themselves from their emotional distress".[32]

Resnick suggests that "the primary motivation to malinger PTSD is financial gain"[33] and, "in this regard, he notes that many of the labels given to PTSD since 1889 suggest malingering.[34] He goes on to state that:

> It is a rare individual who is not influenced to some degree by the possibility that an injury may lead to financial gain (Keiser 1968). Schafer (1986) believes that having a compensable injury promotes a "little larceny" in most litigants.[35]

The most difficult problem, however, is relating the symptoms to the purported stressor. As Taylor points out:

> Evidence that external events may have psychological impact, and result in mental disorder, is long-standing; however, the extent to which it is the events *per se* that is associated with the disorder has been subject to repeated challenge. . . A further problem lies in the threshold for 'usual human experience'. Can there be a universal standard?[36]

Expanding Taylor's first point, Kleinman states that the examiner must determine whether the PTSD:

(1) is a new disorder caused by the recent trauma;

(2) is a previously undiagnosed or undetected PTSD caused by a previous trauma;

(3) has been precipitated by the recent trauma but caused by a previous trauma (more likely if a previous trauma is of greater magnitude than a recent trauma);

(4) has been caused by an interaction of both recent and previous trauma;

(5) has been caused independently by both traumata.[37]

Kleinman implies that a complete trauma history can be helpful in sorting these matters out. Other authors are not so confident. Indeed it is difficult to see (a) how a complete and completely objective trauma history could be obtained, and (b) how any conclusions reached by the examiner, on the basis of the history alone, regarding the respective roles of recent and past traumas, could be anything other than an educated guess.

Expanding Taylor's second point, there is a long-standing, unresolved (and probably unresolvable) debate in the literature about whether or not stress alone can produce the symptoms of PTSD or whether other factors such as the "strength" or otherwise of the individual's pre-morbid personality contributes. "Strength" here refers to the coping mechanisms each individual has developed to deal with stressful situations in the past.

Studies to date have indicated that certain types and degrees of stress, for example rape and torture, are likely to produce symptoms in almost anybody,[38] regardless of their personality strengths, though not necessarily the symptoms of PTSD. What is not clear is the relationship between less severe, though still significant forms of stress, pre-morbid personality and the development of stress-related psychological symptoms. The DSM-IV comes down heavily on the side of the stress itself as the major aetiological factor rather than vulnerability, although it does acknowledge that personality factors and other factors may also contribute in some cases:

> The severity, duration, and proximity of an individual's exposure to the traumatic event are the most important factors affecting the likelihood of developing this disorder. There is some evidence that social supports, family history, childhood experiences, personality variables, and preexisting mental disorders may influence the development of Posttraumatic Stress Disorder. This disorder can develop in individuals without any predisposing conditions, particularly if the stressor is especially extreme.[39]

As McGorry points out, "the DSM definitions shifted the balance in favour of the stressor in accounting for most of the etiological variance" whereas before the shift, in prolonged stress syndromes, "character pathology . . . was seen as the key contributor to persistence of symptoms".[40] McGorry also notes that "subsequent research has highlighted the importance of other variables, notably aspects of the recovery environment, and has led to the formulation of more complex models in which several factors are seen as making potential contributions to the development of frank and/or persistent disorder".[41]

Given the extreme complexity of this subject and the nature of the issues discussed above it is difficult to see how any psychiatrist could be anything other than equivocal about the precise relationship between a particular stressor and the nature of the psychological symptoms under consideration in a civil or criminal case. This is not to deny the fact that stress can produce psychological symptoms of a severe and sometimes disabling nature. There is no doubt that it can and does. The question in each particular case is whether it has and, if so, how the symptoms can be verified, the degree of stress assessed, the nature of the connection demonstrated, and the role of other factors (such as pre-morbid personality and the recovery environment) eliminated.

NOTES

1   One journalist has suggested that it may be just another example of the American "penchant for elevating human problems into psychiatric disorders". Horin, A, "The children who live in no-man's-land", *Sydney Morning Herald* 1 July 1995. For a detailed discussion of the boundary issues between normality and abnormality see McGorry, P, "The clinical boundaries of posttraumatic stress disorder" (1995) 29 *ANZ J Psychiat* 385-393.

2   The high co-morbidity with depression has led some writers to suggest that it is simply a variant of a depressive syndrome. For co-morbidity data, see Helzer, J, Robins, L, McEvoy, L, "Posttraumatic stress disorder in the general population: findings from the Epidemiological Catchment Area Survey" (1987) 317 *New England Journal of Medicine* 1630; Davidson, J, Hughes, D, Blazer, D and George, L, "Post-traumatic stress disorder in the community: an epidemiological study" (1991) 21 *Psychological Medicine* 713; and Kessler, R, Sonnega, A, Bromet, E and Nelson, C, *Post-traumatic Stress Disorder in the National Comorbidity Survey* (1993).

3   Lonie has argued that PTSD is an equivalent of Borderline Personality Disorder, with the differences being simply "that [in the latter] the trauma has either undergone repression or, having been suffered before the establishment of speech, has not been registered in verbal form". Lonie, I, "Borderline Disorder and Post-Traumatic Stress Disorder: An Equivalence?" (1993) 27 *ANZ J Psychiat* 233. See also Gunderson, J and Sabo, A, "The Phenomenological and Conceptual Interface Between Borderline Personality Disorder and PTSD" (1993) 150 *Amer J Psychiat* 19; March, J, "The nosology of posttraumatic stress disorder" (1990) 4 *Journal of Anxiety Disorders* 61; and Gersons, B and Carlier, I, "Post-traumatic Stress Disorder: The History of a Recent Concept" (1992) 161 *Brit J Psychiat* 742.

4   Foa et al, for example, on the basis of a principal-components factor analysis of the symptoms of PTSD in 72 female rape victims and 86 female victims of nonsexual assault, came to the conclusion that there are two patterns of posttrauma symptoms, one characterising PTSD and the second characterising a phobic reaction. Foa, E, Riggs, D and Gershuny, B, "Arousal, Numbing and Intrusion: Symptom Structure of PTSD Following Assault" (1995) 152 *Amer J Psychiat* 116-120.

5   Taylor, P, "Victims and Survivors" in Gunn, J and Taylor, P (eds) *Forensic Psychiatry. Clinical, Legal and Ethical Issues* (1993) p 887.

6   The changes from the DSM-III to the DSM-III-R are outlined in Burges Watson, I, Hoffman, L and Wilson, G, "The Neuropsychiatry of Post-traumatic Stress Disorder" (1988) 152 *Brit J Psych* 165. The changes from the DSM-III-R to the DSM-IV are outlined in Burges Watson, I, "Psychiatry, science and posttraumatic stress disorder" (1995) 29 *ANZ J Psychiat* 2.

7   American Psychiatric Association, *Diagnostic and Statistical Manual of Mental Disorders* (3rd ed; 1980) p 236.

8   American Psychiatric Association, *Diagnostic and Statistical Manual of Mental Disorders* (3rd ed, rev; 1987) p 247.

9   American Psychiatric Association, *Diagnostic and Statistical Manual of Mental Disorders* (4th ed; 1994) p 424.

10   World Health Organization, *The ICD-10 Classification of Mental and Behavioural Disorders* (1992) p 147.

11   Kleinman, S, "Trauma-Induced Psychiatric Disorders and Civil Law", in Rosner, R (ed) *Principles and Practice of Forensic Psychiatry* (1994) p 242.

12   American Psychiatric Association, above n 8 p 247.

13   American Psychiatric Association, above n 9 p 424.

14   Ibid p 427.

15   World Health Organization, above n 10 p 148.

16   American Psychiatric Association, above n 9 p xxiii.

17   Burges Watson et al, above n 6 p 164. Van der Kolk et al consider it has an even longer history: "the traumatic memories that haunt people after experiencing overwhelming terror have always been a central theme in literature, from Homer to Shakespeare". Van der Kolk, B, Herron, N and Hostetler, A, "The History of Trauma in Psychiatry" (1994) 17 *Psychiatric Clinics of North America* 583.

18   Van der Kolk, above n 17 p 583.

19   Stone demonstrates this in his description of the approach used in the treatment of 'shell-shock' at the Tavistock Clinic. According to Stone, the treatment focused on "the psychoanalytic therapy of an inner conflict between fear and duty, in which sadistic impulses had risen to the surface. . . In other words, the war trauma had served primarily to open a tin of libidinous worms and had been reformulated in terms of the patient's early childhood emotional war with members of his family" (Stone, M, cited in Gersons and Carlier, above n 3 p 744). As Gersons and Carlier point out, "The war trauma was thus exchanged for an inner neurotic conflict, and became the point at which treatment began".

20   As van der Kolk et al point out, "Given the vast experience gained during the war, the dedication of the practitioners, and the solid collections of data on the combat neuroses it is astounding how the memory of war trauma was so completely forgotten for the subsequent quarter century". Van der Kolk et al, above n 17 p 592.

21   Ibid p 588.

22   Kardiner described them in his book *The Traumatic Neuroses of War*, published in 1941, eleven years before the emergence of the DSM-I. Cited in van der Kolk et al, above n 17 p 588.

23   Van der Kolk et al (above n 17 p 592) trace the development of the process as follows:

> In 1970, two psychiatrists . . . started "rap groups" with recently returned veterans belonging to Vietnam Veterans against the War in which they talked about their war experiences. These "rap sessions" rapidly spread around the country. . . (With the help of others interested in the subject they combed the literature and more than 700 charts of Vietnam veterans) and arrived at a classification system very close to the one Kardiner had proposed in 1941. As the DSM-III process unfolded there were numerous meetings with the DSM-III Committee, presentations at the American Psychiatric Association culminating, in 1980, with the inclusion of post-traumatic stress disorder (PTSD) in the DSM-III.

24   Ibid p 593.

25   Burges Watson, above n 6 p 2.

26   Hocking, F, "Human Reactions to Extreme Environmental Stress" (1965) II/12 *The Medical Journal of Australia* 481.

27   Kleinman, above n 11 p 243, gives the example of "a mugging in which three young males, one holding a knife, robs a middle-aged woman of her purse. . . One woman may notice the trembling hand of the youth holding the knife, focus on the probable lack of experience of the muggers, conclude that the assailants are likely to bungle a simple mugging and in their panic stab and kill her, and be filled with terror. Another woman may interpret the trembling hand holding the knife as a sign of fear, the youth of the assailants as an indication of a lack of maliciousness – that is, "They are really just boys" – conclude the assailants do not intend to harm her, and not be particularly frightened".

28   Sparr, L and Atkinson, R, "Posttraumatic Stress Disorder as an Insanity Defence: Medicolegal Quicksand" (1986) 143 *Am J Psychiat* 608.

29   American Psychiatric Association, above n 9 p 428. See Furlong, F, "A Biological Marker in Claimed Post-Traumatic Stress Disorder" (1992) 13 *American Journal of Forensic Psychiatry* 41.

30   Id.

31   Raifman, L, "Problems of diagnosis and legal causation in courtroom use of post-traumatic stress disorder" (1983) 1 *Behavioural Science and the Law* 115-130.

32   Kleinman, above n 11 p 243.

33   Resnick, P, "Malingering" in Rosner, R (ed) *Principles and Practice of Forensic Psychiatry* (1994) p 422.

34   Id.

35   Id.

36   Taylor, above n 5 p 887.

37   Kleinman, above n 11 p 243.
38   Hocking, above n 26; Breslau, N, Davis, G and Andreski, P, "Traumatic events and Posttraumatic Stress Disorder in an urban population of young adults" (1991) 48 *Archives of General Psychiatry* 216.
39   American Psychiatric Association, above n 9 p 426.
40   McGorry, above n 1 p 386.
41   Id.

THE PSYCHIATRIST AND THE PERSON BEING ASSESSED

SECTION B

The Assessment

"The basic method of investigation remains what a doctor's mind can make of a patient's mind."[1]

General psychiatry and forensic psychiatry are different in many ways. In both settings the psychiatrist is endeavouring to build up a picture of the state of a person's mind but the referral process, the client, the purpose of the assessment, the circumstances under which the assessment is carried out, the nature of the final report and the use to which it will be put, are all different. This section looks at how these differences might influence the two people involved in the assessment — the psychiatrist and the person being assessed (Chapter 7) — and at how they might affect the assessment process (Chapter 8).

7

THE PSYCHIATRIST AND THE PERSON BEING ASSESSED

THE PSYCHIATRIST

In the practice of forensic psychiatry, the source of referral is not another doctor or mental health professional, but a lawyer or some other legal or judicial agency. The client is not the person referred but the person who does the referring and, depending upon the side they represent and the purpose for which the report is being requested, they may or may not be acting in the interests of the person referred. The client may, in fact, (and usually does) give quite specific instructions to the psychiatrist when requesting an assessment and report and if the psychiatrist agrees to do the report, he or she is bound to follow those instructions.[2] Limiting the purpose of the report in this way limits the amount and type of information that can be provided in a report. The immediate purpose of the examination is not to establish the diagnosis for the purpose of devising and implementing a treatment plan but rather to determine whether the person is suffering from a mental disorder which will interfere with or influence some current judicial (or penal) process or whether the person was suffering from a mental disorder at some time in the past and, if so, the relevance of the disorder for their behaviour at the time. The assessment is sometimes carried out in the psychiatrist's ordinary consulting rooms but it may also be carried out in a secure and hence restrictive setting such as a hospital or prison.[3] The normal factors relating to confidentiality of reports do not apply. The client may or may not decide to use the report. If they do, the report will be used in quite a different way to the way a clinical report is used. As Chiswick points out:

> traditionally psychiatric evaluation proceeds by a global evaluation of all relevant material. Diagnostic formulation depends on taking a comprehensive history and evaluating the patient's mental state. Supplementary data will be gathered, perhaps from a relative or work colleague. By contrast, the approach of criminal lawyers is to select those fragments of the psychiatric findings that support the argument being advanced. Disproportionate emphasis can be placed on this or that item, so that a balanced view that embraces all the data is never properly heard.[4]

Bluglass makes the same point:

90

Psychiatrists would prefer to believe that as experts they can simply offer an informed, independent opinion to the court after careful examination, that is unbiased and unprejudiced. There are however many barriers resulting from the Anglo-Saxon adversarial system of justice which militate against this desirable aim. However much the psychiatrist would prefer to retain a disinterested and impartial stance, his report and the way his evidence is used will inevitably be biased towards enhancing the case of whichever party is requesting it. Most forensic psychiatrists have had the painful experience of learning that their report is not to be used or another expert is to be requested to examine the case, or that the report is not to be shown to the court but selected aspects will be used to assist in eliciting oral evidence. Not infrequently the experts have information that is suppressed by the lawyers in their client's interests, as they see it. In the adversarial arena fragments of clinical material are given exaggerated importance, and extreme positions are adopted; judgements are paraded as objectively determined facts.[5]

If the report is presented in court, the psychiatrist may be subject to cross-examination on the report. As Bluglass notes, this "may tend to place him in a negative and defensive position" especially if the advocate is short on facts but skilled in cross-examination and sets out to "discredit a witness or reduce the value of his evidence".[6] The other side may also present a psychiatric report and their psychiatrist in turn may be cross-examined resulting, at times, in what Morse calls "an appalling 'circus atmosphere'".[7] The cross-examination of both psychiatrists, of course, takes place in the presence of the accused.

The outcome of all this will be the resolution of a legal problem, not the resolution of a medical one.

Between them, Mendelson and Cosgrove sum up succinctly the roots of these problems as follows:

Forensic psychiatry is 'the application of psychiatry to legal issues for legal ends, legal purposes' ... clinical psychiatry ... is the application of psychiatry for therapeutic purposes.[8]

Lawyers and psychiatrists in the basic practice of their professions, are as apart as the poles. There is no area where one impinges on the other.[9]

Wasyliw, Cavanaugh and Rogers have identified five ways in which forensic psychiatrists have been used. Mendelson[10] summarises these as follows:

1 Hired gun. This role is a reflection of the adversarial process, the expert witness providing testimony which is needed by the side which retains his or her services. This involves the distortion of data, and is generally exposed by careful cross-examination.[11][12]

2 Advocate. This type of expert testimony takes place "when personal points of view are given priority". The settings in which this may occur include evidence given in support of a patient's interests, or when certain theories in psychiatry or psychology become an issue in the courtroom. This role is also encouraged by the adversary system, and expert witnesses are frequently

chosen because of their theoretical orientation or well-known views on a particular matter of relevance to the case.[13 14]

3   Impartial expert. This requires the review of all data, including that which may be adverse to the client represented by the solicitor who has retained the expert witness. This is the role traditionally taken by the court-appointed expert. Using Stone's terminology, this is the role of "neutral scientific friend(s) of the court" . . . this is a legitimate role, provided that the forensic psychiatrist's testimony is factually based and the opinion can be supported by an accepted body of professional knowledge pertinent to the specific discipline of psychiatry.[15]

4   Consultant. In this role, the forensic expert witness evaluates the applicability of research data, as it relates to a particular legal issue. Thus, the function of the witness is to define the scope and limitations of "expert input into the case".

5   Ivory tower. In this role the expert witness addresses public policy issues.

Ideally, the forensic psychiatrist would be entirely impartial, "be able to testify on both sides of the fence" and "be comfortable in testifying for defence counsel as well as for plaintiff's counsel".[16] Unfortunately this does not always turn out to be the case even when the forensic psychiatrist is striving for impartiality. The outcome of the Buffalo Creek disaster demonstrates this very clearly:

Zusman and Simon (1983) studied claims of psychological damages for 207 children and 381 adults who were each evaluated by plaintiff and defense psychiatrists. This disaster formed a natural experiment for studying differences between clinicians based on the retaining attorneys. Plaintiff psychiatrists found 69 per cent of the adults suffering from severe impairment with no real hope of recovery. This is in marked contrast with defense psychiatrists who found 24 per cent of the same defendants to have no disorder and only 19 per cent suffering from a severe disorder and nonresponsive to treatment. Further, the level of diagnostic agreement was appallingly low (that is, 12 per cent for specific diagnosis and 21 per cent for general diagnostic category).

Zusman and Simon concluded that this was not a deliberate attempt at advocacy and distortion. They believed that the involved psychiatrists were not 'hired guns' since the clinicians were all university-based, had little financial investment in forensic evaluations, and had evidently been hired without 'opinion shopping'. Rather, the researchers concluded that there was an unintentional distortion because of a phenomenon which they labelled forensic identification. Forensic identification refers to the unintentional process by which clinicians adopt the fact pattern or theory of attorneys with whom they have initial contact. This process skews their clinical findings and distorts their conclusions.[17]

Stanley notes a similar but more serious phenomenon:

Unfortunately but inevitably the psychiatrist, far more than any other medical expert, is drawn into the fray. He is drawn into the arena of battle between the litigants. There has been the tendency for psychiatrists engaged in civil litigation work to be used by solicitors in what I regard as at least an unfortunate if not an unprofessional way. It has resulted in a significantly high proportion of such psychiatrists . . . being branded as belonging to one camp or the other — they are either for the plaintiffs or the defendants. . . A psychiatrist so branded becomes part of 'the team' . . . psychiatrists are seen as 'wearing the guernsey' for the party who is paying them. As a result their objectivity and their professional integrity is subjected to considerable attack.[18]

Although Stanley is discussing the situation in the civil jurisdiction, much of what he says applies equally to the criminal jurisdiction.

Cosgrove cites an article which appeared in the New Yorker about the trial of John Hinckley for the attempted assassination of President Reagan, which sums up the way in which forensic psychiatrists can be drawn, wittingly or unwittingly, into the support of a particular legal point of view as the result of the judicial process:

Next to the central tug-of-war, which concerned John Hinckley's sanity, the one between psychiatry and the law was the most intense in the trial . . . the stark choice between a conviction and a finding of not guilty by reason of insanity pushed the doctors, and their differing opinions, to opposite poles and identified them with one option or the other.[19]

Stone sums up some of the risks of forensic psychiatry as follows:

1   There is a risk that one will go too far and twist the rules of justice and fairness to help the patient.

2   There is an opposite risk, that one will deceive the patient in order to serve justice and fairness.

3   There is the danger that one will prostitute the profession as one is alternatively seduced by the power of the adversarial system and is assaulted by it.[20]

Bowden notes a further risk. Psychiatrists may have their own private agendas, quite independent of the case they are considering, in the form of personal views about the appropriateness or not of the judicial process and the penal system and they may use their reports to "emphasize causes or . . . idiosyncratic beliefs". He warns against psychiatrists "assuming the mantles of arbiter of cultural values or social engineer".[21]

Another problem is that psychiatry, and even sub-specialities such as forensic psychiatry, now encompasses so many areas and topics that no individual psychiatrist, however learned or dedicated he or she may be, and however many academic qualifications he or she may have, can justifiably lay claim to being an expert in every or even any field of psychiatry. Expertise in psychiatry is rapidly becoming expertise in narrower and narrower areas.

Given the problems that exist, what should the role of the forensic psychiatrist in court be? There are a number of different views on this. At one extreme is the view that the forensic psychiatrist has little or no role. According to Menninger, an eminent American psychiatrist, "what all courts should do, what society should do, is to exclude all psychiatrists from the courtrooms".[22] According to Stone, "the forensic psychiatrist outside the therapeutic context is meddling in alien business" and is not in any way qualified to provide "true answers to the legal and moral questions posted by the law".[23]

Putting aside this rather extreme point of view, there does appear to be increasing agreement, both as a result of court decisions and throughout the literature, that psychiatrists, like cobblers, should stick to their lasts, that is, that they should confine themselves to what they are trained to do which is to provide advice on the diagnosis and treatment of established mental disorders. The courts have made it quite clear that in the absence of any mental disorder (and, as Barclay points out, "the demonstration of psychodynamics, however sophisticated, does not establish that a mental disorder . . . exists"[24]) forensic psychiatrists have little or no role to play in courtroom proceedings. Bluglass summarises the situation as follows:

> The rule that an expert's advice is admissible to provide scientific information that is outside the experience or knowledge of the judge and jury means for psychiatry that the subject of the evidence is presumed to be abnormal. 'Jurors do not need psychiatrists to tell them how ordinary folk who are not suffering from mental illness are likely to react to the stresses and strains of life' said Lawton LJ (*R v Turner* 1975). It is not normally permissible therefore for a psychiatrist to comment on the intent of an accused person; that is the role of the jury. . . Evidence that the accused's ability to form an intent was disturbed, or that he lacked intent (or mens rea) as a result of mental disorder, may on the other hand properly be allowed. Similarly, psychiatric evidence about the reactions of 'normal' people to provocation will be inadmissible.[25]

Even if the defendant does have a mental disorder, however, there are still questions about whether psychiatrists should be asked to give an opinion on such matters as intent and responsibility. This issue has been argued at length elsewhere so there is no need to pursue it here, except to reiterate that "intent" and "responsibility" are legal terms and not psychiatric terms. They do not have any basis in psychiatry. As Milte et al point out, what this has resulted in is "much semantic juggling in an endeavour to fit a square psychological peg into an essentially round criminal law hole".[26] With regard to the issue of "mental responsibility", Milte et al comment that it "is entangled in a morass of ethical and moralistic issues defying objective analysis".[27] With regard to the issue of "intent", Durkheim suggested in the nineteenth century that it is "too intimate a thing to be interpreted by another person".[28] Bartholomew notes that Briscoe has also "cast great doubt on the question as to whether the psychiatrist has any real role in assessing 'intent'"[29] and cites his own evidence in a Victorian case in support of this position:

> I don't think anyone, being a clinical psychologist or a psychiatrist or anyone else bar a crystal gazer, can talk about the capacity of anyone under any circumstances in terms of intent. . . [Short of unconsciousness] I don't think any of us have the capacity to offer an expert opinion as to whether or not an intent — whether it be general or specific — can be formed . . . that is when I think we have begun to

'invent' psychiatry and it is a phrase I have used before, and this bothers me. It is no longer expert evidence. It has become magic.[30]

What all this gets down to is the point raised earlier; that psychiatrists should confine themselves to what they are trained to do. Although he does not consider it an exhaustive list, Cosgrove suggests the following:

1   Identify and describe the function of the accused's mind at the time of examination.

2   Draw any proper inferences (either not involving or specifically acknowledging evidence which points elsewhere) as to the function of the accused's mind in the period surrounding the performance of the proscribed act.

3   Identify possible malfunctioning at the actual time of performance of the proscribed act.

4   Point to any evidence indicating disturbance of cognition or volition at that time.[31]

With regard to point 4, however, he notes that:

a psychiatrist cannot, as a matter of science, identify and describe the degree of cognition and volition possessed by an accused person at the precise time of commission of an act proscribed by the law. The utmost that he can do is to diagnose the existence of a disorder of the mind which could disturb the processes of cognition and volition and point to behaviour which may suggest the existence of such disturbance.[32]

Unfortunately, Cosgrove does not say what he means by the term "function of the accused's mind". Presumably he is asking whether the symptoms of a psychiatric disorder are present and, if so, the nature of those symptoms and their relationship, if any, to the proscribed act. If this is what he means, it is a reasonable summary of what the role of the forensic psychiatrist might be. There are, however, problems with retrospective inferences about the state of a person's mind at some time in the distant past. These are discussed below. In addition, the psychiatrist may be able to provide useful information about the treatment options available and their relative rates of success.

Although most of the above deals with the role of the forensic psychiatrist in the criminal jurisdiction, most of what has been said applies to the civil jurisdiction as well except that "the questions which the forensic expert witness may legitimately answer"[33] will be governed by the nature of the case. In the assessment of personal injury claims, for example, Lasky has suggested that the psychiatrist's task is to answer the following questions:

1   Is there a mental disorder?

2   If there is a mental disorder, what is the diagnosis in terms of DSM-III?

3   What are the findings which support the diagnosis?

4   What disabilities are present, described in terms of impairment of function in the labour market?[34]

As pointed out in Section A, the diagnostic categories in the DSM–IV and the ICD–10 have many limitations and caution must be exercised in using them. In most cases a description of the symptoms is far more valuable for forensic purposes (or, for that matter, for ordinary clinical purposes) than the application of a diagnostic label. This problem aside, however, the list is a sensible one in that the questions asked are precise and limited and the answers lie within the expertise of the psychiatrist (although as Mendelson points out the response to question 4 may need a more structured approach than is currently available).

If the questions that are put to a forensic psychiatrist are limited in this way to those that are clearly within the psychiatrist's expertise to answer, a number of the problems that currently occur at the psychiatry/law interface would be resolved (although there would still be some problems arising out of the adversarial process and the imprecise nature of psychiatry as a science).

THE PERSON REFERRED FOR ASSESSMENT

Even when a non-forensic patient is referred to a psychiatrist for assessment certain problems can be anticipated. As I have pointed out elsewhere:

> Any patient being psychiatrically assessed will have certain expectations of what his or her role, as a patient, should be and these expectations will vary according to the patient's previous exposure to psychiatric treatment and according to the purposes for which the assessment is being carried out. The patient will also have certain expectations of what a psychiatrist is and of what a psychiatrist does. These expectations and the conventions that surround them will inevitably influence what the patient says or does in the interview situation. This, of course, is a hazard in any professional interview. It is not confined to psychiatric interviews.[35]

In addition to this, there are a number of emotional distorting factors, known as transference factors, that are thought to exist at the unconscious level, that can influence very profoundly the way a person may respond to the psychiatrist assessing and treating them. These feelings, which can include both positive feelings (such as love) and negative feelings (such as hate), can be of varying intensity. They arise out of feelings that first develop in childhood towards significant people in the child's life. In the course of assessment and treatment they may be transferred onto the psychiatrist. The patient then reacts to the psychiatrist in the same way they would have reacted to the original person towards whom they developed these feelings if that person had been present instead of the psychiatrist. If they are negative feelings or very strong positive feelings they may significantly distort the patient-psychiatrist interaction and relationship.

In the case of a forensic assessment there are additional factors still. There is always the possibility of the patient intentionally misleading the psychiatrist, especially when the psychiatrist's report is based, as it frequently is, on one or two interviews of relatively short duration. The patient may lie to the psychiatrist by deliberately avoiding mentioning significant events in the history or by describing things that never happened. Facts, fantasies, half-truths and outright lies may be blended together in such a way that it is impossible to sort them out without independent corroboration. Even in hospital practice, where a person is under observation 24 hours a day, seven days a week, it can sometimes take days of assessment and the input of a number of professional groups — psychiatrists, psychologists, social workers, occupational therapists and nursing staff — to reach a consensus of opinion about the person's mental state. And even then it is possible for the entire clinical team to be misled as the literature on pseudo-patients aptly demonstrates.

The first major study on pseudo-patients was conducted by Rosenhan,[36] a professor of psychology and law at Stanford University in the early 1970s. Rosenhan and seven other sane experimental subjects presented themselves to 12 different psychiatric hospitals complaining of hearing voices. They did not complain of any other psychiatric symptoms and answered truthfully all questions put to them, except questions about their voices, their name or their occupation. They were all admitted and diagnosed as suffering from either schizophrenia or (in one case) manic-depressive psychosis. Immediately they were admitted they "ceased simulating any symptoms of abnormality". Length of hospitalisation ranged from 7 to 52 days, with an average of 19 days. They were never detected by hospital staff and 11 were discharged with diagnoses of "schizophrenia in remission". This study and subsequent studies of a similar nature illustrate two things. The first is the danger of coming to conclusions about a person's mental state on the first interview. The second is the ease with which mental health professionals can be misled, at least for a short time. What usually lets people down when they are simulating mental disorder is the difficulty of maintaining the pretence for a long period of time. It is relatively easy for a reasonably intelligent person to keep repeating the same story. Indeed, as pointed out earlier, this may be all that is necessary in the case of a person endeavouring to invent a psychiatric explanation for past behaviour. It is much more difficult for someone to maintain the appearance of being mentally disordered or the behavioural manifestations of mental disorder for a long time even when they are psychologically sophisticated enough to know the combination of signs and symptoms (and it is the combination of signs and symptoms that establishes the existence of the mental disorder, not just the presence of individual signs or symptoms) that would normally convince a psychiatrist or other mental health professional of the genuineness of their disorder.[37]

NOTES

1   Hunter, R and Macalpine, I, *Three Hundred Years of Psychiatry* (1963) p viii.

2   According to Bowden, "Erring from the precise instructions of the solicitor can place the psychiatrist in breach of contract so the solicitor can properly decline to pay the agreed fee". Bowden, P, "The written report and sentences" in Bluglass, R and Bowden, P (eds*) Principles and Practice of Forensic Psychiatry* (1990) p 184.

3   As Rappeport points out, "When functioning in such environments and under circumstances which may require that custodial concerns override therapeutic concerns, clearly psychiatrists must operate differently". Rappeport, J, "Differences Between Forensic and General Psychiatry" (1982) 139:3 *Amer J Psychiat* 332.

4   Chiswick, D, "Psychiatric Testimony in Britain: Remembering Your Lines and Keeping to the Script" (1992) 15 *Int'l J L & Psychiat* 176.

5   Bluglass, R, "The psychiatrist as an expert witness" in Bluglass and Bowden, above n 2 p 163. Alcorn notes that: "Langbein has described expert witnesses as 'saxaphones' because the lawyer, "plays the tune as though the expert were a musical instrument on which the lawyer sounds the desired notes". Cited in Alcorn, D, "Basic Law for Psychiatrists" (1995) Presentation notes for Annual Meeting of the Royal Australian and New Zealand College of Psychiatrists Section of Forensic Psychiatry, Article 1 p 11.

6   Id.

7   Morse, S, "Excusing the Crazy: The insanity defence reconsidered" (1985) 58 *S Calif L Rev* 821.

8   Mendelson, G, "The Scope and Limitations of Psychiatric Expert Testimony" (1990) 10 *Aust For Psychiat B* 11.

9   Cosgrove J, "As We See Ourselves — And As Others See Us" (1985) 3 *Aust For Psychiat B* 2.

10   Mendelson, above n 8 pp 13–14.

11   One of the earliest pieces of forensic psychiatric evidence ever recorded sounds suspiciously like the "hired gun" approach. According to Zilboorg:

> [Hippocrates (4th century BC)] once appeared as expert witness when a woman was brought to court on the indictment of miscegenation and testified that there was nothing criminal or unnatural in the fact that the defendant, although fair skinned, gave birth to a dark skinned child. He claimed that the woman was deeply impressed by the sight of the Ethiopians, that this was sufficient to affect her imagination and thus to influence the color of the offspring, and that she need not have borne her child by an Ethiopian (Zilboorg, G, *A History of Medical Psychology* (1967) p 46).

12   In the nineteenth century case of *Lord Abinger v Ashton* (1873) 17 LR Eq 358 at 374, Jessel MR, while not referring specifically to psychiatric evidence suggested that the "hired gun" role was endemic amongst expert witnesses of the time:

[I]n matters of opinion I very much distrust expert evidence, for several reasons. In the first place, although the evidence is given upon oath, in point of fact, the person knows that he cannot be indicted for perjury, because it is only evidence as to a matter of opinion. So that you have not the authority of legal sanction. A dishonest man, knowing he could not be punished, might be inclined to indulge in extravagant assertions on an occasion that required it. But that is not all. Expert evidence of this kind is evidence of persons who sometimes live by their business, but in all cases are remunerated for their evidence. An expert is not like an ordinary witness, who hopes to get his expenses, but he is employed and paid in the sense of gain, being employed by the person who calls him. Now it is natural that his mind, however honest he may be, should be biased in favour of the person employing him, and accordingly, we do find such bias. . . Undoubtedly there is a natural bias to do something serviceable for those who employ you and adequately remunerate you. It is very natural, and it is so effectual that we constantly see persons, instead of considering themselves witnesses, rather consider themselves as the paid agents of the person who employs them (Cited in Katzmann, A, "Cross-Examination of the Expert Witness" in Winfield, R (ed), *The Expert Medical Witness* (1989) p 55).

13   Some idea of the animosity that exists in some circles over the way psychiatric evidence is sometimes used in court can be gleaned from the following extracts from an article by George Will which appeared in the *Guardian*, 4 July 1982. The article was entitled "Ideology Masquerading as Medicine".

The verdict finding John W Hinckley Jr not guilty by reason of insanity of shooting President Reagan and three other men on March 30, 1981, illustrates three perversities: The most morally indefensible crimes are becoming the most legally defendable. The idea of the individual is being obliterated in order to maximize the rights of the individual. And the quest for the chimera of perfect justice is subordinating the social good, including the rule of law, to the quicksilver axioms of a 'science' that is long on pretenses and short on testable assertions.

Seated atop a ramshackle scaffolding of superstitions, merrily minting nouns that denote nothing, many psychiatrists are today condescending to the American people, chiding them for not comprehending the intellectual marvellousness of the Hinckley verdict. But the verdict will serve the social good only if it generates disgust with the incompatible marriage of psychiatry and law. . . [Psychiatrists] often are hired to put an acre of embroidery around a pinhead of 'fact'. So they bandy diagnostic categories that are as evanescent as snowflakes.

Psychiatry as practised by some of today's itinerant experts-for-hire is this century's alchemy. But no, that simile is unfair to alchemists, who were confused but honest chemists. Some of today's rent-a-psychiatry is charlatanism laced with cynicism.

14   In a severity appeal case in 1990 (*Newey v R* (unreported, 23 August 1990, NSW CCA, 60619/89) material placed before the court included two reports from a consulting psychiatrist. Wood J (Gleeson CJ and Badgery-Parker J agreeing) observed:

Regrettably, it seems to me those reports crossed the line into the field of advocacy. For my part I would emphasise the need for psychiatrists to confine their opinions when offered in sentencing proceedings to their area of expertise. I would wish to discourage the development of any practice whereby such experts venture into advocacy or suggest appropriate outcomes for sentencing judges. That is not to say they should not deal with the effects of incarceration upon an offender or underline the psychiatric disabilities which have existed in the past and which may continue. Their proper role is to place before the court evidence concerning those matters, but otherwise they should refrain from requesting or suggesting that the court take into account particular matters of mitigation, or impose particular sentences. . . ((December, 1990) *Judicial Officers Bulletin* 5).

15   As Bowden puts it:

The psychiatrist should aim at a balanced report saying what can be said psychiatrically about the accused, while at the same time pointing out with equal weight the adverse features. . . [The psychiatrist] should not play down negative attributes and make the most of positive ones to advance a particular case (Bowden, above n 2 p 184).

Resnick suggests, however, that once the psychiatrist is called as a witness, impartiality is difficult to maintain. Resnick states that, "Once (the psychiatrist) has formed an opinion . . . it is only human for him to identify himself with that opinion and hope for the success of the side which supports his conclusions" (Resnick, P, "The Psychiatrist as Expert Witness" cited in "Basic Law for Psychiatrists", above n 5 p 14).

16   Sadoff, R, cited in Mendelson, above n 8 p 14.

17   Rogers, R, "Ethical Dilemmas in Forensic Evaluations" (1987) 5/2 *Beh Sci & L* 150.

18   Stanley, R, "The Psychiatrist as Expert Witness: A Legal Perspective" (1989) 9 *Aust For Psychiat B* 4.

19   Cosgrove, above n 9 p 2.

20   Stone, A, cited in Bluglass, above n 5 p 162.

21   Bowden, above n 2 p 184.

22   Menninger, K, cited in Mendelson, above n 8 p 11.

23   Stone, A, cited in Mendelson, above n 8 p 10.

24   Barclay, W, "Homicide — The Viewpoint of One Forensic Psychiatrist", unpublished paper presented to Conference on Homicide: Patterns, Prevention and Control, Melbourne, 1992.

25   Bluglass, above n 5 p 163. In the judgement in *R v Turner* [1975] 1 QB 834, Lawton J notes that one of the reasons for not allowing psychiatrists to comment on matters that can be decided without the help of an expert is that because their evidence:

is given dressed up in scientific jargon it may make judgment more difficult. The fact that an expert has impressive scientific qualifications does not by that fact alone make his opinion on matters of human nature and behaviour within the limits of normality any more helpful than that of the jurors themselves; but there is a *danger* that they may think it does (at 841, cited in Alcorn, D, above n 5 p 10).

26   Milte, K, Bartholomew, A and Galbally, F, "Abolition of the Crime of Murder and of Mental Condition Defences" (1975) 49 *ALJ* 162.

27   Ibid p 160.

28   Durkheim, E, cited in Scott, P, "Assessing Dangerousness in Criminals" (1977) 131 *Brit J Psychiat* 128.

29   Bartholomew, A, *Psychiatry, The Criminal Law and Corrections. An Exercise in Sciolism* (1986) p 157.

30   Id.

31   Cosgrove, above n 9 p 3.

32   Id.

33   Mendelson, above n 8 p 12.

34   Mendelson, G, "The Rating of Psychiatric Impairment in Forensic Practice: A Review" (1991) 25 *ANZ J Psychiat* 84.

35   Shea, P, "Commentary" in *Proceedings of the Institute of Criminology* No 57, "Shoplifting" (1983) p 73.

36   Rosenhan also reversed the study by telling the staff of "a research and teaching hospital [who] . . . had heard these findings but doubted that such an error could occur in their hospital" that "at some time during the following 3 months, one or more pseudopatients would attempt to be admitted". No genuine pseudopatients presented during this period. Of 193 genuine patients who were admitted during this period, "Forty-one . . . were alleged, with high confidence, to be pseudopatients by at least one member of the staff. Twenty-three were considered suspect by at least one psychiatrist". Rosenhan, D, "On being sane in insane places" (1973) 179 *Sci* 250. See also, Owen, A and Winkler, R, "General Practitioners and Psychosocial Problems. An Evaluation Using Pseudo-patients" (1974) 2 *Med J Aust* 393; Winkler, R, "Research Into Mental Health Practice Using Pseudopatients" (1974) 2 *Med J Aust* 399; Leading Article, "Pseudopatients" (1974) 2 *Brit Med J* 729; McConaghy, N, "Pseudopatients and Evaluation of Medical Practice" (1974) 2 *Med J Aust* 383.

37   The feigning of mental illness is not a recent development in the history of psychiatry. The earliest reference to it occurs in the Bible. David, fleeing from Saul, goes to Achish the king of Gath but, fearful for his life, pretends to be mad. "So he changed his behaviour before then, and feigned himself mad in their hands, and made marks on the doors of the gate, and let his spittle run down his beard" (1 Samuel 21:13). Zilboorg notes that Homer also described a case of feigned mental illness. "Ulysses when he simulated madness would yoke a bull and a horse together, ploughing the sands of the seashore and sowing salt instead of corn." Zilboorg, above n 11 p 37.

8

THE ASSESSMENT PROCESS

A symptom is something that a patient experiences and subsequently describes to the person examining them. A sign is something that the person carrying out the examination observes. In general medicine it is often possible to confirm a symptom by either a sign or a test or both. If a person complains of a temperature, for example, the doctor might note that the person is flushed and sweating and for final confirmation can use a thermometer. Psychiatric examinations are quite different. Some symptoms cannot be confirmed by objective signs or tests. Dissociative amnesia and command hallucinations are two such symptoms. These symptoms and the general problems associated with taking a forensic history and doing a forensic assessment are discussed below.

THE EXAMINATION

The assessment that the psychiatrist carries out has two major elements — the history-taking and the mental state examination. Specific physical and psychological tests may also be required to complete the picture.

Obtaining a history can be a long and difficult process. The psychiatrist is not just concerned with the circumstances surrounding the offence. In order to place the offence in context the psychiatrist has to obtain a full longitudinal history going back to the person's early childhood. Details of all significant events an relationships in the person's life history have to be elucidated and evaluated. This is simply not possible on a single interview. Over 90 years ago a psychiatrist gave the following advice to his colleagues: "Always, if possible, see a presumably insane patient at least twice before completing your diagnosis".[1]

This is especially wise advice in the field in forensic psychiatry. All the significant parts of a person's life history cannot be obtained in one interview and, on reflection, even the material that is obtained at the first interview often needs to be checked with the patient for both veracity and further detail.

The history should be gleaned from as many sources as possible, not just the person who is being assessed.[2] This applies to both general and forensic psychiatry but, in the case of the latter, access to corroborative evidence may be denied (especially if the psychiatrist is employed by the prosecution). Any assessment that is based solely on what the patient says and that does not seek corroborative evidence from outside sources (for example, from the patient's family, friends, workplace, existing police and court reports) will be a screened interview. In other words a psychiatrist, however astute or experienced he or she may be, will only glean a limited amount of information from the patient. And even that information may be subject to distortion. Without corroborative information from outside sources, the psychiatrist will be forced to rely on what the patient says. Assessing the truth of what the patient is saying under these circumstances can be quite difficult.[3] A psychiatrist might suspect, for example, that a story is not true if it is very fanciful or internally inconsistent, but there is no way of being certain about this if corroborative information is absent. All practising psychiatrists have had the experience of listening to a story that sounds not only fanciful but positively bizarre only to learn sometime later that the story was true. Also, there is always the possibility, of course, as pointed out in Chapter 7, that the story is a mixture of fact and fiction, and when we move to the patient's symptoms we move even further into the realm of material that is difficult to verify objectively. Patients with a mental disorder may be hearing voices telling them to steal something from a shop or may feel no longer in control of their own bodies but the psychiatrist has no independent way of verifying this. He or she cannot get inside the patient's head and "read their mind".

Also, history-taking depends upon memory and, sometimes, written records. Both can be, and usually are, very selective. Both can be in error. In both the mentally disordered and the non-mentally disordered memories can and do alter and fade over time. In fact, contrary to the expectations and beliefs of some courts, memories are notoriously faulty. Experimentally, memory is not strictly reproductive. It is not like a video tape that reproduces the exact identical image every time it is turned on. There are a number of theories about how memory is actually recorded in the nerve cells in the brain but, at base, they all agree that it is recorded and stored at the cellular level on biochemical substrates and these, like everything else in the body are turned over regularly and replaced. In the course of replacement small variations can occur in the biochemical substrates. Memories are not just encoded (or laid down), stored in an inviolable manner and then retrieved on demand in the pristine state in which they were laid down. Each process is subject to distortion and, in addition to the three basic processes already mentioned, there is a fourth – reconstruction – which further distorts memory. What occurs at each stage of the process is determined by a number of factors. In relation to memories of events, for example, whether or not something is encoded depends, inter alia, upon whether it is related to either pre-existing knowledge or other events occurring around the same time. Whether something is retrieved depends, inter alia, upon the type and amount of information provided by the cue. Kihlstrom uses the following analogy to describe how memory works:

In describing how memory works, we often resort to the metaphor of a library: Memory traces are books that must be purchased and catalogued; the prospective user must look up the book in the catalog to know where to find it; and for the search to succeed, the book must not have been eaten by worms, or displaced by a careless user. The library metaphor will take us a long way, but the notion of memory retrieval obscures the fact that memories can be distorted, biased, and otherwise altered by changes in perspective and other events that occur after the time of encoding. In the final analysis, memory is not so much like reading a book as it is like writing one from fragmentary notes. The reconstruction principle is of utmost importance . . . because it means that any particular memory is only partly derived from trace information at the time of the event: In the process of remembering, trace information combines with knowledge, beliefs, and inferences derived from other sources.[4]

Kihlstrom also goes on to point out that, on the experimental evidence available, "in the absence of . . . independent corroboration, we have no means of reliably distinguishing between fact and fantasy".[5] To complicate the situation even further, Spiegel and Scheflin note that many of the factors that have traditionally been considered in court to be indicative of the accuracy of a memory are, in fact, no guarantee at all of a memory's accuracy. These include such factors as (a) the amount of detail, (b) the richness of detail, (c) clarity and vividness, (d) emotional involvement, (e) consistency over time, (f) the self-confidence of the person relating the memory, (g) the fact that the person is known to be honest, and (h) the fact that the person has a reputation for having a good memory. [6]

Selectivity is also a problem for the person taking the history. It is, in fact, necessary to be selective. It would be impossible to record a person's entire psychosocial history in all its detail and so certain areas will inevitably be chosen for close examination at the expense of others. Which areas are chosen will depend, in part, upon the purpose for which the history is being taken and the time spent on taking the history. As I have pointed out elsewhere,

> If the psychiatrist is taking notes, what he or she writes down is selective. If the psychiatrist is using a tape recorder what she or he later selects from the transcript of the tape to include in the report is selective. What goes into the report and the way the report is put together is selective. It is impossible not to be selective if the report is going to be both readable and comprehensive.[7]

One of the problems that arises from this is the likelihood, on the part of both the person doing the assessment and the person being assessed, of the negative aspects of a person's life (neglect, abuse, isolation and so on) being emphasised and the positive aspects being neglected or played down. If the diagnosis has already been established there is the further danger that the diagnosis itself may affect both the selection process and the way the history is recorded.[8]

The history by itself is only part of the assessment process. An assessment cannot be completed on the basis of the history alone. The other indispensable part of the assessment is the mental state examination. This is the psychiatric equivalent of the physical examination in a general medical setting. If a person went to their general practitioner complaining of headaches and the doctor told them that the headaches were caused by high blood pressure, without measuring the blood pressure at all, the person would be justified in seeking a second opinion. Just as a general practitioner cannot do a proper assessment without a physical examination of the patient, so a psychiatrist cannot do a proper assessment without doing a mental state examination. There are two elements to the examination: the psychiatrist's observations of the person's thinking, mood and behaviour at the time of the examination and the symptoms the person describes to the psychiatrist. One of the problems that arises in relation to the former is that it is subject to and, indeed, "inseparable from"[9] observer influence and error. Further, as Hunter and Macalpine point out: "There is not even an objective way of describing or communicating clinical findings without subjective interpretation".[10]

Problems that can arise with the symptoms the person describes are illustrated in the sections which follow on dissociative amnesia and command hallucinations.

Without a mental state examination it is not possible to come to any firm or reliable conclusions about the person's mental condition. This is one of the major stumbling blocks of forensic psychiatry because a lot of forensic assessments are carried out for the purpose of determining a person's mental condition at some time in the past. In such cases the only information available to the psychiatrist about the mental state of the person being assessed is what that person can remember and is prepared to tell the psychiatrist and what eyewitnesses to the event, if any, can remember about the person's behaviour. Assessing someone's mental state is a highly technical procedure so unless the eyewitnesses are trained mental health professionals their observations cannot be relied upon. And even if they were trained mental health professionals there is still a danger in the psychiatrist doing the assessment accepting what they say simply because of their professional status. As Birns and Levien point out:

> a psychiatrist attempting to evaluate [a prisoner] . . . may be influenced by earlier, perhaps inaccurate psychiatric evaluations for there is evidence that "initial diagnosis 'may have a profound effect' upon a subsequent diagnosis".[11]

What this means in the case of those forensic examinations that are done weeks and sometimes months after the incident took place, is that they have to be based, to a large extent, upon guesswork and they can never pretend to be anything other than that. They are, at best, educated guesses and, at worst, totally unreliable and misleading inventions. It is up to the court to determine how much weight to give to them but the limitations are both obvious and extreme.

DISSOCIATIVE AMNESIA

Dissociative amnesia has a number of different names. In the DSM–III–R it was called "Psychogenic Amnesia". In the DSM-IV it is called "Dissociative Amnesia" and comes under the general heading of "Dissociative Disorders". Other disorders listed under the same heading are "Dissociative Fugue", "Dissociative Identity Disorder" (formerly "Multiple Personality Disorder"), "Depersonalization Disorder" and "Dissociative Disorder Not Otherwise Specified". In the DSM-IV, dissociative amnesia is described as follows:

> The essential feature of Dissociative Amnesia is an inability to recall important personal information, usually of a traumatic or stressful nature, that is too extensive to be explained by normal forgetfulness. This disorder involves a reversible memory impairment in which memories of personal experience cannot be retrieved in a verbal form (or, if temporarily retrieved, cannot be wholly retained in consciousness). . .

> Dissociative Amnesia most commonly presents as a retrospectively reported gap or series of gaps in recall for aspects of the individual's life history. These gaps are usually related to traumatic or extremely stressful events. . .

> Several types of memory disturbances have been described in Dissociative Amnesia. In localized amnesia, the individual fails to recall events that occurred during a circumscribed period of time, usually the first few hours following a profoundly disturbing event (e.g. the uninjured survivor of a car accident in which a family member has been killed may not be able to recall anything that happened from the time of the accident until 2 days later). In selective amnesia, the person can recall some, but not all, of the events during a circumscribed period of time (e.g., a combat veteran can recall only some parts of a series of violent combat experiences). Three other types of amnesia − generalized, continuous, and systematized − are less common. In generalized amnesia, failure of recall encompasses the person's entire life. . . Continuous amnesia is defined as the inability to recall events subsequent to a specific time up to and including the present. Systematized amnesia is loss of memory for certain categories of information, such as all memories relating to one's family or to a particular person.

> Acute amnesia may resolve spontaneously after the individual is removed from the traumatic circumstances with which the amnesia was associated. . . Some individuals with chronic amnesia may gradually begin to recall dissociated memories. Other individuals may develop a chronic form of amnesia. [12]

In the ICD–10, the disorder is also called "Dissociative amnesia". The description is very similar to that in the DSM–IV, except for the following note: "The extent and completeness of the amnesia often vary from day to day and between investigators, but there is a persistent common core that cannot be recalled in the waking state". [13]

A dissociative fugue is very similar to dissociative amnesia except that it is more extensive and more complete. It is described in the DSM-IV as follows:

> The essential feature of Dissociative Fugue is sudden, unexpected, travel away from home or one's customary place of daily activities, with inability to recall some or all of one's past. This is accompanied by confusion about personal identity or even the assumption of a new identity. . . Travel may range from brief trips over relatively short periods of time (i.e., hours or days) to complex, usually unobtrusive wandering over long time periods (e.g., weeks or months), with some

individuals reportedly crossing numerous national borders and travelling thousands of miles.[14]

Although both the DSM–IV and the ICD–10 consider dissociative amnesia a relatively rare phenomenon, in violent crimes, especially homicide, it appears to be a relatively common phenomenon, with between 25 per cent and 45 per cent of convicted homicide cases claiming amnesia for the offence.[15] In violent crimes other than homicide only about 8 per cent claim amnesia. In nonviolent crimes the prevalence is not known but some studies suggest that it is zero.[16] In violent crimes there is also evidence of impaired recall on the part of the victim (in crimes other than homicide) and the eyewitnesses.[17]

There are a number of theories that can be invoked to explain the origin of dissociative amnesia. Unfortunately, the terminology is far from being either clear or settled. The most commonly accepted theories are those which postulate that an unconscious mental defence mechanism (dissociation) swings into play automatically to remove potentially threatening or distressing feelings and thoughts (in this case, memories) from consciousness to the unconscious. In these theories the term "dissociation" and the term used to describe another unconscious mental defence mechanism ("repression") are sometimes used in a synonymous way as they both have the same end result (the keeping of unacceptable material out of immediate consciousness). Technically, however, they can have different meanings. Dissociation can be conceptualised in the way described above, that is as a force which removes potentially threatening material, especially emotionally charged memories, from consciousness. Repression, on the other hand, can be conceptualised as a force that prevents unacceptable instinctual drives from surfacing into consciousness. As no one knows where or how, or even if, these mechanisms actually operate in the brain the argument is largely academic. To complicate matters, however, "dissociation" can be used in another way. When Freud first used it, before he developed his theory of repressed instinctual drives, he used it in much the same way as Janet used it before him – to describe a splitting in consciousness.[18] This is very much the same concept as is found in the definition contained in the DSM-IV (ie "a disruption in the usually integrated functions of consciousness, memory, identity or perception of the environment").[19]

To complicate the matter even further there is the theory of state dependency which suggests that "an individual who is in an altered mood state when an event is experienced, is more likely to remember that event on a subsequent occasion if he is in the equivalent mood state."[20]

It is important to note that dissociative amnesic states are often mixed states. There may be organic factors in evidence as well and sometimes other psychiatric disorders. Also, a history of chronic alcohol abuse and alcohol and other drug intoxication at the time of the offence is commoner in amnesic cases that nonamnesic cases.[21] In the case of fugue states, for example, Kopelman identified five factors that may predispose to a fugue or be associated with one:

1 A severe precipitating stress, e.g. marital, emotional, financial or battle stress; in the presence of

2 Depressed mood, almost invariably present, and sometimes accompanied by suicidal thoughts; and

3 There is commonly a past history of an organic amnesia resulting from, for example, head injury, alcoholic blackout, or epilepsy.

4 In addition, several authors have noted that these patients are sometimes rather unreliable personalities with a tendency to lie; and

5 An offence may occasionally precipitate a fugue.[22]

There are four difficulties that the concept of dissociative amnesia presents for forensic psychiatry.

First, there are the conflicting psychological theories about how the amnesia occurs (discussed above). Secondly, there is the problem of sorting out the relative importance of the other factors that may be present at the time. Thirdly, there is the problem of determining whether or not the offender is simulating the amnesia or not. Fourthly, there is the problem of "repressed memories". These are discussed below in a separate section. The remainder of this section deals with the problem of simulated or feigned amnesia. Kopelman reviewed a variety of approaches that have been used to try to distinguish between genuine amnesia and simulated amnesia and summarised his findings as follows:

> Power adopted an essentially clinical approach, advising that an investigator should examine closely the character of an amnesia (an abrupt onset or termination may be more likely to indicate feigning), the nature of the crime (a genuine amnesia is more likely to have occurred in the context of a psychiatric disorder, a motiveless and unpremeditated crime, and in the presence of witnesses), and the personality of the offender (his truthfulness on other matters, and the consistency of his account through time, can be checked). This approach seems sensible enough, but the validity of its individual components requires corroboration in a systematic study. Other investigators have tried various psychophysical procedures, such as polygraphy, hypnosis, and amytal administration. . . However, all these procedures are very sensitive to suggestion and their validity is disputed; moreover, the results of amytal abreaction are often disappointing. Parwatikar et al employed a psychometric technique: having found that a discrimination function analysis distinguished amnesic and "confessed" murderers on the basis of alcohol and/or drug intoxication plus MMPI scores for hysteria, hypochondriasis, and depression, [they] suggested that subjects who fail to fit this profile might be simulating — but they did not provide any evidence to support this suggestion. More recently various authors have suggested an experimental approach, arguing that malingerers will tend to overplay their role and perform worse on certain tests than they should do. . . These latter approaches [are] promising but [require] further corroboration in clinical and forensic populations.[23]

Kopelman goes on to suggest that,

there are a number of reasons why this issue may be less clear-cut, and perhaps less critical, than it sometimes appears. First, there may not be any distinct demarcation between conscious malingering and unconscious hysteria. . . Secondly, many amnesic cases have been described in the literature who either have reported their own crime or have failed to take measures to avoid their own capture. . . This makes an account of amnesia as simulation to avoid punishment seem less plausible. . . Thirdly . . . in Britain amnesia per se does not constitute a defense or a barrier to a trial; and it does not by itself affect the accused's fitness to plead or responsibility.[24]

In his third point, Kopelman is referring to the case of Gunther Podola who shot and killed a police officer, suffered a head injury while being captured, and claimed severe retrograde amnesia. Five doctors testified. The possibility of an organic cause was quickly discounted and the question arose as to whether the amnesia was a true dissociative amnesia or simulated. The case eventually went to the Court of Criminal Appeal. The outcome of the court's ruling was that "a person who has a hysterical amnesia for all the circumstances of the alleged offence, but has no other mental abnormality, is held to be fit to plead".[25]

Howard also reviews the problem of simulated amnesia and warns psychiatrists not to give firm opinions on the subject unless they are absolutely certain about their facts. He concludes that:

the majority of cases are likely to prove baffling [and that] it seems likely that many individuals will continue to display an amnesia whose origins are unclear and whose genuineness is in doubt. In such cases the forensic psychiatrist can only suspend judgement, however strong the pressures to do otherwise.[26]

The DSM-IV is quite clear on this point. It states, "There are no tests or set of procedures that invariably distinguish Dissociative Amnesia from Malingering". It adds, however, that "individuals with Dissociative Amnesia usually score high on standard measures of hypnotisability and dissociative capacity".[27]

DISSOCIATIVE AMNESIA AND REPRESSED MEMORIES

The confusion over the terms "dissociation" and "repression", discussed earlier, has become evident again, in recent times, in the literature on "repressed memories". The DSM-IV, for example, notes that:

In recent years in the United States, there has been as increase in reported cases of Dissociative Amnesia that involves previously forgotten early childhood traumas. This increase has been subject to very different interpretations. Some believe that the greater awareness of the diagnosis among mental health professionals has resulted in the identification of cases that were previously undiagnosed. In contrast, others believe that the syndrome has been overdiagnosed in individuals who are highly suggestible.[28]

What the DSM is referring to is the upsurge in cases of repressed/dissociated memories, where the memories have surfaced in later life, sometimes, but not necessarily, under hypnosis. Such memories are usually of sexual mistreatment of the individual concerned although they can be related to other crimes.

In cases of repressed memories the terms "repression" and "dissociation" are being used synonymously. To complicate matters, however, some authors have started to talk about "robust repression" of which there are two forms. The first operates immediately after each traumatic sexual event but does not interfere with memories of intervening events. The second operates at the end of the abuse period and prevents the person from remembering both the traumatic events and the non-traumatic periods in between. Although the theorists who push this idea claim that what they are describing is quite different from repression and dissociation as described earlier, there is very little if any evidence to support the theory.[29]

Other authors have suggested that repression is not a universal mental defence mechanism at all but a personality trait. Some people are repressive, some are not. There is very little support for this theory either.

The veracity or otherwise of recovered repressed memories is a subject that is currently very topical. The major difficulty is that there is no valid way of distinguishing true memories from confabulated memories or memories that have been implanted by suggestion (with or without hypnosis), except for independent corroboration.[30] Spiegal and Scheflin point out, however, that it must be independent physical corroboration as "independent mental corroboration, the memories of others, may also have been contaminated, especially at an earlier time".[31]

COMMAND HALLUCINATIONS

A command hallucination is an auditory hallucination ordering the person who is hearing it to do something. Auditory hallucinations can occur in a variety of mental disorders but they are commonest in schizophrenia. Approximately two-thirds of people with schizophrenia experience auditory hallucinations. Approximately one-third of people presenting with auditory hallucinations from any cause experience command hallucinations,[32] although it is difficult to be sure of their exact prevalence as some people with command hallucinations deny their presence and some people without them, especially forensic patients, report their presence even when they are not there. According to Rogers et al, somewhere between 0 – 15 per cent of people who experience command hallucinations obey their commands.[33] The majority ignore them. As Hellerstein et al point out, however:

> there may be subgroups of patients who are at risk. Patients who have acted violently in the past in response to command hallucinations or patients with previous impulsive or violent behaviour may be at high risk for violent behaviour if command hallucinations occur... Perhaps patients who hear repetitive commands with an intrusive, peremptory quality or for an extended period of time are at a high risk.[34]

110

Rogers found that within a forensic context "5.8 per cent of individuals evaluated for insanity had responded to command hallucinations in committing their criminal offenses".[35] Hellerstein et al found that the majority of command hallucinations were commands to commit suicide (51.7 per cent). Commands to commit homicide were far less common (5.2 per cent).[36] Junginger[37] found that compliance with command hallucinations was more common where the hallucinations were associated with delusions and the hallucinatory voices were ones they could recognise. Rogers et al give the following example of a forensic case involving command hallucinations which illustrates both these points:

> [The] defendant [had] . . . a nonforensic history of command hallucinations spanning a 17-year period. The voice of his deceased grandmother served as an oracle of God and, from the patient's perspective, spoke with absolute authority and transmitted messages with unquestionable clarity. The actual content of these hallucinations consisted of the commands, "save your mother," and "do it now," which others might view as ambiguous but which were perceived clearly by the patient as divine instructions to save his mother from the forces of evil by causing her death. After his arrest, he heard his mother calling his name affectionately and knew unquestionably that she was with God and pleased with his actions.[38]

The problem with command hallucinations in a forensic setting is determining whether or not they are simulated. As Resnick points out, "they are easy to make up in order to support an insanity defence".[39] Rogers et al suggest that very careful clinical assessment and the use of clinical probes can be of help. The clinical assessment should take into account the actual content of the hallucination, the person's interpretation of the content, and the perceived authority of the auditory hallucination.

To assist with the clinical assessment in a forensic setting, Rogers et al have developed clinical guidelines covering five factors:

1 Premorbid criminal behaviour.
2 Chronicity of command hallucinations.
3 Consistency of command hallucinations with the patient's wishes.
4 The patient's relationship to the command hallucinations.
5 The patient's disregard for apprehension by police.[40]

They list a number of questions to be addressed under each heading.

With regard to clinical probes, Rogers et al suggest that the following might be helpful:

1 Bizarre and improbable inquiries (for example, "Do these voices ever sing to you in a foreign language?" or "Does this voice echo or vibrate throughout your entire body?").
2 Inquiries suggesting unrealistic precision (for example, "Does this voice occur only on cloudy days?").

3   Inquiries suggesting an unusual combination with other symptoms (for example, "Have you noticed that when you lose weight you also lose these voices?").

4   Inquiries about how the commands are communicated (for example, "Do these commands ever appear to you visually, as a giant message written across the horizon?" or "Are the commands ever whispered to you from stone walls?").

5   Inquiries regarding unusual sources of these commands (for example, "Have you ever received commands from Jupiter or its moons?").

6   Inquiries about the consequences of not obeying them (for example, "Did you ever have the thought that your body would turn to sand if you did not obey these commands?").[41]

Resnick[42] suggests that information available about the nature of ordinary auditory hallucinations provides a useful benchmark for comparison. He suggests that malingering should be suspected if any of the following are observed:

Continuous rather that intermittent hallucinations.[43]

Vague or inaudible hallucinations.[44]

Hallucinations not associated with delusions.[45]

Stilted language reported in hallucinations

Inability to state strategies to diminish voices.[46]

Self-report that all command hallucinations were obeyed.

Other features of ordinary auditory hallucinations are that they usually decrease if the patient becomes drowsy, they are poorly localised in space, and even if they are localised there is no consistent lateralisation.[47] Even with these benchmarks at one's fingertips, however, and even with careful clinical examination and the use of probes, it is still not always possible to distinguish conclusively between genuine auditory hallucinations and malingering. In psychiatry there are no absolutes and 100 per cent certainty is impossible to attain.

NOTES

1   Shaw, J, *Golden Rules of Psychiatry* (1899) p15.

2   The remainder of this paragraph is taken from Shea, P, "Commentary" in *Proceedings of the Institute of Criminology* No 57, "Shoplifting" (1983) p 73.

3   Assessing whether a person is lying can be quite difficult, even under normal circumstances. Resnick, citing a number of authors, summarizes the literature on the detection of deception. He notes that there may be some "clues to deception" in the manner in which material is presented and in the content of the material presented (e.g. the use of a higher pitched tone, more grammatical errors, more slips of the tongue, more negative statements, more irrelevant statements, more over-generalised or vague statements, more self-manipulating gestures, such as rubbing and scratching,

passive rather than active forms, hedging statements, more discrepancy between verbal and non-verbal communication, more blinking and dilated pupils). None of these, however, are anything other than clues and they must be tempered by a number of other experimental findings, such as "facial expressions offer the least reliable cues for detecting lies"; people listening to the tape recording or reading the transcript of an interview are better judges of lying than people watching and hearing the videotape of the interview (because "visual cues served as distractors"); "liars do not demonstrate less eye contact with interviewers"; "liars do not have shifty eyes"; "people mistakenly think that people are lying when they gaze less, smile less, shift their posture more, speak more slowly, and take longer to answer a question"; "planning a lie ahead of time makes a liar less likely to have to pause for words, and more free to control his tone of voice and other potential clues to the deception"; and "untrained observers can detect lying in strangers only at slightly better than chance levels". Resnick, R, "Assessment of Psychic Harm" (1995) Presentation Notes for Annual Meeting of The Royal Australian and New Zealand College of Psychiatrists Section of Forensic Psychiatry, Article 5, p 8).

4 Kihlstrom, J, "Hypnosis, Delayed Recall, and the Principles of Memory" (1994) XLII *International Journal of Clinical and Experimental Hypnosis* 340.

5 Ibid p 342.

6 Spiegel, D and Scheflin, A, "Dissociated or Fabricated? Psychiatric Aspects of Repressed Memory in Criminal and Civil Cases" (1994) XLII *International Journal of Clinical and Experimental Hypnosis* 419.

7 Shea, P, *Psychiatrists and Psychologists: Use and Usefulness of Their Evidence in Criminal Cases* (1995) p 13.

8 Rosenhan, whose study on pseudopatients was described in the previous chapter, gives an example of how easily this can happen. One of Rosenhan's pseudopatients:

> had had a close relationship with his mother but was rather remote from his father during his early childhood. During adolescence and beyond, however, his father became a close friend, while his relationship with his mother cooled. His present relationship with his wife was characteristically close and warm. Apart from occasional angry interchanges, friction was minimal. The children had rarely been spanked.

As Rosenhan notes, "Surely there is nothing especially pathological about such a history". After the pseudopatient was discharged, however, it appeared in the case summary as follows:

> This white 39-year-old male ... manifests a long history of considerable ambivalence in close relationships, which begins in early childhood. A warm relationship with his mother cools during his adolescence. A distant relationship with his father is described as becoming very intense. Affective stability is absent. His attempts to control emotionality with his wife and children are punctuated by angry outbursts and, in the case of the children, spankings. And while he says that he has several good friends, one senses considerable ambivalence embedded in those relationships also...

As Rosenhan points out:

> The facts of the case were unintentionally distorted by the staff to achieve consistency with a popular theory of the dynamics of a schizophrenic reaction. Nothing of an ambivalent nature has been described in relations with parents, spouse, or friends. To the extent that ambivalence could be inferred, it was probably not greater than is found in all human relationships. It is true that pseudopatient's relationships with his parents changed over time, but in the ordinary

context, that would hardly be remarkable - indeed, it might very well be expected. Clearly, the meaning ascribed to his verbalizations (that is ambivalence, affective instability) was determined by the diagnosis: schizophrenia. An entirely different meaning would have been ascribed if it were known that the man was "normal" (Rosenhan, D, "On being sane in insane places" (1973) 179 *Sci*, p 253).

9   Hunter, R and Macalpine, I, *Three Hundred Years of Psychiatry 1535-1860* (1963) p vii.

10   Id.

11   Birns, H and Levien, J, "Dangerousness: Legal Determinations and Clinical Speculations" (1980) 52/2 *Psychiat Q* 115.

12   American Psychiatric Association, *Diagnostic and Statistical Manual of Mental Disorders* (4th ed; 1994) p 478.

13   World Health Organisation, *The ICD–10 Classification of Mental and Behavioural Disorders* (1992) p 153.

14   American Psychiatric Association, above n 12 p 481.

15   Kopelman, M, "Crime and Amnesia: A Review" (1987) 5/3 *Beh Sci & L* 329.

16   Ibid p 330.

17   Ibid p 336.

18   Van der Kolk, B, Herron, N and Hostetler, A, "The History of Trauma in Psychiatry" (1994) 17 *Psychiatric Clinics of North America*, p 586.

19   American Psychiatric Association, above n 12, p 766. See also Howard, C, "Amnesia" in Bluglass, R and Bowden, P (eds), *Principles and Practice of Forensic Psychiatry* (1990) p 297.

20   Howard, above n 19, p 296.

21   Kopelman, above n 15 p 331.

22   Ibid p 328.

23   Ibid p 334.

24   Ibid p 335.

25   Howard, above n 19 p 293.

26   Ibid p 298.

27   American Psychiatric Association, above n 12, p 480.

28   Ibid, p 479.

29   Ofshe, R and Singer, M, "Recovered-Memory Therapy and Robust Repression: Influence and Pseudomemories" (1994) XLII *International Journal of Clinical and Experimental Hypnosis* 393.

30   In 1993 the American Psychiatric Association Board of Trustees issued a Statement on Memories of Sexual Abuse supporting the need for independent corroboration. It stated: "There is no completely accurate way of determining the validity of reports in the absence of corroborating information" (cited in the XLII International Journal of Clinical and Experimental Hypnosis (1994) 263). In 1994 the American Medical Association Council on Scientific Affairs issued a statement which resulted in the AMA adopting a new policy on the subject of recovered memories which stated, in

part: "The AMA considers recovered memories of childhood sexual abuse to be of uncertain authenticity, which should be subject to external verification" (cited in the (1995) XLII *International Journal of Clinical and Experimental Hypnosis* 117). See also Nash, M, "Memory Distortion and Sexual Trauma: The Problem of False Negatives and False Positives" (1994) XLII *International Journal of Clinical and Experimental Hypnosis* 346; and Ceci, S, Loftus, E, Leichtman, M and Bruck, M, "The Possible Role of Source Misattributions in the Creation of False Beliefs Among Preschoolers" (1994) *XLII International Journal of Clinical and Experimental Hypnosis* 304.

31 Spiegel and Scheflin, above n 6, p 419.

32 Hellerstein, D, Frosch, W and Koenigsberg, H, "The Clinical Significance of Command Hallucinations" (1987) 144/2 *Amer J Psychiat* 219.

33 Rogers, R, Gillis, J, Turner, R and Frise-Smith, T, "The Clinical Presentation of Command Hallucinations in a Forensic Population" (1990) 147/10 *Amer J Psychiat* 1304.

34 Hellerstein et al, above n 32 p 221.

35 Rogers et al, above n 33 p 1304.

36 Hellerstein et al, above n 32.

37 Junginger, J "Predicting compliance with command hallucinations" (1990) 147 *Amer J Psychiat* 245.

38 Rogers, R, Nussbaum, D and Gillis, R, "Command Hallucinations and Criminality: A Clinical Quandary" (1988) 16/3 *B Amer Acad Psychiat & L* 253.

39 Resnick, P, "Malingering" in Rosner, R (ed), *Principles and Practice of Forensic Psychiatry* (1994), p 418.

40 Rogers et al, above n 38, p 255.

41 Ibid p 254.

42 Resnick, above n 39, p 420.

43 Ibid, p 418. Hallucinations are "generally intermittent rather than continuous".

44 Id. "The message [is] usually clear; it [is] vague only 7% of the time".

45 Id. "Hallucinations are usually (88%) associated with delusions".

46 Id. "Frequent coping activities among actual schizophrenics are (1) specific activities (working, watching TV), (2) changes in posture (lie down or walk), (3) seeking out interpersonal contact, and (4) taking medication. Schizophrenic hallucinations tend to diminish when patients are involved in activities".

47 Cutting, J, "Hearing voices" (1989) 298 *Brit Med J* 769.

SECTION C

The Connection Between Mental Disorder and Criminal Behaviour

"If someone commits an offence while suffering from some degree of [mental] disorder it is likely to be assumed by the public at large that the mental condition and the offending act are connected; but this is not necessarily so."[1]

As the above quotation from the report of the Butler Committee indicates, the relationship between mental disorder and criminal activity is far from simple. In this section the problems that arise when attempting to establish such a relationship are explored.

9

MENTAL DISORDER AND CRIMINAL BEHAVIOUR

If someone commits a crime the presence of a concomitant mental disorder can have profound consequences. The victim of the crime, for example, either through sympathy or a feeling that there is no point in doing so, may decide not to pursue the matter. If the police are called they may have the same reaction and, rather than arresting the person and charging them, they may take them home or to hospital (depending upon how serious they consider the mental disorder to be and how serious the crime is). What the mentally disordered person may learn from this is that certain types of criminal behaviour carry virtually no negative sanctions. There may even be some rewards involved.[2] They may receive a great deal of attention and, if they have a chronic mental disorder and are living in the community but would prefer to be in hospital, they may learn that one way of getting back into hospital, even if only for a few days, is to commit a crime. If they are arrested and charged and the offence is only a minor one the charge may be dismissed without a penalty being imposed or with a lesser penalty imposed than would otherwise have been the case. If the crime is a serious one, the presence of a mental disorder may provide a complete defence, resulting in a verdict of not guilty by reason of mental illness. If the charge is murder, the mental disorder may result in a reduction of the charge to manslaughter on the grounds of diminished responsibility.

Now there is no doubt whatever that if a mentally disordered person commits a crime there can be a causal relationship between the two. There is also no doubt whatever that the causal relationship cannot simply be assumed. It must be established. As indicated in the quotation from the report of the Butler Committee at the beginning of this section, the simple coexistence of two sets of phenomena – criminal behaviour and mental disorder – especially for the first time, does not establish a causal relationship. Simply because a person with a depressive disorder or schizophrenia steals something from a shop, this does not necessarily mean that the symptoms of the disorder are the cause of the behaviour. They may be. They may not be. If they are they may be the sole cause or they may be just one of several causes operating together. In the past, some courts have found it convenient to routinely equate coexistence with causality. Provided both sides agree about the existence of the mental disorder and about the assumed connection between it and the criminal behaviour, this provides the court with an excuse for disposing of the case in a lenient manner and ensures that the media treat the case sympathetically. Some courts will undoubtedly go on doing this, especially where the defendant is a prominent public figure, the crime is something minor, like shoplifting, and the mental disorder is depression. And, depending upon the circumstances of the case, this might be a reasonable and humane approach. A closer analysis of the assumed relationship between the disorder and the crime may lead to different conclusions.

There are many ways in which mental disorders and criminal behaviour can be related. They are examined in the remainder of this chapter.

PSYCHOSEXUAL DISORDERS

Among the paraphilias (DSM-IV) or disorders of sexual preference (ICD-10) are several conditions that are both crimes and mental disorders by virtue of the fact that they are defined as such by the criminal law and the major psychiatric classifications respectively. They include pedophilia, necrophilia and zoophilia.

Pedophilia is described in the DSM-IV as follows:

> Over a period of at least 6 months, recurrent, intense sexually arousing fantasies, sexual urges, or behaviors involving sexual activity with a prepubescent child or children (generally aged 13 years or younger).[3]

If the pedophilic tendencies result in actual sexual intercourse with a child under the age of 10, this is a crime. Section 66A of the New South Wales *Crimes Act* 1900 states that: "Any person who has sexual intercourse with another person who is under the age of 10 years shall be liable to penal servitude for 20 years".[4]

Section 66C(1) states that: "Any person who has sexual intercourse with another person who is of or above the age of 10 years, and under the age of 16 years, shall be liable to penal servitude for 8 years".[5]

Zoophilia and necrophilia are classified in the DSM-IV under "Paraphilia Not Otherwise Specified",[6] and in the ICD-10 under "Other disorders of sexual preference".[7] Zoophilia is a preference for sexual relations with animals.[8] Bestiality is actual sexual intercourse with animals.[9] Under the New South Wales *Crimes Act* the penalty for bestiality is penal servitude for 14 years.[10] Although prosecutions for it are uncommon, according to Kinsey 8 per cent of adult males (mainly rural males) and 3.6 per cent of females surveyed admitted to sexual activity with animals at some time in their lives.[11] Necrophilia, or sexual intercourse with a corpse, is extremely rare, although instances have been recorded for over two millennia.[12] Under s 81C of the New South Wales *Crimes Act,* "Any person who: (a) indecently interferes with any dead human body; or (b) improperly interferes with, or offers any indignity to, any dead human body or human remains (whether buried or not), shall be liable to imprisonment for two years".[13]

119

DRUG DEPENDENCY

Drug dependency ("Substance Dependence" in the DSM-IV[14] and "Mental and behavioural disorders due to psychoactive substance use-Dependence syndrome" in the ICD-10[15]) can lead to involvement with criminal activity in a number of ways, depending upon what the drug-dependent person has to do to obtain the drug, the type of dependency the drug produces, the effects of the drug and the withdrawal effects of the drug. In the case of the opioids, for example, the illicit nature of the drugs and their cost may involve the user in a variety of direct criminal activities, such as prostitution and theft, to obtain the money to buy the drugs; activities relating to their manufacture, distribution and sale; and illegal prescribing. Possession itself may be an offence. The greater the degree of physical dependency, psychological dependency and tolerance that the drug produces and the more severe the withdrawal effects, the greater will be the lengths to which the drug-dependent person will go to obtain the drug.

DEPRESSION

When it comes to establishing a causal relationship between a major mental illness, such as depression, and a particular crime, three major difficulties arise.

The first relates to the concept of causality itself. There are semantic problems about what the term means and there are philosophical problems about what constitutes causality even in the physical sciences.[16] This book is not the place to argue these matters but it should be borne in mind in any discussion of causality that such problems exist and that they are unresolved.

The second difficulty relates to the complexity of the human mind and the matters raised in Chapter 2 about the inadequacies of the different theoretical constructs that are adduced to explain mental activity. No human being can ever fully understand what motivates another human being to do anything. At best we can make educated guesses but the nature of these will be determined by our own experiences and understanding of human nature and hence be subjective.

The third difficulty relates to the inadequacies of epidemiological studies. It might be assumed that by doing large-scale surveys of populations, both general and forensic, some statistical correlations between specific mental disorders and specific criminal acts might be found. Unfortunately all epidemiological surveys have methodological problems and the interpretation of their results is fraught with difficulty. Statistics can be very misleading. In the eighteenth century, for example, the social scientist James Hanway seriously suggested that "Since tea has been in fashion, even suicide has become more familiar amongst us than in times past".[17] Even more unfortunately, epidemiological surveys have not demonstrated close correlations between any particular mental disorder and any particular crime (except in the case of the psychosexual disorders described above and in the case of kleptomania described below). At times they have suggested a higher correlation between them than would have been expected by chance but these correlations do not prove causality. They merely indicate avenues that need to be explored. Higgins summarises the difficulties that arise from the use of epidemiological surveys as follows:

> Gunn ... has said that the main problem in discussing any relationship between criminal behaviour and mental disorder is that the two concepts are largely unrelated. Although there is a reasonable risk of acquiring a criminal conviction (particularly in men) and an affective illness or at least an episode of depression (particularly in women), the prevalence of depressive illness in criminals is low and this coupled with the unique difficulties of assessment in forensic practice make any estimate of the rate of affective illness difficult and unreliable, and probably too low. The drawing of any direct relationship between any diagnosis and offence category or behaviour is thus most hazardous. It is therefore not unexpected that the literature is very sparse, consisting for the most part of small and anecdotal studies of highly selected populations, with markedly different criteria of selection, lacking in diagnostic rigour and statistical sophistication, and fixed in the diagnostic habits of their time and country of origin.[18]

Epidemiological studies suggest, for example, that more apprehended and charged shoplifters appear to be suffering from a depressive disorder than would be expected from the prevalence of such disorders in the community at large. Putting aside the methodological problems of establishing the prevalence of depressive disorders in the community at large (including the problems of defining depressive disorders for the purposes of such a study) there is still the problem of establishing the nature of the relationship between a depressive disorder and shoplifting when they are found to coexist. As pointed out earlier in this book, many people suffer from depressive disorders. Only a very small percentage of people with depressive disorders shoplift. The majority of people who shoplift are not depressed. They shoplift for a whole range of reasons. Some of the groups who shoplift are:

1   Alcohol and drug-dependent people who steal things that they can sell to finance their habit.

2   Professionals who make a living out of it.

3   People who steal from need to obtain the necessities of life.

4   People who steal from greed or a desire to maintain social status.

5   Children and adolescents who steal for a variety of reasons including peer group pressure, excitement, alienation, revenge, rebellion, impatience, temptation, resentment, alcohol, drugs, and need for attention. This is usually a passing phase and decreases over time.

6   People who have a mental disorder or are emotionally disturbed.[19]

7   People who are physically ill.

The two largest categories of shoplifters are staff and children. Up to 60 per cent of shoplifting is thought to be done by staff[20] and up to 60 per cent of customer shoplifting by children and adolescents.[21] In a 1982 study of 15-year-old

121

Tasmanian school children "54 per cent of the boys and 44 per cent of the girls in the sample admitted to stealing from a shop in the preceding three years".[22] The National Coalition to Prevent Shoplifting in the United States surveyed "almost 50,000 American students in 1979-80, over 100,000 in 1980-81 and over 76,000 in 1981-82". In the three years studied, 49 per cent, 49 per cent and 43 per cent of students had shoplifted and 17 per cent, 30 per cent and 19 per cent intended to continue shoplifting.[23]

Only a small proportion of shoplifters ever get caught. Of those that do get caught only about half are prosecuted. Of the latter group only a small percentage are mentally disordered (somewhere between 5 per cent and 20 per cent).[24] Of those that are mentally disordered approximately 10 per cent of men and 33 per cent of women are suffering from a depressive disorder.[25] So the statistical correlation between depression and shoplifting is quite low with somewhere between 0.5 per cent and 2 per cent of apprehended male shoplifters and 1.6 per cent to 7 per cent of apprehended female shoplifters suffering from a depressive disorder at the time. As the vast majority of depressed people do not shoplift, the question that has to be asked in the case of a depressed person who has shoplifted is: why did this particular depressed person shoplift at this particular point in time? This is where psychiatric evidence can be of some use to the court. There are four possibilities that need to be explored:

1 That the person had never shoplifted before and that the depression was causally related to the shoplifting. In this case there are a number of possible reasons:

    (a) that the shoplifting resulted from inattention and lack of concentration, or absent-mindedness. This possibility may be heightened if the depressed person is using sedative drugs or alcohol to cope with the depression;[26]

    (b) that it was a "cry for help", "analogous to attempted suicide"; that is, it was an attempt to bring their plight to someone's attention so as to get professional help that they are otherwise unable to seek out for themselves;[27]

    (c) that because of feelings of unworthiness, guilt or sin, which may or may not be of delusional intensity, there was a desire to be caught, punished and suffer. The guilt may be part of an unresolved grief reaction;[28]

    (d) that the excitement of the shoplifting provided a relief from the depression, (a pathological form of the normal behavioural response of going shopping to cheer yourself up when feeling down);[29]

(e) that the depression was associated with sexual deprivation or sexual problems and the shoplifting provided a substitute form of excitement;[30]

(f) that the items stolen had a symbolic significance;

(g) that the shoplifting was an attempt to discredit or to bring disgrace onto the family.[31] According to Gibbens, "all depressed [people] . . . are aggressive, either to themselves or others, and the element of well-concealed resentment and spite is detectable".[32]

In (a), (b), (c), (f) and (g) there may be no attempt to conceal the behaviour. This list, of course, is in no way exhaustive.

2 That the person had not shoplifted before but there was no causal connection between the depression and the shoplifting. In this case one or more of the other reasons for shoplifting (need, greed etc) may provide an explanation.

3 That the person had shoplifted before but that there was a causal connection nonetheless between the depression and this particular episode of shoplifting. In this case any of the reasons listed in (1) above may be operative, either independently or in association with any of the general reasons for shoplifting. This combination may explain why a previously successful shoplifter gets caught.

4 That the person had shoplifted before but that there was no causal connection between the depression and the shoplifting on this occasion.

Determining which of the above applies may, of course, be extremely difficult. It may even be impossible. Unless a person had been caught before it is unlikely that they would want to prejudice their case by admitting to previous shoplifting. What is important is that all the possibilities be at least explored and considered before a decision is reached about the nature of the relationship between the depressive disorder and the shoplifting.

Another set of factors that also need to be taken into account are the environmental factors, including the relationship between an invitation to buy and an invitation to steal. As I have pointed out elsewhere:

> Shops generally display their goods as openly and invitingly as possible. There is a whole psychology concerned with the selling of goods. It involves making them as attractive and accessible as possible . . . there may be a relationship, as yet unexplored in any depth in the literature, between the psychology of selling and the psychology of stealing.[33]

This requires detailed research.

The difficulty of sorting out the factors listed above can best be illustrated by the following case history.[34] "Mrs Jones" was a 50-year-old woman who had been charged with stealing a dress from a shop. She was referred by her lawyer for a psychiatric assessment. The initial assessment was carried out by a psychiatrist at the outpatient department of the hospital. The history he obtained and the assessment he made were along the following lines:

> There was no indication that Mrs Jones had ever shoplifted in her life before. She was in her late middle age and living in reasonably comfortable circumstances though not rich. Prior to her marriage in her mid twenties she had worked in a secretarial position in a busy insurance company. She had not worked since her marriage which, as far as could be determined, had been reasonably happy though not very eventful. She had three children in rapid succession, all of whom had grown up, married and left home. Two had children of their own whom she rarely saw. The psychiatrist who saw her was of the opinion that she was starting to feel some of the stresses of late middle age, especially the isolation, loss of physical attractiveness (she had always taken a great deal of pride in her appearance) and loss of contact with her children. In the month prior to the shoplifting episode her sister and one of her close friends had died. The sister had been ill for some time and her death was expected and in some sense a relief to the family. The friend's death was quite unexpected. The dress Mrs Jones stole from the shop wasn't the sort of dress she would normally wear herself and it wasn't even her size. She couldn't remember taking the dress and in fact she had some difficulty remembering exactly what had happened.

The psychiatrist who saw her thought she may have had a masked depression. She was admitted to the ward in which I was working and subsequently became my patient. She was in hospital for three weeks and attended small group sessions daily. At the sessions she repeated the same story she had given to the psychiatrist who first saw her and her repetition of the story was always consistent and convincing. Because of the possibility of depression she was given some antidepressant medication. After three weeks in hospital she was discharged at her own request. She was seen as an outpatient for three months and the medication was gradually tapered off. I did not see her again for four years. The next time she presented she had a clear-cut and severe depression which appeared to have been precipitated by a mild heart attack. Her depression lifted with medication. She was in hospital on this occasion for six weeks. As her depression lifted she gave me quite a different story about the shoplifting incident. She had, she claimed, been shoplifting most of her life. It started in her childhood, which was rather impoverished, as a way of obtaining things she could not afford to buy and it continued intermittently into adulthood. It was one of the few activities in her somewhat dull married life that gave her a degree of excitement. The things she stole in later life were mostly clothes. They were not usually for herself but for her children, her grandchildren and sometimes friends. When she was giving them to her friends she would say things like "this dress is too small for me" or "not my style" and so on. She rationalised her activities on the grounds that the goods she stole were mainly for others. She knew that it was wrong to steal but she did not feel a great deal of remorse or guilt all the same. The store in which she was finally caught was a shop from which she had stolen on several occasions before. It was not that she had grown suddenly careless. Her modus operandi was quite sophisticated and for many years quite successful. It was just that the store had changed its security procedures.

SCHIZOPHRENIA

Much of what was said above by way of introductory remarks in the case of depression applies in the case of schizophrenia, except that the definitional problems are greater (see Chapter 3) and the methodological problems are greater. Because there are no large-scale epidemiological surveys of the population at large which allow the relationship between schizophrenia and criminality to be adequately addressed, studies are mostly confined to surveys of the prevalence of schizophrenia in gaol populations or the prevalence of criminality (usually measured in terms of the conviction rate) amongst schizophrenic residents or former residents of psychiatric hospitals. If these studies are to be valid, matched control groups must be used. Many studies simply compare the prevalence of criminality amongst schizophrenic patients or the prevalence of schizophrenia amongst convicted criminals with the same prevalences in the population at large. Unfortunately the population at large does not usually have the same demographic characteristics as the prison and hospital populations being studied and some of the different demographic characteristics (age, sex, marital status, place of living, race and social class) in the different populations may themselves be factors that account for some of the differences in the prevalence rates. Even if suitable control groups are used, however, and significant differences are found between the sample and control populations, factors other than the presence of the mental disorder itself may be adduced to account for the differences, factors such as policy decisions and alterations in the network of services available for the treatment of patients. Modestin and Amman, summing up a number of studies in this area, note that:

> The presumed increase in the criminality rate of the psychiatric population has been considered to be a consequence of deinstitutionalisation and the criminalisation of the mentally ill, who are transferred into the penal system instead of being cared for by the mental health system.[35]

To "deinstitutionalisation" we may add "early discharge policies". It has also been suggested that the mentally disordered have higher arrest rates than the non-mentally ill, "being disproportionately liable to detection and arrest after their offence".[36] Against this, however, is the suggestion that "some trivial charges may be dropped in the case of the mentally ill",[37] and the possibility that some mentally ill may be diverted to a hospital or out-patient clinic rather than being charged.

In what appears to be unique study, Modestin and Amman looked at the prevalence of criminality (as measured by convictions) among an unselected sample of 1265 Swiss in-patients and a matched control group drawn from the general population. They found that, with sociodemographic factors controlled, "no, or only marginal relation to crime could be demonstrated in 'true' mental illness such as schizophrenia".[38] What they also found was that the major contributor to a higher conviction rate was the use of alcohol or drugs. They suggested, however, that a reason for the "marginal relation to crime", especially in the case of male schizophrenics, could be the fact that in Switzerland deinstitutionalisation is not advanced and schizophrenic men particularly spend more time in hospitals which would limit their "opportunity to become criminal".[39] What this study and the accompanying discussion illustrates is that the relationship between schizophrenia and crime is multifactorial and a simple one-to-one correspondence can never be assumed to exist.

Another study which illustrates the importance of carefully examining the data before coming to any final conclusions is that of Rice and Harris. In 1992 they published a study comparing criminal recidivism among schizophrenic and non-schizophrenic offenders using matched pairs.[40] The schizophrenic group consisted of people who had been admitted to a maximum security hospital after being acquitted on the grounds of mental illness and who met the DSM-III criteria for schizophrenia. The matched comparison group was chosen from patients admitted to the same institution during the same period for brief pretrial assessment, but who did not have schizophrenia. Contrary to what they expected from the literature, Rice and Harris initially found that schizophrenic offenders had a lower recidivism rate; that is, they were less likely to offend upon release than the non-schizophrenic offenders. They also found that within the schizophrenic group there was no difference in the recidivism rate between people with paranoid schizophrenia, and those with other types of schizophrenia and no difference between people whose index offences were committed in response to a delusion and whose index offences were not. On analysing their data further they found that non-schizophrenic offenders had a higher rate of alcohol abuse and as alcohol had been shown to be related to crime and violence in a number of studies they did a statistical correction for this factor. When this was done they found no difference in the recidivism rate between the schizophrenic group and the non-schizophrenic group. Comparing their study with those that had found a difference, they came to the conclusion that a significant differentiating factor was the active and extended follow-up that their subjects received. They were only discharged when their symptoms were under control (usually with psychotropic drugs) and if their symptoms started to flare up again and get out of control they could be returned to the maximum security hospital. In the other studies florid symptoms were usually present in the cohort studied. Rice and Harris concluded that, "compared to the factors known to predict recidivism among offenders in general, current psychotic symptomatology is a relatively weak, though statistically significant, predictor of crime among schizophrenic offenders".[41]

With regard to mental disorder in general, however, they concluded that "the relationships among diagnosis, crime and violence are unclear". As Tidmarsh points out: "[It] is not possible to produce a scientifically satisfying account of the relationship between schizophrenia and crime as it stands today, still less is it possible to draw firm conclusions about the past".[42]

The purported connection between schizophrenia and homicide illustrates the problem of establishing a clinical connection once a statistical connection is determined. According to Tidmarsh:

> the lifetime incidence of schizophrenia calculated for European populations is around 0.85 per cent and England has an age-corrected prevalence of 0.44 per cent. . . If therefore a sample [of a population] contains a significantly greater proportion of schizophrenics identified by modern methods, an explanation is needed.[43]

The prevalence of schizophrenia among people who commit homicide varies from country to country and within the same country from year to year. In some studies it is as low as 3 per cent. In others it is as high as 15 per cent. The difficulty with comparing studies from different countries is that both the definition of homicide and the diagnostic criteria for schizophrenia differ from country to country and from study to study. On any criteria, however, the prevalence of schizophrenia in populations of people who have committed homicide does appear to be significantly higher than in the population at large, so the connection needs to be examined. Clinical studies suggest that of the large collection of symptoms that have been described, from time to time, as being part of the schizophrenic syndrome, two in particular – delusions and hallucinations – (in the case of delusions, delusional jealousy and, to a lesser extent, delusions of being loved, and in the case of hallucinations, somatic hallucinations but not command hallucinations) have a higher correlation with homicide than other symptoms.[44] It would be quite reasonable, therefore, for a psychiatrist to suggest that in the case of a man with schizophrenia who has delusions of jealousy and kills his wife, the delusions and the killing are causally related, and to back this statement up by pointing to some of the epidemiological and clinical evidence that indicates some correlation between the two. Persuasive as this may be, it is still only a matter of opinion. A number of other factors have to be taken into account:

1 There are many reasons why people murder their spouses other than delusional jealousy, (such as money and self defence). Any of these may be operating in the person with delusional jealousy.[45]

2 Homicidal urges can arise in schizophrenia without any connection to a delusional system.[46]

3 Most people with delusional jealousy do not kill their spouses, although approximately half of them assault them.[47]

4   Delusional jealousy can exist for years or even for the person's lifetime without any concomitant violent behaviour.

So the coexistence of delusional jealousy and homicidal behaviour does not necessarily mean that the first caused the second. The question is whether there are other factors which could have contributed and, in many cases, there are. Some people with schizophrenia, for example, are drug dependent and alcohol dependent as well. Some have brain damage. People with schizophrenia, however it is defined, are all subject to the whole range of usual psychosocial stresses that other people in the community are, although their responses may be influenced by their schizophrenic symptomatology. They are also subject to additional psychosocial stresses imposed by their disorder. Some or all of these may play a significant role in the homicidal behaviour. Unfortunately there is no scientific way of determining the relative importance of any of the factors that might be identified and there is no way of knowing whether all or only some of the factors have been identified.

KLEPTOMANIA

The DSM-IV describes kleptomania as follows:

> The essential feature of Kleptomania is the recurrent failure to resist impulses to steal items even though the items are not needed for personal use or their monetary value. The individual experiences a rising subjective feeling of tension before the theft and feels pleasure, gratification, or relief when committing the theft. . . The objects are stolen despite the fact that they are typically of little value to the individual, who could have afforded to pay for them and often gives them away or discards them. Occasionally the individual may hoard the stolen objects or surreptitiously return them. Although individuals with this disorder will generally avoid stealing when immediate arrest is probable (e.g., in full view of a police officer), they usually do not preplan the thefts or fully take into account the chances of apprehension. The stealing is done without assistance from, or collaboration with, others. . . Individuals with Kleptomania experience the impulse as ego-dystonic and are aware the act is wrong and senseless. The person frequently fears being apprehended and often feels depressed or guilty about the thefts.[48]

In the DSM-IV it is listed under the general heading of "Impulse-Control Disorders Not Elsewhere Classified", a group of disorders whose central feature is "the failure to resist an impulse, drive or temptation to perform an act that is harmful to the person or to others".[49]

The ICD-10 calls it "pathological stealing" and describes it in similar terms. In the ICD-10 it is listed under "Habit and impulse disorders".[50] In the ICD-9 it was listed as a "Compulsive conduct disorder".[51]

Goldman describes it as an "irresistible impulse to steal unneeded objects".[52] McElroy et al state that:

> Since the early nineteenth century, it has been recognized that a small but distinct subgroup of thieves impulsively or compulsively steal worthless or un-needed

objects, or objects easily obtainable by legitimate means. This behaviour [is] now called kleptomania.[53]

A leading article in the *Lancet* in 1991 stated that:

> The reasons for impulsive stealing are unknown, but may reflect the availability of merchandise: the frequency of the disorder rose when department stores were introduced into Paris at the turn of the century. This compulsion may be a defence against some other form of less acceptable impulse, such as behaviours with a psychosexual origin.[54]

The use of the terms "impulsive" and "compulsive", apparently interchangeably in some of the above quotations, raises some difficulties because they are understood, in psychiatry, to have different meanings, at least in psychodynamic terms, and the descriptions in the DSM-IV and the ICD-10 suggest a meaning close to the psychodynamic concept of compulsion.

From the psychodynamic point of view, stealing on impulse occurs when normal personality controls over acquisitive drives or urges are poorly developed (as in the case of the psychopathic personality) or when they are temporarily out of action (due to drugs, alcohol, illness, powerful emotions or peer group pressure). There is little or no attempt to resist the impulse at either the conscious or unconscious level and no subsequent feelings or guilt or remorse (unless the personality controls are only temporarily out of action for the reasons just given).

Compulsive behaviour is quite different. An impulse to steal is common. A compulsion to steal is not. Impulsive behaviour results from the absence of certain control mechanisms. Compulsive behaviour results from the excessive and pathological use of certain unconscious defence mechanisms. What the compulsive behaviour is trying to defend against or ward off is not an acquisitive drive or urge but something quite different such as a sexual drive or urge. Compulsive behaviour is an attempt to deal with anxiety by diverting whatever unconscious drives or unconscious material is threatening to break through into consciousness (and hence causing the anxiety the person is experiencing), into a form of behaviour that ties up the unconscious material and hence relieves the anxiety.

This psychodynamic explanation is usually applied to simple repetitive acts rather than more complex behaviours such as theft, although there is some evidence to support its application to the latter in the case of kleptomania.[55] Certainly the description of the mounting tension before the act and its relief with the committal of the offence is much more akin to the description of a compulsive act than the description of an impulsive act. According to the DSM-IV, compulsions are "repetitive behaviours ... the goal of which is to prevent or reduce anxiety or distress".[56]

There are also, however, a large number of other etiological explanations, ranging from other psychodynamic theories, to organic theories, to behavioural theories.[57] McElroy et al suggest that it may be part of an "affective spectrum disorder".[58] Goldman suggests that although "no unified psychological theory regarding kleptomania's etiology"[59] can be identified at the present time, a composite clinical picture can be built up along the following lines:

> The average person suffering from kleptomania is a 35-year-old married woman who has been apprehended for the theft of objects she could easily afford and does not need. Her stealing began at age 20 and she has been caught several times. . . Her acts of theft bring her great relief from tension, and she may attempt to force herself to remain indoors for fear that she will steal. Despite her sense of entitlement about the thefts, she feels remorse and almost never seeks treatment on her own. Perhaps because of guilt or shame or because she is fearful of losing the opportunity to steal, she feels compelled to keep it a secret. She seems to suffer from a powerfully necessary, pervasive, repetitive, and ultimately self-destructive act. A personal history reveals that she is unhappily married, may have sexual difficulties, and has been dysphoric and moody for many years. She very likely has had a tumultuous and stressful childhood. Furthermore, she may have a personality disorder.[60]

The DSM-IV notes that three typical courses have been described: "sporadic with brief episodes and long periods of remission; episodic with protracted periods of stealing and periods of remission; and chronic with some degree of fluctuation".[61]

Kleptomania has had an interesting history in the psychiatric literature. St Augustine wrote in his *Confessions*, "Yet I lusted to thieve and did it compelled by no hunger, nor poverty".[62] Although first named in the early nineteenth century:

> court cases, personal accounts, and anecdotal reports throughout the ages have underscored the curious nature of this type of stealing. . . In 1799, for example, a wealthy woman appeared before a British magistrate charged with the theft of a piece of lace. Some years later . . . Benjamin Rush remarked on the otherwise high moral character of afflicted individuals and further commented on the theft of a seemingly unneeded object. . . According to Gibbens and Prince, Esquirol and Marc coined the term "kleptomania" in 1838 to describe the behaviour of several kings who stole worthless items.[63]

Marc defined kleptomania as follows: "A conscious urge to steal in an individual in whom there is no ordinary disturbance in consciousness. The individual concerned frequently strives against this urge, but by its nature it is irresistible".[64]

Duncan, in 1853, in his book, *Popular Errors on the Subject of Insanity Examined and Exposed*, noted that lawyers were somewhat critical of the diagnosis. In his chapter on "Cleptomania" he stated:

> The existence of such a form of insanity . . . though almost universally admitted by medical writers, has been called in question by some of our highest legal authorities, who insist that no case ought properly to be referred to that denomination which does not exhibit some evidence of the existence of a palpable delusion affecting the patient's understanding, or some undoubted lesion of his reasoning powers.[65]

Duncan went on to describe the difference between ordinary thieving and kleptomania as follows:

[Kleptomania] is not prompted by the wants of the individual, neither is it practised with any view to the subsequent use in any way of the article that has been stolen. A thief steals only such things as are immediately applicable to the supply of his own pressing wants, or are convertible into the means of supplying them.[66]

The doubt about the existence of kleptomania that Duncan described in the mid-nineteenth century persists to the present day with some authors still doubting its existence. Bluglass, for example, states that it is rare or nonexistent and that "shoplifting almost never has associations of this kind".[67] Goldman, on the other hand, reviewing the literature on shoplifting in 1991, came to the conclusion that kleptomania "may account for a substantial proportion of the staggering 40 billion dollars in business losses attributed to shoplifting (in the United States) each year".[68] This is supported by a leading article in the *Lancet* which points out that:

studies of shoppers indicate that about 10 per cent steal. This proportion translates into 140 million thefts, every year, and since 4 per cent of shoplifters satisfy criteria for kleptomania the number of kleptomaniacs in society is large, and often unrecognised.[69]

The DSM-IV suggests that it is "a rare condition that appears to occur in fewer than 5% of identified shoplifters" and that it is "much more common in females".[70]

The fact that kleptomania has been recognized as a mental disorder for so long, that it is listed in both the DSM-IV and the ICD-10 and described in both classifications in very similar terms, that there is a fairly typical clinical picture that can be identified with it, and that psychiatrists see patients who fit this clinical picture, suggests that it should continue to be recognised as a genuine psychiatric entity, even though its etiology is far from settled at the present time.

POST-TRAUMATIC STRESS DISORDER

The problems of establishing a diagnosis of PTSD were dealt with in Chapter 6. Since its appearance in the DSM-III, a diagnosis of PTSD has mainly been used as an entree to treatment programmes and as a basis for compensation claims. Occasionally, however, it has been presented as the basis for either an insanity defence or a sane automatism defence for various violent offences, including murder. To date, it appears to have been used rather sparingly[71] but even its occasional use raises a number of important theoretical and practical issues. As Sparr and Atkinson point out:

Establishing a valid link between posttraumatic stress disorder and criminal behaviour is an imposing task. At least two levels of causation have to be investigated: 1) causal connection between the traumatic stressor and psychiatric symptoms and 2) causal connection between psychiatric symptoms and the criminal act.[72]

The problems of establishing the first level of causal connection were discussed in Chapter 6. This section deals with the problems of establishing the second level.

In the United States, a number of cases in which PTSD has been used as a defence have involved Vietnam veterans and the basis of the defence has usually been that, at the time of the offence, the person was suffering from flashbacks of traumatic combat events that the person had actually experienced during the war. What this means is that the flashback either occurred spontaneously, that is without any particular external trigger, or, more typically, that the situation which resulted in the offence being committed had features which were reminiscent of the particular combat events and triggered the flashback. Once the memory of the combat events came forward into the person's consciousness, the experience of the current event became a reliving of aspects of the original event and the person then reacted accordingly, that is they reverted, automatically, without any conscious control over what they were doing, and usually without any awareness of what they were doing, "to the class of survival behaviors learned in combat".[73] As one defence psychiatrist described it, at this stage the person is on "automatic pilot".[74] It should be reiterated at this point that although dissociation is the mechanism that is commonly adduced to explain such behaviour, the term "dissociation" has several different meanings in the literature depending upon whether or not the dissociated material is considered to be part of the conscious mind (and the result of splitting) or part of the unconscious mind (See Chapter 8). It should also be noted that there may be aetiological and phenomenological differences in the nature of the various dissociative states described. For example, in the case of a non-veteran who has a flashback to a former traumatic episode, reversion to a "class of survival behaviours learned in combat" would be an impossibility. A distinction also has to be made between a defence based on a PTSD flashback and a defence based on stress-induced dissociative amnesia not associated with PTSD[75] such as a 'psychological blow'.[76] Black has proposed the following criteria for assessing whether or not (in Vietnam veterans) a particular form of behaviour is flashback-induced or not.

(1) The flashback behavior is unpremeditated and sudden. (2) The flashback behavior is uncharacteristic of the individual. (3) There is a retrievable history of one or more intensely traumatic combat events that are reenacted in the flashback episode. (4) There may be amnesia for all or part of the episode (itself quite difficult to verify). (5) The flashback behavior lacks current motivation. (6) The stimuli for the flashback behavior may be current or environmental features that are reminiscent of original experiences in Vietnam. (7) The patient is mostly unaware of the specific ways he has repeated and reenacted war experiences. (8) The choice of victim may be fortuitous or accidental. (9) The patient has, or has had other symptoms of PTSD.[77]

On the basis of cases in which Vietnam veterans have attempted to use PTSD flashbacks as a defence against murder and in which it was later discovered that their claims to extensive combat experience were completely fictitious, Sparr and Atkinson suggest that all claimed combat experiences be verified through collateral and, preferably, official sources before they are acted upon. In spite of all precautions, however, problems remain when PTSD flashbacks are put forward as a defence. The difficulties are well summed-up in the following two quotations, the first from Sparr and Atkinson, the second from Kleinman: "The symptoms of posttraumatic stress disorder are mostly subjective and nonspecific, have been well publicized, and are relatively easy to imitate",[78] and "Dissociative states can last only seconds and leave little to no detectable traces".[79]

NO MENTAL DISORDER

Sometimes, when no mental disorder can be identified, the psychosocial history is presented instead, with certain features highlighted. These are usually features that emphasise the deprived nature of the person's childhood and upbringing, such as poverty, neglect, physical and mental abuse, isolation, lack of suitable role models, physical illness and so on. At times the purpose of this can be difficult to determine. Often it appears to lie somewhere between an attempt to explain the person's behaviour and an attempt to provide an excuse for it. Whatever the purpose, a deprived psychosocial history must be treated with a great deal of caution, first because of the problems outlined in Section B with regard to history-taking generally, and secondly, because of the difficulty of establishing a connection between past experiences and present behaviour.

Few people would doubt that the two are related in some way and that childhood experiences contribute something to a person's adult personality. There is, however, a great deal of dispute about whether or not one's personality is entirely formed by one's childhood experiences (Freud thought it was) or whether it goes on changing and developing, sometimes quite radically, throughout one's life in response to continual exposure to new learning situations (as the behaviourists believe). In any case, only the most dedicated determinist would deny that a person has a choice in the way they behave and at least some personal responsibility[80] for the lifestyle they lead, the situations they find themselves in and the actions they take.

Many people have deprived backgrounds of one sort or another. Only a small proportion of them commit crimes. People from backgrounds that do not appear to be deprived also commit crimes. So a deprived background is not necessarily a precursor to criminal activity and an apparently stable childhood does not act as a barrier to it. Also, people can and do rise above the circumstances of even the most deprived childhoods (possibly even because of them) and go on to form stable relationships and to make significant contributions to society. As Chaplow et al point out, forensic psychiatry reports that purport to establish links between a person's upbringing and a particular crime committed some time later in adult life, especially those reports that fall into the category of "facile over-generalisations", may even prove detrimental to a person's case. As Chaplow et al note, "A judge and jury members who may have had ... deprived upbringings may not be impressed!".[81]

It is not the role of psychiatrists in court to excuse behaviour. Their role is to attempt to explain behaviour. Whatever explanation they offer will always be a hypothetical explanation, not scientific fact, and it will be grounded in one or other of a number of hypotheses about the origins of normal and abnormal human behaviour. It is up to the court to decide whether to accept the explanation the psychiatrist offers or not. It is also up to the court to decide whether or not the explanation, or part of it, provides an excuse, or partial excuse, for that behaviour and if so what effect this should have on the sentencing process. The danger of an abuse explanation is that it can easily metamorphose, in the psychiatrist's report, into an abuse excuse which, if accepted, can metamorphose once again, at a later stage of the person's life, into a justification for all similar behaviours and, hence, an abnegation of all personal responsibility for such behaviours. This is part of the "my syndrome made me do it" defence or the "I am the victim of – fill in the blank – and couldn't help myself"[82] school of rationalisation. Some of the more recent syndromes offered in United States courts as an explanation/excuse/rationalisation for criminal behaviour include "urban survival syndrome" and "black rage". And as Slade points out: "at a time when Americans have moved from the self-absorbed Me Generation to the self-absolved Not Me Generation, [even] the Devil is increasingly appearing in court these days as a defence with a psychological pedigree".[83]

Monahan asks, somewhat cynically, "If we allow urban psychosis as a defence to crime, what would be next? Suburban psychosis, marked by a pathological fear of lawnmowers and barbecues?".[84]

Fortunately, both the judges and juries appear to be becoming cynical as well. As Monahan points out, "When [such defences] are raised, juries still tend to roll their eyes and convict".[85] Pringle suggests that the abuse excuse "may have hit its high point and be on the wane".[86]

CONCLUSION

If a person who is mentally disordered commits a crime it does not necessarily follow that there is a causal relationship between the two, except in the case of kleptomania and mental disorders that are crimes by definition. To establish a causal relationship, the precise nature of the connection between the disorder and the crime must be demonstrated.[87] As part of this process all the factors that might have led a person who is not mentally disordered to commit a similar crime under similar circumstances must also be taken into consideration. Because human behaviour and human motivation are so complex, the end result of this process will be a list of possible contributory factors, some related to the mental disorder, some not. At this point there is no scientific way of determining the relative importance of the various factors. Science gives way to educated guesses. There is also no way of guaranteeing that the factors identified are the only factors that need to be taken into account. The psychological factors operating at the unconscious level may never be known.

NOTES

1   Department of Health and Social Security, *Report of the Committee on Mentally Abnormal Offenders* (1975) p 57.

2   See, for example, Shea, P, commentary in *Proceedings of the Institute of Criminology* No 57 "Shoplifting" (1983) p 76.

3   American Psychiatric Association, *Diagnostic and Statistical Manual of Mental Disorders* (4th ed, 1994) p 528. See also, Glasser, M, "Paedophilia", in Bluglass, R and Bowden, P (eds), *Principles and Practice of Forensic Psychiatry* (1990) p 739.

4   *Crimes Act* (No 40) 1900 p 47.

5   Id.

6   American Psychiatric Association, above n 3 p 532.

7   World Health Organization, *The ICD-10 Classification of Mental and Behavioural Disorders* (1992) p 220.

8   Hucker, S, "Necrophilia and other unusual philias", in Bluglass and Bowden, above n 3 p 723.

9   Bluglass, R, "Bestiality", in Bluglass and Bowden, above n 3 p 729.

10   Above n 4 p 57.

11   Hucker, above n 8 p 723.

12   Ibid p 724. According to Hucker:

    It appears that sexual interference with the dead was known and abhorred by the Egyptians as Herodotus (484-425 BC) noted. . . "When the wife of a distinguished man dies, or any woman who happens to be beautiful or well known, her body is not given to the embalmer immediately, but only after a lapse of three or four days. This is a precautionary measure to prevent the embalmers from violating her corpse. . ." However, male corpses may have been treated differently, as a pseudo- copulation ritual was performed with the mummy to restore the dead man's virility.

13   Above n 4 p 57.

14   American Psychiatric Association, above n 3 p 176.

15   World Health Organization, above n 7 p 24.

16   Hospers, J, *An Introduction to Philosophical Analysis* (1967) p 279-320.

17   Goldney, R and Burvill, P, "Trends in Suicidal Behaviour and its Management" (1980) 14 *ANZ J Psychiat* 1.

18   Higgins, J, "Affective Psychoses", in Bluglass and Bowden, above n 3 p 346.

19   Faulk identifies a number of psychiatric disorders that may be associated with shoplifting apart from depression. See Faulk, M, *Basic Forensic Psychiatry* (1994) pp 86-91.

20   Challinger, D, "Theft From Retail Stores – An Overview" in *Proceedings of the Institute of Criminology* No 57, above n 2 p 11.

21   Ibid p 17.

22   Warner, C, "A Study of the Self-Reported Crime of a Group of Male and Female High School Students" (1982) 15 *ANZ J Crim* 255. See also Jackson, M, "The Motives of Children who Yield in Temptation to Steal Situations" (1970) 3 *ANZ J Crim* 231. Jackson surveyed a sample of 120 Grade 6 schoolchildren: 99 per cent "had at some time stolen and . . . 75 per cent said they would yield again in at least one of a set of hypothetical temptation situations, including shoplifting". Cited in Ray, J, "Is the Ned Kelly Syndrome Dead? – Some Australian Data on Attitudes to Shoplifting" (1981) 14 *ANZ J Crim* 249.

23   National Coalition to Prevent Shoplifting, *National Research Report, Summary* (1981), cited in Challinger, above n 20 p 14.

24   Bluglass, R, "Shoplifting", in Bluglass and Bowden, above n 3 p 790.

25   Id. See also Gibbens, T, Palmer, C and Prince, J, "Mental Health Aspects of Shoplifting" (1971) 3 *Brit Med J* 612.

26   Ibid p 791.

27   Id.

28   Hume, F, "Mental Health Aspects of Shoplifting", in *Proceedings of the Institute of Criminology*, above n 2 p 59.

29   Bluglass, above n 24 p 792. See also Neustatter, W, *Psychological Disorder and Crime* (1953) p 188.

30   Ibid p 791. See also Fenichel, O, *The Psychoanalytic Theory of Neurosis* (1966) p 371. Fenichel describes the case of 'A woman of forty, who constantly reverted to thievery, reported that she was sexually excited whenever she stole and that she even experienced orgasm at the moment she accomplished her theft. In sexual intercourse she was frigid; while masturbating, she would imagine that she was stealing.'

31   Ibid p 792.

32   Gibbens, T, "Shoplifting" (1981) 138 *Brit J Psychiat* 347.

33   Shea, above n 2 p 71. See also Brown, D, "Commentary" in *Proceedings of the Institute of Criminology*, above n 2 p 50-51. According to Brown, "A number of writers report a clear economic calculus that too low a shoplifting rate indicates insufficiently alluring display and marketing techniques". Brown goes on to cite MacDonald from the Retail Traders of Victoria who stated "One of the first slogans I learned in retailing nearly 19 years ago was that 'If it can't be stolen, it won't be sold'".

34   "Mrs Jones" is a fictitious name. The remainder of this section on depression is taken from Shea, above n 2 p 74-75.

35   Modestin, J and Ammann, R, "Mental Disorders and Criminal Behaviour" (1995) 166 *Brit J Psychiat* 667.

36   Ibid p 672.

37   Ibid p 673.

38   Ibid p 674.

39   Ibid p 673.

40   Rice, M and Harris, G, "A Comparison of Criminal Recidivism Among Schizophrenic and Nonschizophrenic Offenders" (1992) 15 *Int'l J L & Psychiat* 406.

41   Ibid p 397.

42   Tidmarsh, D, "Schizophrenia" in Bluglass and Bowden, above n 3 p 321.

43   Ibid p 322.

44   Ibid p 333. See also Bowden, P, "Homicide" in Bluglass and Bowden, above n 3 p 513. Bowden cites a study which showed that 12 per cent of male and 3 per cent of female insane murderers admitted to Broadmoor between 1936 and 1955 were morbidly jealous. It should be noted that delusional jealousy is not confined to schizophrenia but can occur in a variety of other mental disorders, including depressive disorders, alcohol-related disorders, paranoid psychoses, and organic psychoses.

45   Ibid p 334.

46   Ibid p 333. According to Tidmarsh, "Unexplained and overwhelming homicidal urges apparently unconnected to any delusional system and sometimes accompanied by enough insight for the patient to seek help are an uncommon but disquieting clinical reality".

47   Mullen, P, "Morbid jealousy and the delusion of infidelity", in Bluglass and Bowden, above n 3 p 830.

48   American Psychiatric Association, above n 3 p 612.

49   Ibid p 609.

50   World Health Organization, above n 7 p 213.

51   World Health Organization, *International Classification of Diseases* (1977) p 208.

52   Goldman, M, "Kleptomania: Making Sense of the Nonsensical" (1991) 148 *Amer J Psychiat* 986.

53   McElroy, S, Hudson, J, Pope, H and Keck, P, "Kleptomania: clinical characteristics and associated psychopathology" (1991) 21 *Psych Med* 93.

54   Leading Article, "Kleptomania" (1991) 337 *Lancet* 1090.

55   Goldman, above n 52 p 992.

56   American Psychiatric Association, above n 3 p 418.

57   Goldman, above n 52 p 989-995.

58   McElroy et al, above n 53 p 104-106. See also McElroy, S, Pope, H, Hudson, J, Keck, P and White, K, "Kleptomania: A Report of 20 Cases" (1991) 148 *Amer J Psychiat* 652.

59   Goldman, above n 52 p 994.

60   Id.

61 American Psychiatric Association, above n 3 p 613.

62 Ibid p 986.

63 Id.

64 McElroy et al, above n 53 p 93.

65 Duncan, J, "Popular errors on the subject of insanity examined and exposed", cited in Hunter, R and Macalpine, I, *Three Hundred Years of Psychiatry* (1963) p 1007.

66 Id.

67 Bluglass, above n 24 p 793.

68 Goldman, above n 52 p 986.

69 Leading Article, above n 54.

70 American Psychiatric Association, above n 3 p 613.

71 Applebaum, P, Jick, R, Grisso, T, Givelber, D, Silver, E and Steadman, H, "Use of Posttraumatic Stress Disorder to Support an Insanity Defense" (1993)150 *Amer J Psychiat* 229. Applebaum et al surveyed the court records of 8163 defendants who pleaded not guilty by reason of insanity and found that only 0.3 per cent of them had diagnoses of PTSD. In the cases in which pleas based on PTSD were used, "they were no more likely to succeed than pleas based on any other diagnosis".

72 Sparr, L and Atkinson, R, "Posttraumatic Stress Disorder as an Insanity Defense: Medicolegal Quicksand" (1986)143 *Amer J Psychiat* 610.

73 Id.

74 Kleinman, S, "Trauma-Induced Psychiatric Disorders in Criminal Court" in Rosner, R (ed), *Principles and Practice of Forensic Psychiatry* (1994) p 217.

75 Slovenko suggests that a defence based on a stress-induced dissociative state (other than a PTSD flashback) is "the most frequent type of testimony given by forensic psychiatrists in criminal cases". Slovenko, R, "Posttraumatic Stress Disorder and the Insanity Defence" (1994) 151 *Amer J Psychiat* 152. Appelbaum et al dispute this. Appelbaum, P, Grisso, T, Givelber, D, Jick, R, Silver, E and Steadman, H, "Dr. Appelbaum and Colleagues Reply" (1994) 151 *Amer J Psychiat* 153.

76 For a discussion on the leading Australian case on the "psychological blow" sane automatism defence, see Febbo, S, Hardy, F and Findlay-Jones, R, "Dissociation and Psychological Blow Automatism in Australia" (1993-94) 22 *Int J Ment Health* 39-59.

77 Blank, A, "The unconscious flashback to war in Vietnam veterans: Clinical mystery, legal defense, and community problem" in Sonnenberg, S, Blank, A and Talbott, J (eds), *The Trauma of War: Stress and Recovery in Vietnam Veterans* (1985), cited in Kleinman, above n 74.

78 Sparr and Atkinson, above n 72 p 608.

79 Kleinman, above n 74 p 218.

80 "Responsibility" is used here in the moral sense not the legal sense.

81 Chaplow, D, Peters, J and Kydd, R, "The Expert Witness in Forensic Psychiatry" (1992) 26 *ANZ J Psychiat* 628.

82   Monahan, J, cited in Slade, M, "My syndrome made me do it . . . the latest US defence", *Sydney Morning Herald,* 11 June 1994. (Originally printed in the *New York Times*).

83   Id. Pringle, in an article entitled "Why an abuse excuse is the ultimate ruse", notes that the "abuse excuse" has created quite a large industry in the United States.

> Defence lawyers, who used to create doubts about the accusations made against their clients, now seek to paint the accused as a victim. To help this exercise, hundreds of small firms of psychologists, social workers, family therapists and other arcane experts are busily, and expensively, advising lawyers across the country. One such practitioner is Allan Campo, who lives in Louisiana. He predicts, "a lot of murderers will get off over the next ten years" because of the abuse excuse. He describes his job as "not trying to shape the testimony, only its presentation". He makes sure the lawyers he advises "tell the story as well as possible". Pringle, P, *Sydney Morning Herald*, 23 February 1994, p 13.

84   Monahan, above n 82.

85   Id.

86   Pringle above n 83. See also Rosenbaum, R, "Staring into the Heart of the Heart of Darkness", the *New York Times Magazine*, 4 June 1995, Section 6 p 36.

87   In the case of serious crimes these principles were first enunciated in the nineteenth century. In 1800 Hadfield attempted to assassinate George III. He did so in the belief that God wanted him to sacrifice his life to prevent the world from coming to an end. He could not kill himself and so he decided to kill the king, believing that he would then be arrested, tried for treason and hung which, in turn, would result in the salvation of the world. His bullet missed the king by about twelve inches. (Forshaw, D and Rollin, H, "The history of forensic psychiatry in England" in Bluglass, R and Bowden, P (eds), *Principles and Practice of Forensic Psychiatry* (1990) p 83). At this point in English law the defence of insanity required the person to be suffering from "idiocy" or "total alienation of the mind (perfect madness)". In addition, as a result of these, the person had to be so deprived of his reason that he was not conscious of what he was doing or was unable to distinguish right from wrong. Hadfield's counsel, Thomas Erskine, tried to change the law. He wanted to replace "perfect madness" with "partial madness" (ie delusions alone) and he wanted to replace the concepts of not knowing what one was doing or not knowing right from wrong with the principle of establishing a connection between the symptoms of the mental disorder and the crime. He said to the court: "I must convince you not only that the unhappy prisoner was a lunatic, within my own definition of lunacy, but that the act in question was the immediate unqualified offspring of the disease" (From Erskine's speech in the defence of Hadfield, cited in "The State Trials Report. The Queen Against Daniel McNaughton, 1843" in West, D and Walk, A (eds) *Daniel McNaughton His Trial and the Aftermath* (1977) p 36).

In 1843 McNaughton shot Edward Drummond, the private secretary of the British Prime Minister, Sir Robert Peel, apparently in the mistaken belief that Drummond was Peel. McNaughton suffered from persecutory delusions. He believed that he was being persecuted, inter alia, by the Catholic Church and the Tories. His counsel, Cockburn, adopted the same line of argument that Erskine used in Hadfield's case. He said:

The question is . . . whether under that delusion of mind he did an act which he would not have done under any other circumstances, save under the impulse of the delusion which he could not control, and out of which delusion alone the act itself arose (from Cockburn's speech in defence of McNaughton, cited in West and Walk p 44).

In spite of the fact that, like Hadfield, McNaughton was found not guilty on the grounds of mental illness, the law did not change in the direction advocated by both Erskine and Cockburn. Instead, as a result of the deliberations of the judges in the House of Lords following McNaughton's case, the law stayed much the same as it was in the seventeenth century except that the phrase "defect of reason from disease of the mind" was substituted for "idiocy" and "total alienation of the mind". In 1954 Judge Bazelon in the United States, attempted to introduce the principle again in a formulation that became known as the "product rule" (*Durham v United States* 214 F 2d 862, DC Cir 1954). It held that an accused person is not criminally responsible if his unlawful act was the product of a mental disease or defect. As Bazelon put it:

> The purpose of this decision was to grant the psychiatrist his hundred year old request to be allowed to tell what he knows and, just as importantly, what he does not know about the phenomenon of human behavior rather than face demands for conclusions resting on ethical, moral, and legal considerations beyond his expertise (Bazelon, D "The Perils of Wizardry" (1974) 131 *Am J Psychiat* 1319).

Unfortunately, according to Bazelon:

> "the purpose of the Durham decision was not fulfilled. Psychiatrists continued adamantly to cling to conclusory labels without explaining the origin, development or manifestations of a disease in terms meaningful to a jury. The jury was confronted with a welter of confusing terms such as personality defect, sociopathy, and personality disorder. What became more and more apparent was that these terms did not rest on disciplined investigation based on facts and reasoning, as was required for the fulfilment of the Durham decision. I regret to say that they were largely used to cover up a lack of relevance, knowledge and certainty in the practice of institutional psychiatry... First of all, psychiatrists did not acknowledge the limits of their expertise. Secondly, they failed to confront honestly and openly the conflicts that impaired their competence even when their expertise was sufficient and relevant. (Id).

SECTION D

Dangerousness

"We strive after accurate prediction of dangerousness because this would quell our anxieties, enable us to draw clear lines between the dangerous and non-dangerous, and avoid the necessity of continuing contact with and concern for them. But no such magical process will be possible".[1]

Dangerousness is hard to define. It is also hard to predict. As Mullen points out, psychiatrists are often called upon to make judgements on the future dangerousness of mentally disordered subjects in civil commitment procedures, in the criminal courts, and during the decision process on the release of offenders,[2] *and yet, as will be demonstrated in this section, their track record in predicting dangerousness is generally rather poor. Pollock and Webster suggest that through "judicial default" they are "increasingly being cast in roles that are beyond the limits of their expertise".*[3]

This section considers this problem. Chapter 10 looks at the concept of dangerousness itself and at the various ways in which the term is used. Chapter 11 considers the relationship between mental disorder and dangerousness. Chapter 12 deals with the prediction of dangerousness in mentally disordered people and the role of psychiatrists in this.

10

THE CONCEPT OF DANGEROUSNESS

"Dangerousness is a dangerous concept". Scott explains why:

> It is difficult to define, yet very important decisions are based upon it; it is a term which raises anxiety and which is therefore peculiarly open to abuse. . . . The label, which is easy to attach but difficult to remove, may contribute to its own continuance, or may even become a convention for avoiding responsibility.[4]

Some of the difficulties of defining dangerousness are illustrated in the following quotations:

> A "dangerous" individual is simply "anyone whom we would, all things considered, prefer not to encounter on the streets".[5]

> In England recently there has been the case of Peter Sutcliffe, the so-called Yorkshire Ripper. As far as is known he killed thirteen women and attempted to kill six others. This had been carried out over a period of five years, and in view of his strange mental state it was very likely to continue, thus making Sutcliffe a highly dangerous man by anybody's standards. Nevertheless other individuals have killed as many people and are as likely to kill again, for example, the drunken bus driver who drives his coach into a ravine, the negligent engine driver who passes a red signal, the industrialist who by ignoring safety regulations creates a factory explosion or a high death rate from poisoning by a contaminant. Clearly all such people are dangerous but they are not as high on the public priority list for anti-dangerousness measures as Mr. Sutcliffe. . . He didn't just kill people, he terrorized the whole community of several million people. Maybe this terror is partly what is meant by the man in the street when he describes the Yorkshire Ripper as "the most dangerous man in England".[6]

> Why is it that when someone mentions "dangerous offenders" we do not immediately think of drunken drivers, keepers of unsafe factories, tippers of toxic waste, vendors of unsafe cars or harmful pharmaceutical products? Dangerousness is a thoroughly ambiguous concept and we may well ask whether it has any place in the administration of criminal justice.[7]

> Dangerousness is best left undefined or vaguely delineated.[8]

In making any assessment of dangerousness it is necessary, therefore, to be as clear as possible about what the term means in the specific context in which it is being employed. This, in turn, involves delineating and defining the individual elements that make up the definition.

In the forensic field, two types of concepts and definitions are encountered – legal ones and clinical ones. The two are quite different as Pollock and Webster point out:

> Legal dangerousness and clinical dangerousness are two very different concepts and often the legal idea of dangerousness is at odds with present-day scientific theories of human behaviour. Shah notes that, from the perspective of the law, dangerousness is viewed "as stemming largely from within the person; that is it is viewed as a stable and fairly consistent characteristic of the individual". Current thinking in personality and social psychology . . . however, regards all behaviour, dangerous or otherwise, as determined by complex interactions between environmental factors and personality variables. Because of these differences in perspective, rarely are there definitive scientific answers to legal questions about dangerousness.[9]

An example of the legal perspective is Walker's proposed typology of dangerousness:

> The first type is the individual who harms others only if sheer bad luck brings him/her into a situation of provocation or sexual temptation. . . The second type is the individual who gets into such situations not by chance but by following inclinations. Examples are men who, having killed or seriously injured women with whom they have been cohabiting, seek similar relationships after they have been discharged. . . The first two types can fairly be called only "conditionally dangerous". The third, however, consists of individuals who are consciously on the look-out for opportunities. One might call them "opportunity-seekers". The fourth type is the "opportunity-maker" . . . I am not suggesting that there is a sharp distinction between these [last] two kinds of behaviour. . . My point is that [they are both] . . . unconditionally dangerous.[10]

As far as legal definitions of dangerousness are concerned, the problem is that mental health statutes tend to avoid using the term and, even when they do use it, they do not define it. The elements of a definition, however, can sometimes be gleaned from the wording of the legislation or from judicial interpretations of it. This can be illustrated by looking at the New South Wales mental health legislation. The *Mental Health Act* 1958 (NSW) did not use the term "dangerous" or any of its variants. Its definition of a "mentally ill person", however, stated:

> 'Mentally ill person' means a person who owing to mental illness requires care, treatment or control for his own good or in the public interest, and is for the time being incapable of managing himself or his affairs and "mentally ill" has a corresponding meaning.[11]

The phrase "in the public interest" was not defined in the Act but it was assumed by the people with day-to-day responsibility for the operation of the Act that is subsumed the concept of "dangerousness to others" and this was the informal interpretation used for many years in magistrate's inquiries held under s 12(9) of the Act and Tribunal examinations carried out under s 12(14). It was not until 1983, however, that a judicial interpretation confirmed this. In *CF v TCML*, Powell J stated that:

> a person 'requires care, treatment or control . . . in the public interest' if it appears that there is a real risk that, unless such care treatment or control be given or exercised, the person could so conduct himself or herself as to inflict significant injury on some person, or cause significant damage to property, or otherwise commit or cause the commission of some significant breach of the peace; it would not, however, be sufficient, in my view, that the person's conduct or probable conduct constituted or would constitute a mere nuisance and annoyance.[12]

Even though Powell did not use the term "dangerous" or any of its variants it would be reasonable to assume that "a real risk that . . . the person could so conduct himself or herself as to inflict significant injury on some person" would be an interpretation of what "dangerous to others" would mean.

In the *Mental Health Act* 1990 (NSW), the term "danger" (and a variant "endangered") is used but only in relation to the release of forensic patients. Section 90(3), for example, which deals with leave of absence of forensic patients from a hospital states:

> The Tribunal may not make a recommendation unless it is satisfied that, having regard to the leave proposed to be granted, the safety of the patient or any member of the public will not be seriously endangered if the leave of absence is granted.[13]

The definition of a mentally ill person in the 1990 Act does not contain the term "dangerous" or any of its variants but the concept is incorporated into the second arm of the definition as follows:

> A person is a mentally ill person if the person is suffering from mental illness and, owing to that illness, there are reasonable grounds for believing that care, treatment or control of the person is necessary:
>
> (a)   for the person's own protection from serious physical harm; or
>
> (b)   for the protection of others from serious physical harm,
>
> and a person is also a mentally ill person if the person is suffering from mental illness which is characterised by the presence in the person of the symptom of a severe disturbance of mood or the symptom of sustained or repeated irrational behaviour indicating the presence of that symptom and, owing to that illness, there are reasonable grounds for believing that care, treatment or control of the person is necessary for the person's own protection from serious financial harm or serious damage to the person's reputation.[14]

Unfortunately, having a precise legal definition does not necessarily mean precision in decision-making. This was demonstrated in a study carried out in Arizona in 1984. Forty psychiatrists were given the case histories of 16 patients and were asked to rate them according to their dangerousness to themselves and others. The case histories were taken from an earlier World Health Organisation study (discussed below in Chapter 12). In addition to the case histories, half the psychiatrists were given copies of the definitions in the Arizona Commitment Law

144

relating to dangerousness to self and others. The researchers' hypothesis was that this would increase the reliability of psychiatrist raters. The result was quite different to what they had anticipated: "Psychiatrists who used the statute summary were less consistent in their predictions of dangerousness than were those who did not use it, especially when the patient had a history of violence".[15]

Two of the most commonly cited definitions are Scott's: "Dangerousness . . . is an unpredictable and untreatable tendency to inflict or risk serious, irreversible injury or destruction, or to induce others to do so. Dangerousness can, of course, be directed against the self",[16] and the definition in the report of the Butler Committee: "Dangerousness [is] a propensity to cause serious physical injury or lasting psychological harm".[17]

Both of these lean towards the legal concept of dangerousness in that they appear to site the dangerousness in the person and to identify it as some inherent characteristic of the person's personality, arising from either physical factors (such as brain damage or biochemical defects) or psychological factors or both, rather than seeing it as the outcome of a complex interplay of interpersonal, intrapersonal and situational factors and both have been heavily criticised. Tidmarsh, for example, has objected to the phrase "unpredictable and untreatable"[18] in Scott's definition while Scott, in turn, has criticised the inclusion of psychological harm in the Butler Committee's definition. According to Scott:

> [while] psychological damage is very real and is frequently noted as a result of aggression . . . psychological harm, especially that which is lasting, is so very difficult to distinguish from pre-existing idiosyncratic vulnerability, so intangible and so easy to simulate, that it will offer, at present, insuperable difficulties.[19]

Faulk is also critical of the Butler Committee's definition, noting the "lack of precision in the terms such as 'serious' injury or 'lasting' psychological harm".[20] The limitations of the legal model are obvious. The clinical model identifies dangerousness, not simply as an intrapersonal trait but as the result of the interplay between three sets of factors – intrapersonal, interpersonal and situational. The intrapersonal factors are the same as those identified in the legal model, that is they are either physical factors or psychological factors or both and the psychological factor can be either conscious or unconscious. The interpersonal factors involve, inter alia, a consideration of the role of the victim and the role of any other person who may have been present (either at or around the time of the violence). As I point out elsewhere, however:

> The clinical model's comprehensiveness, unfortunately, is one of it's weaknesses. To identify every single element – intrapersonal, interpersonal and situational – and to take all of them into account in one's deliberations would be an impossible task. . . [Moreover, it] is a very subjective task that is influenced by both conscious and unconscious factors . . . [and] the problems of . . . determining the relative importance of each of the individual factors and their importance vis-a-vis one another . . . is an even more highly subjective procedure. Hence, although the

clinical interactional approach is a much more comprehensive and meaningful approach to the issue of dangerousness than the statistical/legal approach, its very comprehensiveness limits its usefulness, just as its subjectivity limits its validity.[21]

Given the fact that the term "dangerousness" is so difficult to conceptualise and to define it would be better, for forensic purposes, if the term was dropped altogether and the concept of "harm" was substituted. The type and degree of harm could then be specified and an attempt could be made to estimate the risk of that type of harm occurring or recurring. One model of harm that could be used for this purpose is the following:[22]

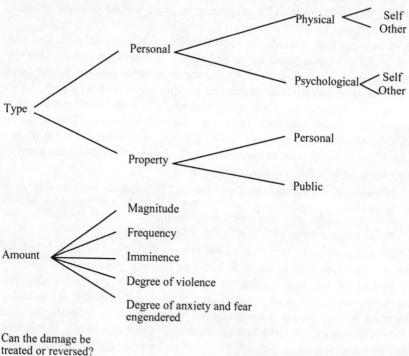

Even with a reasonably well-articulated model such as this, there are still problems:

(a) of measurement (how do you measure degrees of psychological harm or the degree of fear engendered?), (b) of weighting (is physical harm more serious than psychological harm? Is personal harm more serious than property harm? Is physical harm to others more serious than physical harm to oneself?), and (c) of inclusion (should harm to animals be included? Should such factors as treatability or reversibility . . . be included or excluded? If so, how do you measure them and assess them?).[23]

As far as any of these factors are concerned, the psychiatrist's role should be limited to giving the court an opinion on the degree of psychological damage that has occurred and on whether or not it can be treated.

The risk of the harm occurring or recurring and the assessment of the risk is discussed in Chapter 12.

NOTES

1   Scott, P, "Assessing Dangerousness in Criminals" (1977) 131 *Brit J Psychiat* 140.

2   Mullen, P, "Mental Disorder and Dangerousness" (1984) 18 *ANZ J Psychiat* 8.

3   Pollock, N and Webster, C, "The clinical assessment of dangerousness", in Bluglass, R and Bowden, P, (eds) *Principles and Practice of Forensic Psychiatry* (1990) p 489.

4   Scott, above n 1 p 127.

5   Birns, H and Levien, J, "Dangerousness: Legal Determinations and Clinical Speculations" (1980) 52(2) *Psychiatric Quarterly* 108.

6   Gunn, J, "An English Psychiatrist Looks at Dangerousness" (1982) 10:3 *Bulletin of the American Academy of Psychiatry and the Law* 144.

7   Floud, J, "Dangerousness and Criminal Justice" (1982) 22:3 *British Journal of Criminology* 214.

8   Mullen, above n 2 p 9.

9   Pollock and Webster, above n 3 p 489.

10   Walker, N, "Dangerous Mistakes" (1991) 158 *Brit J Psychiat* 754.

11   *Mental Health Act* 1958 (NSW), p 6.

12   *CF v TCML* (unreported, NSW Sup Ct Protective Division, No S.21 of 1983, Transcript of judgement at 5).

13   *Mental Health Act* 1990 (NSW), p 40.

14   *Mental Health Act* 1990 (NSW) p 6.

15   Beigel, A, Berren, M and Harding, T, "The Paradoxical Impact of a Commitment Statute on Prediction of Dangerousness" (1984) 141:3 *Amer J Psychiat* 373. According to Beigel et al, this was the result of cognitive dissonance.

> Information which is contrary to an existing belief tends to be either ignored or modified in some way. . . After reading each case, the psychiatrists formed an immediate impression as to whether or not the individual was dangerous. Those psychiatrists who did not have the statute to review rated the individual according to this initial impression, which was more consistent across raters. Those psychiatrists who had reviewed the law, however, reported that after forming an initial decision, they used the law in a mediation process. For example, some of these psychiatrists said in follow-up interviews that in some cases where they judged the patient to be dangerous, they found the patient did not fit any of the legal criteria for dangerousness. Hence, they rated the patient as less dangerous than their initial impression suggested. Other psychiatrists faced with similar conflicting cognitions tended to ignore the law and responded consistently with their original 'gut' impressions.

16   Scott, above n 1 p 128.

17   Department of Health and Social Security, *Report of the Committee on Mentally Abnormal Offenders* (1975) p 57.

18   Tidmarsh, D, "Implications from research studies" (1982), cited in Faulk, M, *Basic Forensic Psychiatry* (1984) p 271.

19   Scott, above n 1, p 128.

20   Faulk, above n 18, p 272.

21   Shea, P, "Mental Disorders and Dangerousness" (1993-94) 22 *Int J Ment Health* 77.

22   This analysis is adapted from Brooks, A, "Defining the dangerousness of the mentally ill: involuntary civil commitment" in Craft, M and Craft, A, (eds) *Mentally Abnormal Offenders* (1984), cited in Prins, H, "Dangerous People or Dangerous Situations? – some further thoughts" (1991) 31:1 *Medicine, Science and the Law* 27.

23   Shea, P, "A danger to themselves and others" (1995) 11 *Open Mind* 17.

11

THE RELATIONSHIP BETWEEN MENTAL DISORDER AND DANGEROUSNESS

As pointed out in Section A, "mental disorder" is a very broad term covering a wide range of disparate mental disorders, each of which has a number of different symptoms. Each person who suffers from a mental disorder will respond in their own way to the symptoms they experience. Some symptoms could increase the risk of dangerousness in some people in certain circumstances. Others could decrease the risk. Others still might have no relationship to dangerousness whatever. The problem, which is currently unresolved, is to determine which symptoms fall into each category. Unfortunately the literature is conflicting.

Up to the early 1980s it was generally thought that, on balance, mentally disordered people were no more (or less) dangerous than non-mentally disordered people. The general public may have thought otherwise[1] but this was the general opinion in the literature. In most studies dangerousness was measured by episodes of criminal and/or violent behaviour.[2] Cohen, for example, in 1980, looked at the crime rate amongst patients who had been discharged from psychiatric hospitals. He reviewed 12 major studies and noted that some of them showed a lower rate of criminal activity than in the population at large, some showed a higher rate and some showed no difference. He came to the conclusion that all the studies were methodologically flawed and that the question of whether former patients were more dangerous than members of the general public remained unresolved.

In 1983, Monahan and Steadman,[3] reviewing the literature to that time, came to the conclusion that mental disorder was not a predictive factor for dangerousness and that the factors that could be used to predict criminal and/or violent behaviour in the mentally disordered and the non-mentally disordered were the same (ie age, sex and previous offences).

Since then a number of conflicting studies have appeared and by 1992 Monahan had changed his mind and had come to the conclusion that "mental disorder may be a robust and significant risk factor for the occurrence of violence", although he also concluded that "compared with magnitude of risk associated with the combination of male gender, young age, and lower socioeconomic status. . . the risk of violence presented by mental disorder is modest".[4]

Teplin, on the other hand, in an article entitled "The Criminality of the Mentally Ill: A Dangerous Misconception"[5] describes a study carried out in a large Northern American city in which she and five clinical psychology graduates directly observed 1072 police-citizen encounters for 2200 hours over a 14-month period. A symptom checklist for severe mental disorder was used. What Teplin found was that people with signs of serious mental disorder "were not suspected of serious crimes at a rate disproportionate to their numbers in the population [and that the] patterns of crime for mentally disordered persons and for non-mentally disordered persons were substantially similar". Teplin concluded that such data "help dispel the myth that the mentally ill constitute a dangerous group prone to violent crime".[6]

Some of the studies that identified mental disorder as a predictive factor for criminal and/or violent behaviour also identified schizophrenia as the major mental disorder involved.

Cirincione et al reviewed the literature on the relationship between schizophrenia and violence and came to the following conclusions:

> Research seeking to establish a link between schizophrenia and violent behaviour has . . . been inconclusive. Some studies indicate that patients diagnosed as schizophrenic are more violent than other patients. . . Others disagree. Krakowski, Jaeger and Valavka (1988) reviewed seven recent studies . . . and found four that reported paranoid schizophrenics to have higher rates of violence than those with other diagnoses, two that reported paranoid schizophrenics to have lower rates of violence than those of other diagnoses, and one that reported no difference. Taylor has stated that, "There is no doubt that schizophrenics are capable of violent behaviour and there any certainty about the relationship between schizophrenia and violence ends".[7]

An article which is frequently quoted as demonstrating a significant relationship between psychiatric disorder and violence is the article by Swanson et al which analyses data from the National Institute of Mental Health's Epidemiologic Catchment Area (ECA) survey. Being an epidemiologic survey of selected samples of household residents the ECA survey lacks many of the methodological problems discussed earlier in Chapter 9. It was the largest community study of the prevalence of psychiatric disorders ever undertaken in the United States.

> Representative sample surveys of adult household resident populations were carried out in New Haven, Baltimore, St Louis, Raleigh-Durham, and Los Angeles. Structured diagnostic interviews were conducted between 1980 and 1983 with 3000 to 5000 household residents at each site. . . The core of the interview at all five sites was the Diagnostic Interview Schedule (DIS). The DIS is a structured interview designed for use by trained lay persons. [It] generates DSM-III diagnoses.[8]

150

Swanson et al realised that some of the questions in the diagnostic sections of the survey could be used to explore the relationship between mental disorder and certain forms of violent behaviour. Four of the questions they identified came from the diagnostic section for antisocial personality disorder (items 1-4). The fifth came from the diagnostic section for alcohol abuse or dependence disorder (item 5). The five items were:

1) Did you ever hit or throw things at your wife/husband/partner? If so, were you ever the one who threw things first, regardless of who started the argument? Did you hit or throw things first on more than one occasion?

2) Have you ever spanked or hit a child, (yours or anyone else's) hard enough so that he or she had bruises or had to stay in bed or see a doctor?

3) Since age 18, have you been in more than one fight that came to swapping blows, other than fights with your husband/wife/partner?

4) Have you ever used a weapon like a stick, knife, or gun in a fight since you were 18?

5) Have you ever gotten into physical fights while drinking?[9]

A respondent was counted as being positive for violent behaviour if he or she endorsed at least one of the five items and said that some such behaviour occurred during the 12 months preceding the interview. Specific recency for Item 5 was not included in the surveys conducted in New Haven and St Louis, so the data from these two sites were excluded from the study. This left a data base of approximately 10,000 respondents. The results were as follows:[10]

Diagnosis	Violence
No disorder	2.05%
Schizophrenia or schizophreniform disorder	8.36%
Schizophrenia plus some other disorder	12.7%
Alcohol abuse or dependence	24.57%

The study, of course, only looks at schizophrenia as a single category and does not distinguish between the various sub categories of schizophrenia.

One conclusion that has been drawn from this study is that violence among schizophrenics in the community is 4 to 6 times higher than in the normal population, (depending on whether schizophrenia alone is being considered or a combination of schizophrenia plus some other disorder). This is one way of looking at the data. Another conclusion that might be drawn is that most people with schizophrenia in the community (87 per cent to 92 per cent) are not violent (at least as measured on the five items listed above).

One of the problems with the studies quoted so far is that they look at the relationship between broad diagnostic categories and violence or criminal behaviour. As indicated earlier, it is the relationship between the symptoms of mental disorders (and/or the degree of disability or impairment they cause) and the undesirable behaviour in question that needs to be explored if the courts are to be provided with an explanation of the behaviour.

Resnick summarises the literature on the relationship between symptoms and violence as follows:

1. Persecutory delusions are more likely to be acted on than other delusions.

2. Threat/control-override symptoms associated with increased aggression include: (a) Mind feels dominated by forces beyond your control, (b) Feelings that thoughts are being put into your head, (c) Feelings that there are people that you wish to harm.

3. Men whose schizophrenia follows an almost exclusively delusional course are more likely to be violent that those whose schizophrenia is associated with other symptoms.

4. Persons with delusional misidentification syndromes may be more likely to be dangerous than other delusions disorders or schizophrenia.

5. Command hallucinations are more likely to be complied with if they are associated with an hallucination-related delusion or if the voice is familiar.[11]

In a major study currently in progress – the MacArthur Risk Assessment Study, which commenced in 1988 – attempts are being made to delineate the "risk factors" or "cues" associated with one specific form of violent behaviour (violence directed towards another person) in the mentally ill.[12] Risk factors are defined in the study as the variables that other studies and experienced clinicians have nominated as possible predictors of violent behaviour. They include factors in common with the population at large as well as factors specific to people with mental illness. The factors have been grouped into four major groups (called "cue domains"). Some of the factors being investigated are demographic (age, sex, social class). Some are a matter of historical record (family history, work history, educational history, history of hospitalisation in mental institutions, history of crime and violence). Some require clinical assessment (personality, cognitive factors, diagnoses, symptoms, level of functioning and substance abuse). Some relate to situational or environmental factors (eg perceived social stress, social support, means for violence).

A large part of the preliminary work for the study has been involved with developing ways of carrying out the various types of assessment required. The study proper involves a 12-month follow up of 1000 patients discharged from three different hospitals. What the researchers carrying out the study are hoping is that when the study is completed they will be able to narrow down the long list of cue factors they currently have into a smaller group of "robust factors" to which they will be able to assign statistical probabilities. It is not anticipated that any definitive answers will come out of this study (apart from the need for more research) but, hopefully, it will provide a list of factors that such research should focus on (as well

152

as some probability estimates that can be used, in the meantime, to assist decision-making about future risk).

What the list of "risk factors" reminds us is that the relationship between mental disorders (and the symptoms of mental disorders) and violence is not a simple one-to-one relationship. Many other concurrent factors may be involved.

In 1993 the National Institute of Mental Health (USA) convened a conference of leading researchers, consumers, family members and mental health administrators. The topic was "Treatment of Violent Mentally Ill Persons in the Community: Issues of Policy, Services and Research". The consensus findings of the conference, along with evidence from more recent research material, were summarised in a 1994 pamphlet drafted by the John D and Catherine T MacArthur Foundation Research Network on Mental Health and the Law, under the direction of John Monahan. The pamphlet was entitled: "What Do We Know About Mental Disorder and Violence?". Its findings were as follows:

1. Compared with the risk associated with alcoholism and other drug abuse, the risk associated with major mental disorders, such as schizophrenia and affective disorder, is small. Compared with risk associated with the combination of male gender, young age, and lower socioeconomic status, the risk of violence presented by mental disorder is modest.

2. The bottom line from recent research is that "the studies to date have shown an increased risk for violence among [certain] individuals with mental illness compared to the general population; mental illness increases the likelihood of having a violent incident". But, "the absolute risk posed by mental illness is small, and only a small proportion of the violence in our society can be attributed to the mentally ill".

3. "Clearly, mental health status makes at best a trivial contribution to the overall level of violence in society".

4. Substance abuse presents much greater risks for violence than does mental disorder.

5. The type and level of symptoms and disabilities are more important than diagnoses for understanding, treating, and preventing violent behaviour in persons with mental illnesses.

6. Violence among persons with mental illnesses may be caused by many of the same factors producing violence in the general public (e.g. people become violent when they feel threatened and when they use alcohol and drugs excessively).

7. In efforts to predict and treat violence, it is important to recognise that risk fluctuates over time. Risk is not a static personality trait; violent behaviour is a product of the interactions between an individual and his or her environment. The level of risk depends on many factors other than mental disorder that vary, thus increasing or decreasing risk of violence by persons with mental illnesses.

8. To the degree that support services are available, are used, and are effective, persons with mental illnesses pose no greater threat to the community than

other individuals. If these elements are not in place, some persons with mental illnesses may commit violent acts that will lead to their arrest.[13]

Finally, it must be remembered that the concurrent presence of the symptoms of a mental disorder and the occurrence of violent or criminal behaviour in the same person does not mean that the two are automatically connected. As indicated in Section C, such a relationship must be demonstrated, not simply assumed.

NOTES

1   See, for example, Steadman, H and Cocozza, J, "Selective reporting and the public's misconceptions of the criminally insane" (1978) 41 *Public Opinion Quarterly* 523.

2   Cohen, C, "Crime Among Mental Patients – A Critical Analysis" (1980) 52:2 *Psychiatric Quarterly* 100.

3   Monahan, J and Steadman, H, "Crime and mental disorder: An epidemiological approach" in Morris, T, (ed) *Crime and justice: An annual review of research* (1983).

4   Monahan, J, "Mental disorder and violent behaviour" (1992) 47 *American Psychologist* 519.

5   Teplin, L, "The Criminality of the Mentally Ill: A Dangerous Misconception" (1985) 142:5 *Amer J Psychiat* 593.

6   Id.

7   Cirincione, C, Steadman, H, Robbins, P and Monahan, J, "Schizophrenia as a Contingent Risk Factor for Criminal Violence" (1992) 15 *Int'l J L & Psychiat* 348.

8   Swanson, J, Holzer III, C, Ganju, V and Tsutomu Jono, R "Violence and Psychiatric Disorder in the Community: Evidence From the Epidemiologic Catchment Areas Surveys" (1990) 41 *Hospital and Community Psychiatry* 762

9   Ibid, p 763.

10   Ibid, p 765.

11   Resnick, P, "Psychiatric Prediction of Violence" (1995) Presentation Notes for Annual Meeting of the Royal Australian and New Zealand College of Psychiatrists Section of Forensic Psychiatry, Article 9, pp 8-9.

12   The remainder of this section is taken mainly from Shea, P, "A danger to themselves and others" (1995) 11 *Open Mind* 18. See also Monahan, J and Steadman, H (eds) *Violence and Mental Disorder* (1994).

13   John D and Catherine T MacArthur Foundation Research Network on Mental Health and the Law, *What Do We Know About Mental Disorder and Violence?* (1994).

12

THE PREDICTION OF DANGEROUSNESS

The prediction of dangerousness is not an exact science and it probably never will be. As pointed out in Chapter 2, no two individuals can ever be exposed to exactly the same set of circumstances and no single individual can be exposed to exactly the same set of circumstances twice.

Floud, looking at the prediction of dangerousness in legally sane offenders is particularly pessimistic.

> [We] sifted a considerable quantity of theoretical argument and empirical evidence bearing directly or indirectly on the state of the art of assessing "dangerousness". We reached a conclusion which is not surprising, in so far as it amounts to saying that, since it is impossible to be sure how people will behave in the future, if only because of the working of chance, any attempt to apply precautions selectively against some persons for the sake of others is bound to be more or less wide of the mark. What is surprising — and very alarming — is to discover just how wide of the mark it turns out to be, whenever it is possible to put predictive judgments to the test by following the post-release careers of "dangerous" offenders. Statisticians have calculated the probabilities; so many judgments of dangerous falsified by the offender's subsequent behaviour (that is to say, by his failure to cause further grave harm) and so many judgments of safe falsified by the further serious offences he commits. Not surprisingly, it tends to be the critics of protective sentencing who worry about the former and members of the general public who worry about the latter. But the former figure, the proportion of falsified judgments of dangerous, even at its lowest, is so uncomfortably high that no-one engaged in making predictive judgments in the administration of justice can fail to be impressed — or, more likely, depressed.[1]

Floud also points out that "few serious offenders repeat their serious offences".[2]

The situation with regard to the prediction of dangerousness in mentally disordered people is also rather gloomy at the present time except with regard to short-term predictions in emergency civil commitments. (The shorter the period of time for which the prediction is made, the higher the predictive success rate).[3]

Psychiatrists are especially poor at predicting dangerousness, except for the short-term predictions mentioned above. Studies conducted in the 1970s suggested that psychiatrists were wrong about 70 per cent of the time.[4] The American Civil

Liberties Union placed it even higher. One group of studies that are particularly relevant in this regard are those that were conducted on the Baxstrom case. In 1958, Baxstrom was given a three-year sentence for attacking a police officer. While serving his sentence he was found to be insane and transferred to a state institution for the criminally insane. Although his sentence expired in December 1961, he was kept in the institution under the provisions of the Correction Law. He appealed against his continued detention and in February 1966, in *Baxstrom v Herod*, the Supreme Court held that:

> [the] petitioner had been denied 'equal protection of the laws' guaranteed by the Fourteenth Amendment by virtue of his continued detention in a facility for the criminally insane, beyond the expiration date of his sentence and without benefit of judicial review available to civilly committed persons.[5]

As a result of the court decision, Baxstrom was transferred to an ordinary state psychiatric hospital along with 966 other prisoner patients who had also been confined in facilities for the criminally insane in New York State. They were transferred between March and August 1966. As the report of the Butler Committee points out, "all these patients had previously been denied transfer by experienced psychiatrists from the Department of Mental Hygiene on the grounds that they were too disturbed or potentially dangerous".[6] It was anticipated that they would continue to be dangerous and to cause problems when transferred to the civil hospitals and on subsequent release into the community. These predictions did not come true.

> By the end of February, 1967, 147 had been discharged into the community and only seven had been found difficult enough to warrant a judicial commitment to special security. Of those released there was, by the end of 1967, only one record of subsequent arrest, and that was for minor theft. . . Research workers who followed up a 20 per cent sample of the Baxstrom men and all of the Baxstrom women for four years found that 20 per cent of the men and 26 per cent of the women were recorded as having assaulted people. . . 49 per cent of the men and 53 per cent of the women had either remained in or been returned to hospital. Ten per cent of the men and 13 per cent of the women had died by the end of the four-year period.[7]

As the Butler Report points out, however, there may have been more assaults if the people released had been younger. The mean age on transfer was 46 for men and 48 for women. The men had been detained, on average, for 13 years and the women for 17. Also, many of them had committed relatively minor crimes before admission.

Other studies, similar to the Baxstrom studies, have led to similar results.[8]

In a different type of study, researchers compared two groups of people — those considered by psychiatrists to be dangerous and those considered not to be dangerous. This study was set up to examine the outcome of the introduction of a new section of the New York Criminal Procedure Law (s 730.50) which made it mandatory for all felony defendants found to be incapable of standing trial to be assessed for dangerousness. The new section did not contain any criteria on which the prediction of dangerousness could be based. This was left to the psychiatrists. The researchers examined both groups on a number of variables and found that they were similar on all except one — "the defendant's current alleged offense". From this they concluded that:

> since a lay person provided with only the alleged offense could have made predictions very similar to those of the psychiatrists, the apparent use of this factor raises the question of the supposed special expertise brought to bear by psychiatrists in the prediction of dangerousness.[9]

The researchers subsequently followed up the defendants through their institutional career and out into the community to check on the accuracy of the psychiatrists' predictions. They concluded:

> On the basis of all these indicators ... the psychiatric predictions of dangerousness were not at all accurate. There was no significant difference between the two groups on any of the measures of assaultiveness examined. Those defendants evaluated by the psychiatrists as dangerous were no more dangerous than those evaluated as nondangerous.[10]

In 1984, Montandon and Harding reported a study in which 193 raters from 6 countries assessed 16 case histories for their degree of dangerousness. Of the 193 raters, 62 were psychiatrists, 52 were penal justice professionals (judges, magistrates, lawyers and police officers), 42 were medico-social professionals (doctors other than psychiatrists, nurses, social workers) and 37 were non-professionals. The 26 case histories were chosen from 42 that were submitted from all the participating countries. There were four cases with histories of violence associated with mental illness; four with histories of violence but no mental illness; five with histories of mental illness but no violence; and three with histories of neither violence nor mental illness. The results were as follows:

> The level of agreement between raters was generally low, the level of 60 per cent being reached for only 4 cases out of 16. Psychiatrists did not reach a higher level of agreement on the ratings of dangerousness than non-psychiatrists. Psychiatrists had a tendency to rate individuals as more dangerous than did non-psychiatrists. . . Psychiatrists were the least likely to indicate no danger even for cases with no mental illness and no violent behaviour.[11]

Given the track record of psychiatrists in predicting dangerousness, and the results of studies such as those cited above, Monahan, in 1984, suggested that:

> More studies concluding that psychiatrists and psychologists are relatively inaccurate clinical predictors of whether mentally disordered offenders who have been institutionalized for lengthy periods will offend once more are not needed. There are so many nails now in that coffin that I propose we declare the issue officially dead. Rather, what we need are, first, studies that vary the methods of prediction to focus on actuarial techniques, including those that incorporate

clinical information in statistical tables and those that provide statistical tables to clinicians as an additional source on which to base clinical judgments; second, studies that vary the factors used in making predictive decisions to include situational items such as characteristics of the family environment, the work environment, and the peer group environment in which the individual is to function; and, third, studies that vary the populations upon which predictive technology is brought to bear, to include short-term predictions made in the community.[12]

Unfortunately, as Prins pointed out in 1990: "There are no statistical or actuarial measures [yet] available that offer the prediction of dangerousness in either so-called normal or mentally disordered offenders with any degree of certainty".[13]

Pollock and Webster, moreover, while agreeing that actuarial methods might improve the predictive powers of psychiatrists, give a number of very cogent reasons why "actuarial approaches cannot provide an ultimate solution to the problem of prediction in the clinical assessment of dangerousness".

> For one thing, clinical assessment is about the individual, not populations, and the danger of the purely statistical approach is that the person's individuality will be obscured or trivialised by actuarial tables. . . Saying that 500 out of 1000 people in a particular group will be violent is not the same as saying that there is a 50 per cent chance a particular individual in this group will be violent. This individual either will or will not be violent; either he is one of the 500 or he is not. What does the clinician mean when he says there is a 50 per cent chance a person will be violent? It would seem that the percentage is not an evaluation of the subject's dangerousness but is the clinician's self-evaluation of how often his predictions will come true.

> Actuarial methods in clinical practice also raise serious ethical questions. . . The application of base-rate statistics inevitably biases the clinician's interpretation of the clinical data and unless great care is exercised the ethical problems involved will merely be disguised. As Monahan (1981) warns us, "clinical prediction sometimes functions as a 'laundering' of actuarial prediction by hiding the nature of the variables used in the prediction from public view".

> Perhaps an even more serious ethical problem with the actuarial approach is that the prediction remains more or less immutable.[14]

The last point is particularly important for, as Lucas points out: "The repeating of an opinion over the years can contribute to the creation of myths about particular individuals and play a part in the manufacture of a 'dangerous person'".[15]

In spite of these dangers, actuarial information, once it becomes available, would still seem to offer a better baseline for making predictions than totally unsupported clinical judgement.[16]

Risk assessment and risk management are, in fact, what the courts should be concerned with in the future, not the prediction of some indefinable and vague criterion such as dangerousness, and accurate risk assessment depends very much

158

upon the availability of adequate statistical data and the application of actuarial techniques. As Floud points out:

> We can measure risk - actuaries make a profession of it. Risk is, in principle, a matter of fact; but danger is a matter of judgement or opinion - a question of what we are prepared to put up with. People tolerate enormous risks without perceiving them as dangers, when their fears are not aroused or when it suits their convenience.[17]

In the United States, risk assessment and risk management have become increasingly important issues in recent years because of a series of cases that have articulated "various 'duties' owed by the mental health professional either to the patient or to third parties, including the duty to warn, the duty to protect and the duty to predict".[18] Negligent-release cases have already led to substantial damages being awarded against clinicians and hospitals.[19]

The MacArthur Risk Assessment Study, discussed in Chapter 11, is the sort of study that will contribute to the development of the statistical data on which risk assessment can be based. Eventually risk assessment and risk management will become disciplines in their own right.

In the meantime, the psychiatrist's role in this area is necessarily limited. The factors that can be used to assess the risk of a particular type of harm occurring or recurring will vary according to whether or not a previous harmful act has occurred. If it has not, then the psychiatrist's role is very limited because, we do not have any accurate way, as yet, of determining the combination of symptoms and circumstances that might predict the risk of harmful behaviour in the absence of a history of previous harmful behaviour. Kvaraceus's aphorism that "nothing predicts behaviour like behaviour"[20] applies to the behavioural manifestations of mental disorders as well as to behaviour in general. In the absence of previous harmful behaviour the psychiatrist is confined to predictions based on (a) the very limited statistical information available, especially that relating to the statistical relationship between individual symptoms and particular types of harmful behaviour, with all the dangers that predictions based on such data hold, and (b) clinical impressions,[21] subjective as these may be. As Schwartz points out, the problems here are manifold.

Schwartz examined the case of a 25-year-old man who stabbed to death a 16-year-old boy who was on his way to school. The killer, who had had extensive psychiatric treatment for schizophrenia, did not know his victim, made no attempt to cover up the crime and could not see that he had done anything wrong. As Schwartz points out (and as indicated earlier in this section) an act of violence results from a combination of internal psychological factors and external environmental factors (including provocation). According to Schwartz:

> For violence to occur, there must be sufficient provocation that is meaningful to the individual; in general, the more mentally ill the individual, the less external provocation necessary, and the more difficult it may be for anyone else to

understand the relevance of what the individual perceives as provocation. There must also be sufficient lack of reality testing or morality or self-control, or any combination of these, so that the individual, now provoked, either sees nothing wrong with his behaving violently or does it so impulsively that he cannot stop himself in time. All these factors, however, are poorly defined and imprecisely measurable, and the prediction of violence beforehand is therefore necessarily uncertain.[22]

In the presence of previous harmful behaviour, especially repeated harmful behaviour, (and especially repeated harmful behaviour in a hospital),[23] the psychiatrist is on more certain, but still shaky ground as even the presence of previous harmful behaviour is no guarantee of future harmful behaviour. So what is the role of the psychiatrist as an expert witness, at the present time, in the assessment of risk in a patient with a previous history of harmful behaviour? The factors that have to be taken into account (in line with the clinical model discussed earlier) are:

1 The nature and particular combination of factors (intrapersonal, interpersonal and situational) that are considered to have contributed to the previous harmful behaviour.

2 Whether any of these factors can be prevented from recurring.

Gunn suggests that the psychiatrist's role should be limited to consideration of some of the intrapersonal factors, specifically the role of a mental disorder. According to Gunn:

> The first step is to decide whether the patient concerned has a demonstrable mental disorder. The next is to try and determine the connection, if any, between the aggressive or feared behaviour and the mental disorder. If it is clear there is no connection, that should be the end of the prognostic statement. If a connection between the disorder and the violence is hypothesized, however, then the details of that connection should be spelled out. The more direct the link between the violence and the mental disorder, the more the prognosis of the disorder becomes the prognosis of the violence. For example, a man is subject to recurrent depressive episodes during which he becomes deluded to the point where he believes that life is useless, he is worthless, and the only practical remedy is to kill himself and destroy his world. During one such episode he kills his wife and tries to kill himself. He has no other history of violence so it is reasonable to regard him as not dangerous during his well phases, but as potentially suicidal and perhaps homicidal if the psychotic depression returns, and, also, to regard a future close relationship with a woman with especial concern.[24]

Pollock and Webster envisage a broader role. They suggest that although a psychiatrist has "no necessary expertise in the area of predicting dangerousness":

> Nontheless, by evaluating the patterns of events associated with the individual's dangerous behaviour in the past, the clinician may be able to discern a constellation of factors to be used in outlining the circumstances under which dangerous behaviour might recur.[25]

160

As long as this is translated into the language of risk assessment and as long as the factors identified are in an area in which the psychiatrist can properly be considered to be an expert (ie to have special expertise) this may also be a legitimate role for the psychiatrist.

With regard to the question of preventability, the psychiatrist's role should be limited to a discussion of the full range of treatment and management options available where a mental disorder has been identified. This should include a realistic appraisal of the relative effectiveness of the various options.

CONCLUSION

1. In the court room psychiatrists should resist being drawn into making predictions about the dangerousness of mentally disordered people. They should limit themselves to providing the court with as much clinical information as they can, along the lines suggested by Pollock and Webster and Gunn and leave the question of dangerousness for the courts to decide.

2. Lawyers, in turn, should refrain from asking psychiatrists specific questions about dangerousness. They should respect the fact that dangerousness is not "a medical or psychological concept",[26] that psychiatrists have no particular expertise in this area and that their track record in predicting dangerousness is, on the available evidence, poor.

3. At some stage in the future risk assessment and risk management will have developed to the point where prediction is more of a science than an art. By that stage the role of the psychiatrist will, hopefully, be clearer.

NOTES

1   Floud, J, "Dangerousness and Criminal Justice" (1982) 22/3 *Brit J Crim* 217.

2   Ibid p 216.

3   See, for example, McNiel, D and Binder, R, "Predictive Validity of Judgments of Dangerousness in Emergency Civil Commitment" (1987) 144:2 *Amer J Psychiat* 197. McNiel and Binder found that two-thirds of patients judged to be dangerous on admission engaged in at least one assault-related event within 72 hours of admission compared with one-third of patients judged not to be dangerous. See also Rofman, E, Askinazi, C and Fant, E, "The Prediction of Dangerous Behaviour in Emergency Civil Commitment" (1980) 137:9 *Amer J Psychiat* 1061. It should also be noted with regard to in-patients that various rating scales, including self-rating scales, for measuring the risk of violence have been developed. The success rate is extremely variable. See, for example, Plutchik, R and van Praag, H, "A Self-Report Measure of Violence Risk, II" (1990) 31:5 *Comprehensive Psychiatry* 450.

4   Monahan, J, "The Prediction of Violent Behaviour: Toward a Second Generation of Theory and Policy" (1984) 141:1 *Amer J Psychiat* 10.

5   Birns, H and Levien, J "Dangerousness: Legal Determinations and Clinical Speculations" (1980) 52/2 *Psychiat Q* 117.

6   Department of Health and Social Security, *Report of the Committee on Mentally Abnormal Offenders* (1975) p 61.

7   Id.

8   See, for example, Thornberry, T and Jacoby, J, *The Criminally Insane: A Community Follow-up of Mentally Ill Offenders* (1979), cited in Mullen, above n 2 p 15. In this study, "a similar group of 438 patients released in Pennsylvania . . . showed a similar 14% rate of assault in the four years following release".

9   Cocozza, J and Steadman, H, "The failure of psychiatric predictions of dangerousness: clear and convincing evidence" (1976) 29 *Rutgers Law Review* 1096.

10   Ibid p 1098.

11   Montandon, C and Harding, T, "The Reliability of Dangerousness Assessments — A Decision Making Exercise" (1984) 144 *Brit J Psychiat* 149.

12   Monahan, above n 34 p 13.

13   Prins, H, "Dangerousness: a review", in Bluglass, R and Bowden, P, (eds) *Principles and Practice of Forensic Psychiatry* (1990) p 503.

14   Pollock, N and Webster, C, "The clinical assessment of dangerousness" in Bluglass, R and Bowden, P (eds), *Principles and Practice of Forensic Psychiatry* (1990) p 492.

15   Lucas, W, "Review for Release: The Use and Misuse of Psychiatric Opinion" in Gerull, S and Lucas, W (eds), *Serious Violent Offenders: Sentencing, Psychiatry and Law Reform* (1993) p 239.

16   Gunn, J, "Dangerousness" in Gunn, J and Taylor, P (eds) *Forensic Psychiatry. Clinical, Legal and Ethical Issues* (1993) p 633.

17   Floud, J, "Dangerousness and Criminal Justice" (1982) 22/3 *Brit J Crim* 213.

18   Poythress, N Jr, "Avoiding Negligent Release: A Risk-Management Strategy" (1987) 38 *Hospital and Community Psychiatry* 1051. See also Monahan, J, "Limiting Therapist Exposure to Tarasoff Liability. Guidelines for Risk Containment" (1993) *American Psychologist* 242.

19   Monahan notes that in several of the cases in which he had served as an expert witness, "a treating clinician has learned of his or her patient's violence from the media and shortly thereafter has gone to the patient's chart and inserted new (but factually correct) material tending to support the reasonableness of the decisions that the clinician has made". Monahan, above n 18, p 248.

20   Kvaraceus, W, The Community and the Delinquent, cited in Walker, N, "Dangerous Mistakes" (1991) 158 *Brit J Psychiat* 753.

21   As Ingleby puts it, "clinical judgement is a blank cheque which can be filled in with any amount of tacit biasis and unwritten rules". Ingleby, D, "Understanding 'Mental Illness'" in Ingleby, D (ed), *The Politics of Mental Health*, (1981) p 30.

22   Schwartz, D, "Some Problems in Predicting Dangerousness" (1980) 52/2 *Psychiat Q* 82.

23   Noble and Rodger, for example, found that of 470 assaults committed at the Bethlem and Maudsley Hospitals, 405 were committed by 72 patients. Noble, P and Rodger, S, "Violence by Psychiatric In-Patients" (1989) 155 *Brit J Psychiat* 384.

24   Gunn, J, "An English psychiatrist looks at dangerousness" (1982) 10/3 *Amer Acad Psychiat & L* 149.

25   Pollock and Webster, above n 14, pp 494-495. One of the factors that might be considered here is the role of others in precipitating the harmful behaviour and this includes both the role of the victim and the role of bystanders. As Link et al point out, "It may be that inappropriate actions by others to psychotic symptoms are involved in producing the violent/illegal behaviour". Link, B, Andrews, H and Cullen, F, "The Violent and Illegal Behaviour of Mental Patients Reconsidered" (1992) 57 *American Sociological Review* 275.

26   Floud, J, cited in Bottoms, A and Brownsword, R, "The Dangerousness Debate After the Floud Report" (1982) 22:3 *British Journal of Criminology* 231.

CONCLUSION

The Court of Criminal Appeal has called for a criminal law review after quashing three murder convictions against a Sydney woman who stabbed to death her sister-in-law and two daughters. In a judgment handed down yesterday [her] appeal was upheld and her murder conviction substituted with the lesser verdict of manslaughter. . . Justice Gleeson said the only issue at the trial was [her] state of mind at the time of the killings. He said seven psychiatrists had testified and all had reached different conclusions. "The jury had before them opinion that [she] was schizophrenic, and opinion that [she] was not schizophrenic; opinion that [she] was suffering from a major depressive illness, and opinion that [she] was not suffering from depression. . ." [Justice Gleeson] said that section 23A of the *Crimes Act* depended upon concepts which medical experts found ambiguous and "perhaps unscientific". "The fact that, as the present case shows, there can be such conflicting expert opinion about the application to a given case of the legal principles of diminished responsibility is a matter of concern", Justice Gleeson said.[1]

This news item from the *Sydney Morning Herald* illustrates clearly the three problem areas that limit the use and usefulness of psychiatric evidence in court — psychiatry itself, the law and the legal process.

The problem with psychiatry, as demonstrated in Section A, is that, for all its striving to be one, it is not a science. The Oxford philosopher Anthony Kenny proposed four criteria for determining whether or not a discipline is a science:

1   *Consistency.* Different experts must not regularly give conflicting answers to questions central to the discipline.

2   *Method.* There should be agreement about the appropriate procedures for gathering information within the discipline which will be capable of replication between experts.

3   *Accumulation.* The knowledge within the discipline must be established as proven and accepted by each generation as part of the accumulation of facts basic to the discipline.

4   *Prediction.* The discipline must predict the not yet known from the already known.[2]

On these criteria, psychiatry is not a science at all.[3] Its language is confused and behind each word in it there are multiple theoretical constructs competing for control of the language. Because of these multiple theoretical constructs, any explanation about the cause of a person's behaviour will be a hypothetical explanation based on the particular hypothesis or hypotheses about normal and abnormal behaviour that the psychiatrist concerned espouses at that particular point in time. As long as the language remains unsettled and as long as the several theoretical bases upon which that language is structured remain in conflict, psychiatry will never be a unified science. When the problems that arise from this are coupled with the problems discussed in Sections B, C and D, serious doubts must arise about the value of forensic psychiatric evidence and about the way in which such evidence is currently used in court. Indeed, given these problems, it would seem logical for forensic psychiatric evidence to be restricted to (a) a statement about whether or not the signs or symptoms of mental disorder were present at the time the psychiatrist examined the person and, if so, their nature and severity, and (b) if required, a statement about treatment options and their relative effectiveness. This would mean that the use of forensic psychiatric evidence would be somewhat curtailed as retrospective analysis of a person's mental state at some time in the past could not be used in evidence, unless the person was being treated by a psychiatrist at the time of the offence. Given the present state of the law, this is not a viable option. Inter alia, mental illness defences and diminished responsibility necessitate the introduction of such evidence. As Slovenko points out with regard to the American jurisdiction, "in criminal cases, failure to engage an expert may constitute ineffective assistance of counsel warranting reversal of a conviction".[4]

Until the law is changed (and given the state of the law with regard to the mental illness defence and diminished responsibility, especially since *Byrne*[5] and *Veen*,[6] this is a very desirable option), psychiatric evidence based on a retrospective analysis (mainly educated guesswork) of suspect and inevitably deficient and flawed information will continue to be used in court. And as long as the adversarial system persists, the charm, charisma, confidence,[7] appearance[8] and presentation of the expert (plus their ability to stand up to cross-examination) will continue to be influential factors in determining whether the evidence presented is accepted or not.[9]

Psychiatry is not about to become a unified science. The law is not about to change. Lawyers, psychiatrists and judges alike have been calling for change for many years, the occasional prestigious report recommending change has appeared, and nothing has happened. The only areas, therefore, in which change seems even remotely possible at the present time are the ways in which psychiatric evidence is used in court and the legal process itself. Many proposals for improving the former have been put forward. Some are definitely worth further consideration as they would go a long way towards improving the quality of the expert psychiatric evidence provided:

1 The increased use of court-appointed experts[10] (although, as Slovenko points out, court-appointed experts are not always free from bias).[11]

2 Employment of expert assessors.[12]

3 Return of the special jury (of experts).[13]

4 Giving of group expert evidence.[14] This would satisfy Brent's requirement that "testimony should be treated as a scholarly endeavour

and experts should be encouraged to seek peer review of their opinions".[15]

5 Pre-trial consultation between forensic psychiatrists, including pre-trial exchange of forensic psychiatric reports.[16]

6 Mandatory tabling in court of all forensic psychiatric and forensic psychological reports commissioned by both the defence and the prosecution.

With regard to the legal process itself, there is a model for change available which has much to recommend it – the Queensland Mental Health Tribunal system which has been in operation since 1985. This system removes the determination of the state of a person's mind at the time of the offence and whether they have a psychiatric defence because of it[17] from the court which is trying the offence to an independent Tribunal consisting of a Judge of the Supreme Court, assisted by two psychiatrists. As Dodds points out:

> Many of the problems encountered by criminal courts when dealing with mentally ill offenders are obviated by the Mental Health Tribunal system. . . Although court rules and procedures are maintained in a dignified and formal manner at tribunal hearings there is a less tense atmosphere, and cross examinations of medical witnesses are conducted in an inquisitorial way in contrast to the adversarial way in criminal trials. . . [The] tribunal tries to avoid aggressive defences or prosecutions and discourages the practice of having witnesses for the prosecution cancelling out witnesses for the defence. The tribunal is a commission of inquiry and witnesses are asked to assist the tribunal and not to be one sided or partisan in favour of the side paying for their opinions.[18]

This system does not solve the inherent deficiencies of psychiatric evidence discussed in this book but it does go a long way towards eliminating some of the more unsatisfactory aspects of the adversarial legal process.

Until changes are made the onus must remain on psychiatrists, the courts and lawyers to do all they can themselves to remedy the deficiencies of the present situation. Psychiatrists should endeavour to remain neutral and objective and should resist the pressures placed upon them (a) to step outside their proper (and limited) area of expertise, and (b) to align themselves with the party who engages them. If they wish to work in the field of forensic psychiatry they should bear in mind, at all times, Diamond's dictum that, "the psychiatrist is no mere technician to be used by the law as the law sees fit, nor is the science, art, and definitions of psychiatry and psychology to be redefined and manipulated by the law as it wishes".[19]

They should also, however, be prepared to acknowledge the limitations of their evidence and knowledge.

The courts should be critically aware at all times of the limitations of the psychiatric evidence presented to them and should ensure that such evidence is used responsibly and not simply as a form of window dressing or as a convenient way of abdicating the court's own decision-making responsibilities.[20] The courts might also start considering the true nature of psychiatric evidence and whether or not it meets the normal tests for the admission of scientific evidence.[21] Although the courts tend to be more critical these days of psychiatric and psychological evidence on "cutting edge topics", such as the admissibility of evidence of repressed memories, they rarely apply the same critical scrutiny to routine and more traditional psychiatric evidence, even when, as the Californian Supreme Court noted in 1984, "the subject matter is as esoteric as the reconstitution of a past state of mind or the prediction of future dangerousness".[22] Lawyers from both sides should use psychiatrists appropriately and sparingly and, unless the law calls for it, not as psychohistorians or because of their history-taking skills,[23] and especially not as "hired guns" or "advocates" for a particular point of view. Lawyers working in this field should also equip themselves with the knowledge which would enable them to examine the evidence of psychiatrists and psychologists more thoroughly than is customarily the case. As Greig points out:

> It is incumbent on lawyers to examine the validity and reliability of empirical data. FA Whitlock's statement that "it is perfectly proper for psychiatrists to ask that their evidence should be taken seriously however far-fetched some of their pronouncements may at times appear" is no longer appropriate.[24]

This, of course, is somewhat of a wish-list. The reality is that for a long time to come psychiatric evidence will be used in court in much the same unsatisfactory and inappropriate way as it has been in the past (and with much the same results). The keys to change are education (of psychiatrists, lawyers and the judiciary alike) and debate. Hopefully this book will act as a catalyst for the type of dialogue that is needed to initiate change, even if that change is a long way away.

NOTES

1   *Sydney Morning Herald* 16 February 1993.

2   Kenny, A, cited in Bluglass, R, "The psychiatrist as an expert witness" in Bluglass, R and Bowden, P, (eds), *Principles and Practice of Forensic Psychiatry* (1990) p 162.

3   Although Kenny considers psychiatrists to be 'men of science' (because psychiatry is a branch of medicine and medicine is a 'paradigm case' of a science) the fact is that psychiatry does not fulfil Kenny's definition.

4   Slovenko, R, "The Lawyer and the Forensic Expert: Boundaries of Ethical Practice" (1987) 5/2 *Beh Sci & L* 124.

5   *R v Byrne* [1960] 2 QB 396.

6   *Veen v The Queen* (1979) 143 CLR 458; *Veen v The Queen (No 2)* (1988) 62 ALJR 224.

7   Confidence rather than overconfidence appears to be the relevant factor. This was first noted by Burrows in 1828 who stated, in a chapter dealing with "medical evidence in juridical enquiries" in his book *Commentaries on the Causes, Forms, Symptoms and Treatment, Moral and Medical, of Insanity* p 715:

> A medical witness should certainly be rather diffident than forward in giving his evidence in cases of disputed insanity. If too confident, he will be immediately, and not perhaps improperly, suspected of being a partisan, and having a stronger interest in the event than meets the eye. He should, therefore, shape his conduct and speech equally to avoid shewing that degree of diffidence which betrays ignorance, and that degree of earnestness which evinces a feeling beyond the exercise of a mere professional office.

Scientific support for this opinion came in 1992 in a study by Rogers et al. According to this study:

> Testimony with an expressed confidence of 80 per cent appears to exert a greater influence on perceptions of sanity/insanity than at either 60 per cent or 100 per cent... Expressed confidence also appeared to affect the perceived clarity of testimony and its believability. When testimony is proffered without attendant doubts (ie 100 per cent condition), subjects were very clear regarding its conclusions. This finding appears common-sensical, since testimony offered in absolute terms is generally unambiguous. In addition, the expert was seen as more believable at the 80 per cent and 100 per cent conditions than at the 60 per cent condition. This finding is somewhat puzzling because the less certain expert (ie 60 per cent conditions) appears to be very forthcoming about the frailities of his opinion. However, an alternative explanation is that subjects were simply unconvinced by the uncertain testimony while not doubting the expert's integrity (Rogers, R, Bagby, R and Chow, M, "Psychiatrists and the Parameters of Expert Testimony" (1992) 15 *Int J L & Psychiat* 394).

8   According to Resnick:

> Studies reveal that wearing conservative clothing substantially increases the psychiatrist's credibility in court. Male psychiatrists should wear dark suits. Solid colours confer greater authority. Female psychiatrists appear most credible if they wear solid-colored suits with skirts that fall below the knee. Conservative dresses with contrasting blazers are also effective. Both male and female witnesses should avoid wearing jewellery or anything ostentatious (Resnick, P, "Guidelines for Courtroom Testimony" in Rosner, R (ed) Principles and Practice of Forensic Psychiatry (1994) p 36).

Resnick also suggests that:

> Ties of small repeating patterns, such as diamonds are best... Paisley patterns are not viewed as serious, and bow ties evoke distrust. Persons wearing tinted glasses are not trusted. Facial hair is generally viewed negatively; persons with goatees are especially distrusted (Resnick, P, "Court Testimony as an Expert Witness" (1995) Presentation Notes for Annual Meeting of the Royal Australian and New Zealand College of Psychiatrists, Section of Forensic Psychiatry Article 4 p 32).

9   According to Slovenko, "what the lawyer wants in an expert medical witness . . . are the looks of Robert Redford, the knowledge of Michael DeBakey, and the presence of Ronald Reagen [sic]". Slovenko also cites the Federal Public Defender in Chicago as saying that, for psychiatric testimony, he would "get someone with a foreign accent and Freud as his middle name". Slovenko, above n 4 p 125.

10   Bluglass, above n 2 p 166.

11   Slovenko, above n 4 p 147.

12   Bluglass, above n 2 p 166.

13 Id.

14 Id.

15 Brent, R, cited in Mendelson, G, "The Scope and Limitations of Psychiatric Expert Testimony" (1990) 10 *Aust For Psychiat B* 13.

16 Cosgrove, J, "As We See Ourselves — And As Others See Us" (1985) 3 *Aust For Psychiat B* 3.

17 Specifically, the Mental Health Tribunal determines:

1. Whether there is a dispute of facts that would make it unsafe for the tribunal to make a finding of unsoundness of mind.

2. Whether a person charged with an indictable offence and subsequently referred to the tribunal has a psychiatric defence of unsoundness of mind at the material time.

3. In the case of murder when the accused is found not of unsound mind, whether there is a defence of diminished responsibility.

4. When it is the finding of the tribunal that court proceedings should continue, whether the patient is fit to stand trial.

Dodds, A, "The Queensland Mental Health Tribunal", paper published by the Mental Health Tribunal, Queensland Health Department (undated, circa 1994) p 24.

18 Ibid p 33.

19 Diamond, B, "The forensic psychiatrist: Consultant v. activist in legal doctrine" (1992) 20 *Bulletin of the American Academy of Psychiatry and the Law* 119.

20 See, for example, Slovenko, above n 4 p 124.

In some cases the courts want psychiatric testimony as window dressing. Decisions on civil commitment, child custody, and also on criminal responsibility are difficult and uncomfortable to make. Such decisions, however, have to be made and the courts, mindful of public opinion, often abdicate their decision making responsibility to psychiatrists or want to decorate their decision with psychiatric testimony. It's passing the buck, so to speak.

21 See Philipsborn, J, "On Firm Ground? A Discussion of the Current Law of Foundation for the Expression of Opinions by Psychiatrists and Psychologists" (1994) 15 *American Journal of Forensic Psychiatry* 53.

22 *People v McDonald* 37 (Cal 3d) 35 at 373 (1984). Cited in Philipsborn, above n 21 p 59.

23 Stanley, R, "The Psychiatrist as Expert Witness: A Legal Perspective" (1989) 9 *Aust For Psychiat B* 4.

24 Greig, D, "Expert Evidence – Book Review" (1994) 28 *ANZ J Psychiat* 543.

BIBLIOGRAPHY

Akiskal, H and Mc Kinney, W, "Overview of recent research in depression. Integration of ten conceptual models into a comprehensive clinical frame" (1975) 32 *Archives of General Psychiatry* 285-305.

Alcorn, D, "Basic Law for Psychiatrists" (1995) Presentation Notes for Annual Meeting of The Royal Australian and New Zealand College of Psychiatrists Section of Forensic Psychiatry, Article 1, 1-11.

Aldrich, C, *An Introduction to Dynamic Psychiatry*, New York: McGraw-Hill Book Company, 1966.

Altman, E and Jobe, T, "Phenomenology of Psychosis" (1992) 5 *Current Opinion in Psychiatry* 33-37.

American Medical Association Council on Scientific Affairs, "Report on Memories of Childhood Abuse" (1995) XLIII *International Journal of Clinical and Experimental Hypnosis* 114-117.

American Psychiatric Association Board of Trustees, "Statement on Memories of Sexual Abuse" (1994) XLII *International Journal of Clinical and Experimental Hypnosis* 261-264.

American Psychiatric Association, *Diagnostic and Statistical Manual: Mental Disorders*, Washington: American Psychiatric Association, 1952.

— *Diagnostic and Statistical Manual of Mental Disorders* (2nd ed), Washington: American Psychiatric Association, 1968.

— *Diagnostic and Statistical Manual of Mental Disorders* (3rd ed), Washington: American Psychiatric Association, 1980.

— *Diagnostic and Statistical Manual of Mental Disorders* (3rd ed, rev), Washington: American Psychiatric Association, 1987.

— *Diagnostic and Statistical Manual of Mental Disorders* (4th ed), Washington: American Psychiatric Association, 1994.

Andreasen, N, "Scale for the Assessment of Thought, Language and Communication (TLC)" (1986) 12/3 *Schizophrenic Bulletin* 473-482.

Appelbaum, P, Grisso, T, Givelber, D, Jick, R, Silver, E and Steadman, H, "Dr Appelbaum and Colleagues Reply" (1994) 151 American Journal of Psychiatry 153.

Applebaum, P, Jick, R, Grisso, T, Givelber, D, Silver, E and Steadman, H, "Use of Posttraumatic Stress Disorder to Support an Insanity Defense" (1993) 150 *American Journal of Psychiatry* 229-234.

Arieti, S (ed), *American Handbook of Psychiatry*, New York: Basic Books, 1974.

Arieti, S and Bemporad, J, "The Psychological Organization of Depression" (1980) 137/11 *American Journal of Psychiatry* 1360-1365.

Barclay, W, "Diminished Responsibility: The Third Leg", unpublished paper delivered to the Section of Forensic Psychiatry of the Royal Australian and New Zealand College of Psychiatry, 1991.

170

—   "Homicide – The Viewpoint of One Forensic Psychiatrist", unpublished paper delivered to a Melbourne Conference on Homicide: Patterns, Prevention and Control.

Bartholomew, A, *Psychiatry, The Criminal Law & Corrections: An Exercise in Sciolism*, Bundalong: Wileman Publications, 1986.

Bazelon, D, "The Perils of Wizardry" (1974) 131 *American Journal of Psychiatry* 1317-1322.

Beigel, A, Berren, M and Harding, T, "The Paradoxical Impact of a Commitment Statute on Prediction of Dangerousness" (1984) 141/3 *American Journal of Psychiatry* 373-377.

Birns, H and Levien, J, "Dangerousness: Legal Determinations and Clinical Speculations" (1980) 52/2 *Psychiatric Quarterly* 108-131.

Black, D and Boffeli, T, "Simple Schizophrenia: Revisited" (1990) 31/4 *Comprehensive Psychiatry* 344-349.

Blackburn, R, "On Moral Judgements and Personality Disorders: The Myth of Psychopathic Personality Revisited" (1988) 153 *British Journal of Psychiatry* 505-512.

Bleuler, E, *Textbook of Psychiatry*, New York: The MacMillan Company, 1924.

Bluglass, R, "The Psychiatrist as an Expert Witness"; "Bestiality"; "Shoplifting"; chapters in Bluglass, R and Bowden, P (eds), *Principles and Practice of Forensic Psychiatry*, Edinburgh: Churchill Livingstone, 1990.

Bluglass, R and Bowden, P (eds), *Principles and Practice of Forensic Psychiatry*, Edinburgh: Churchill Livingstone, 1990.

Boeringa, J and Castellani, S, "Reliability and Validity of Emotional Blunting as a Criterion for Diagnosis of Schizophrenia" (1982) 139/9 *American Journal of Psychiatry* 1131-1135.

Bottoms, A and Brownsword, R, "The Dangerousness Debate After the Floud Report" (1982) 22/3 *British Journal of Criminology* 229-254.

Bowden, P, "Homicide" and "The Written Report and Sentences" in Bluglass, R and Bowden, P (eds), *Principles and Practice of Forensic Psychiatry*, Edinburgh: Churchill Livingstone, 1990.

Breslau, N, Davis, G and Andreski, P, "Traumatic events and Posttraumatic Stress Disorder in an urban population of young adults" (1991) 48 *Archives of General Psychiatry* 216-222.

Brown, D, Commentary in *Proceedings of the Institute of Criminology* No 57 "Shoplifting", Sydney: Institute of Criminology, 1983.

Brown, J, *Freud and the Post-Freudians*, Harmondsworth: Penguin Books Ltd, 1961.

Brown, L, "A Psychologist's Perspective on Psychiatry in China" (1980) 14 *Australian and New Zealand Journal of Psychiatry* 21-35.

Burges Watson, I, "Psychiatry, science and posttraumatic stress disorder" (1995) 29 *Australian and New Zealand Journal of Psychiatry* 2-5.

Burges Watson, I, Hoffman, L and Wilson, G, "The Neuropsychiatry of Post-traumatic Stress Disorder" (1988) 152 *British Journal of Psychiatry* 164-173.

Burrows, G, *Commentaries on the Causes, Forms, Symptoms, and Treatment, Moral and Medical, of Insanity*. Original edition 1828. Special edition privately printed for the members of the Classics of Psychiatry & Behavioral Sciences Library.

Carpenter, P, "Descriptions of Schizophrenia in the Psychiatry of Georgian Britain: John Haslam and James Tilly Matthews" (1989) 30/4 *Comprehensive Psychiatry* 332-338.

Catts, S, "A biological basis to schizophrenia – have we learnt anything?" (1995) 4 *Psyche* 2-3.

Ceci, S, Loftus, E, Leichtman, M and Bruck, M, "The Possible Role of Source Misattributions in the Creation of False Beliefs Among Preschoolers" (1994) XLII *International Journal of Clinical and Experimental Hypnosis* 304-320.

Chaika, E, "Thought Disorder or Speech Disorder in Schizophrenia" (1982) 8/4 *Schizophrenia Bulletin* 587-591.

Challinger, D, "Theft from Retail Stores: An Overview", in *Proceedings of the Institute of Criminology* No 57 "Shoplifting" Sydney: Institute of Criminology, 1983.

Chaplow, D, Peters, J and Kydd, R, "The Expert Witness in Forensic Psychiatry" (1992) 26/4 *Australian and New Zealand Journal of Psychiatry* 624-630.

Chiswick, D, "Psychiatric Testimony in Britain: Remembering Your Lines and Keeping to the Script" (1992) 15 *International Journal of Law and Psychiatry* 171-177.

Ciompi, L, "Is there really a Schizophrenia? The Long-Term Course of Psychotic Phenomena" (1984) 145 *British Journal of Psychiatry* 636-640.

Cirincione, C, Steadman, H, Robbins, P and Monahan, J, "Schizophrenia as a Contingent Risk Factor for Criminal Violence" (1992) 15 *International Journal of Law and Psychiatry* 347-358.

Cocozza, J and Steadman, H, "The Failure of Psychiatric Predictions of Dangerousness: Clear and Convincing Evidence" (1976) 29 *Rutgers Law Review* 1084-1101.

Cohen, C, "Crime Among Mental Patients – A Critical Analysis" (1980) 52/2 *Psychiatric Quarterly* 100-107.

Cooper, D, *Psychiatry and Anti-Psychiatry*, London: Granada, 1970.

— *The Grammar of Living*, London: Penguin, 1976.

Cooper, J, "On the Publication of the *Diagnostic and Statistical Manual of Mental Disorders:* Fourth Edition (DSM-IV)" (1995) 166 *British Journal of Psychiatry* 4-8.

Cosgrove J, "As We See Ourselves – And As Others See Us" (1985) 3 *Australasian Forensic Psychiatry Bulletin* 1-4.

Crow, T, "Aetiology of Schizophrenia" (1994) 7 *Current Opinion in Psychiatry* 39-42.

Cutting, J, "Hearing voices" (1989) 298 *British Medical Journal* 769-770.

Davidson, J, Hughes, D, Blazer, D and George, L, "Post-traumatic stress disorder in the community: an epidemiological study" (1991) 21 *Psychological Medicine* 713-721.

Davies, W and Feldman, P, "The Diagnosis of Psychopathy by Forensic Specialists" (1981) 138 *British Journal of Psychiatry* 329-331.

Department of Health and Social Security, *Report of the Committee on Mentally Abnormal Offenders*, London: HMSO, 1975, .

Der, G, Gupta, S and Murray, R, "Is Schizophrenia Disappearing?" (1990) 335 *The Lancet* 513-516.

Diamond, B, "The forensic psychiatrist: Consultant v activist in legal doctrine" (1992) 20 *Bulletin of the American Academy of Psychiatry and the Law* 119-132.

Dodds, A, "The Queensland Mental Health Tribunal", paper published by the Mental Health Tribunal, Queensland Health Department (undated, circa 1994).

Dolan, B and Coid, J, *Psychopathic and Antisocial Personality Disorders*, London: Gaskell, 1993.

Ellard, J, "Did Schizophrenia Exist Before The Eighteenth Century?" (1987) 21 *Australian and New Zealand Journal of Psychiatry* 306-314.

—   "New White Elephants for Old Sacred Cows; Some Notes on Diagnosis" (1992) 26/4 *Australian and New Zealand Journal of Psychiatry* 546-549.

—   "Schizophrenia: Here Today, Gone Tomorrow?" (1985) 28/1 *Modern Medicine of Australia* 9-13.

—   "The Madness of Mental Health Acts" (1990) 24 *Australian and New Zealand Journal of Psychiatry* 167-174.

Eysenck, H, "Behaviour Therapy and the Philosophers" (1979) 17 *Behaviour Research and Therapy* 511-514.

Faulk, M, *Basic Forensic Psychiatry*, Oxford: Blackwell Scientific Publications, 1994.

Fenichel, O, *The Psychoanalytic Theory of Neurosis*, London: Routledge & Kegan Paul Ltd, 1966.

Finlay-Jones, R, "Psychopathic Disorder" (1991) 4 *Current Opinion in Psychiatry* 850-855.

Floud, J, "Dangerousness and Criminal Justice" (1982) 22/3 *The British Journal of Criminology* 213-228.

Foa, E, Riggs, D and Gershuny, B, "Arousal, Numbing and Intrusion: Symptom Structure of PTSD Following Assault" (1995) 152 *American Journal of Psychiatry* 116-120.

Forshaw, D and Rollin, H, "The history of forensic psychiatry in England" in Bluglass, R and Bowden, P (eds), *Principles and Practice of Forensic Psychiatry*, Edinburgh: Churchill Livingstone, 1990.

Forth, A, Hart, S and Hare, R, "Assessment of psychopathy in male young offenders" (1990) 2 *Psychological Assessment* 342-344.

Freedman, A, Kaplan, H and Sadock, B (eds), *Comprehensive Textbook of Psychiatry-II*, Baltimore: The Williams & Wilkins Company, 1975.

Furlong, F, "A Biological Marker in Claimed Post-Traumatic Stress Disorder" (1992) 13 *American Journal of Forensic Psychiatry* 41-47.

Gersons, B and Carlier, I, "Post-traumatic Stress Disorder: The History of a Recent Concept" (1992) 161 *British Journal of Psychiatry* 742-748.

Gibbens, T, "Shoplifting" (1981) 138 *British Journal of Psychiatry* 346-347.

Gibbens, T, Palmer, C and Prince, J, "Mental Health Aspects of Shoplifting" (1971) 3 *British Medical Journal* 612-615.

Glasser, M, "Paedophilia" in Bluglass, R and Bowden, P (eds), *Principles and Practice of Forensic Psychiatry*, Edinburgh: Churchill Livingstone, 1990.

Goldman, M, "Kleptomania: Making Sense of the Nonsensical" (1991) 148 *American Journal of Psychiatry* 986-996.

Goldney, R and Burvill, P, "Trends in Suicidal Behaviour and its Management" (1980) 14 *Australian and New Zealand Journal of Psychiatry* 1-15.

Greig, D, "Expert Evidence – Book Review" (1994) 28 *Australian and New Zealand Journal of Psychiatry* 543-544.

Gunderson, J and Sabo, A, "The Phenomenological and Conceptual Interface Between Borderline Personality Disorder and PTSD" (1993) 150 *American Journal of Psychiatry* 19-27.

Gunn, J, "An English Psychiatrist Looks at Dangerousness" (1982) 10/3 *Bulletin of the American Academy of Psychiatry and the Law* 143-153.

— "Dangerousness" in Gunn, J and Taylor, P (eds), *Forensic Psychiatry. Clinical, Legal and Ethical Issues*, Oxford: Butterworth-Heinemann, 1993.

Gunn, J and Taylor, P (eds), *Forensic Psychiatry. Clinical, Legal and Ethical Issues*, Oxford: Butterworth-Heinemann, 1993.

Hafner, R, "Behaviour Therapy For The Neuroses: Some Conceptual And Practical Problems" (1981) 15 *Australian and New Zealand Journal of Psychiatry* 287-300.

Hamilton, M, "Frequency of Symptoms in Melancholia (Depressive Illness)" (1989) 154 *British Journal of Psychiatry* 201-206.

— "Mood Disorders: Clinical Features" in Kaplan, H and Sadock, B (eds) *Comprehensive Textbook of Psychiatry* (5th ed), Baltimore: Williams & Wilkins, 1989.

Hare, E, "Schizophrenia as a Recent Disease" (1988) 153 *British Journal of Psychiatry* 521-531.

Hare, R, *The Hare Psychopathy Checklist-Revised*, Toronto:Multi-Health Systems, 1991.

Harrison, G and Mason, P, "Schizophrenia – Falling Incidence and Better Outcome?" (1993) 163 *British Journal of Psychiatry* 535-541.

Hart, S, Hare, R and Forth, A, "Psychopathy as a Risk Marker for Violence: Development and Validation of a Screening Version of the Revised Psychopathy Checklist" in Monahan , J and Steadman, H (eds), *Violence and Mental Disorder*, Chicago: The University of Chicago Press, 1994.

Hays, P, "The Nosological Status of Schizophrenia" (1984) I *The Lancet* 1342-1345.

Hellerstein, D, Frosch, W and Koenigsberg, H, "The Clinical Significance of Command Hallucinations" (1987) 144/2 *American Journal of Psychiatry* 219-221.

Helzer, J, Robins, L and McEvoy, L, "Posttraumatic stress disorder in the general population: findings from the Epidemiological Catchment Area Survey" (1987) 317 *New England Journal of Medicine* 1630-1634.

Henderson, D and Gillespie, R, *A Text-Book of Psychiatry for Students and Practitioners*, London: Oxford University Press, 1950.

Higgins, J, "Affective Psychoses" in Bluglass, R and Bowden, P (eds), *Principles and Practice of Forensic Psychiatry*, Edinburgh: Churchill Livingstone, 1990.

Hocking, F, "Human Reactions to Extreme Environmental Stress" (1965) II/12 *The Medical Journal of Australia* 477-483.

Hoenig, J, "The Concept of Schizophrenia: Kraepelin-Bleuler-Schneider" (1983) 142 *British Journal of Psychiatry* 547-56.

— "Schneider's First Rank Symptoms and the Tabulators" (1984) 25/1 *Comprehensive Psychiatry* 77-87.

Holzman, P, "Thought Disorder in Schizophrenia: Editor's Introduction" (1986) 12/3 *Schizophrenia Bulletin* 342-347.

Hospers, J, *An Introduction to Philosophical Analysis*, London: Routledge & Kegan Paul, 1967.

Howard, C, "Amnesia" in Bluglass, R and Bowden, P (eds), *Principles and Practice of Forensic Psychiatry*, Edinburgh: Churchill Livingstone, 1990.

Hucker, S, "Necrophilia and Other Unusual Philias" in Bluglass, R and Bowden, P (eds), *Principles and Practice of Forensic Psychiatry*, Edinburgh: Churchill Livingstone, 1990.

Hume, F, "Mental Health Aspects of Shoplifting: A Retrospective Analysis of 135 Referrals to Bondi Junction Community Health Centre" in *Proceedings of the Institute of Criminology* No 57 "Shoplifting", Sydney: Institute of Criminology, 1983.

Hunter, R and Macalpine, I, *Three Hundred Years of Psychiatry 1535-1860*, London: Oxford University Press, 1963.

Ingleby, D, "Understanding 'Mental Illness'" in Ingleby, D (ed) *Critical Psychiatry The Politics of Mental Health,* Harmondsworth, Penguin Books Ltd, 1981.

Jablensky, A, Hugler, H, von Cranach, M and Kalinov, K, "Kraepelin revisited: a reassessment and statistical analysis of dementia praecox and manic-depressive insanity in 1908" (1993) 23 *Psychological Medicine* 843-858.

John D and Catherine T MacArthur Foundation Research Network on Mental Health and the Law, *What Do We Know About Mental Disorder and Violence?* (1994) Policy Research Associates (pamphlet).

Junginger, J, "Predicting Compliance With Command Hallucinations" (1990) 147 *American Journal of Psychiatry* 245-247.

Kaplan, H and Sadock, B (eds), *Comprehensive Textbook of Psychiatry*, Fifth Edition, Baltimore: Williams & Wilkins, 1989 .

Kardiner, A, *The Traumatic Neuroses of War*, New York: Hoeber, 1941.

Katzmann, A, "Cross-Examination of the Expert Witness" in Winfield, R (ed), *The Expert Medical Witness*, Sydney: The Federation Press, 1989.

Kendler, K and Diehl, S, "The Genetics of Schizophrenia: A Current, Genetic-Epidemiologic Perspective" (1993) 19/2 *Schizophrenia Bulletin* 261-285.

Kessler, R, Sonnega, A, Bromet, E and Nelson, C, *Post-traumatic Stress Disorder in the National Comorbidity Survey*, Ann Arbor: Institute for Social Research, 1993.

Kihlstrom, J, "Hypnosis, Delayed Recall, and the Principles of Memory" (1994) XLII *International Journal of Clinical and Experimental Hypnosis* 337-344.

Kiloh, L, "Non-Pharmacological Biological Treatments of Psychiatric Patients" (1983) 17 *Australian and New Zealand Journal of Psychiatry* 215-225 .

King, D and Cooper, S, "Viruses, Immunity and Mental Disorders" (1989) 154 *British Journal of Psychiatry* 1-7.

Kleinman, S, "Trauma-Induced Psychiatric Disorders in Criminal Court" in Rosner, R (ed), *Principles and Practice of Forensic Psychiatry*, New York: Chapman & Hall, 1994.

Kluft, R, "First-Rank Symptoms as a Diagnostic Clue to Multiple Personality Disorder" (1987) 144/3 *American Journal of Psychiatry* 293-298.

Kopelman, M, "Crime and Amnesia: A Review" (1987) 5/3 *Behavioural Sciences and the Law* 323-342.

Lanin-Kettering, I and Harrow, M, "The Thought Behind the Words: A View of Schizophrenic Speech and Thinking Disorders" (1985) 11/1 *Schizophrenia Bulletin* 1-7.

Leach, A, "Negative Symptoms" (1991) 4 *Current Opinion in Psychiatry*, 18-22.

Leading Article, "Is Schizophrenia a Psychosis or a Neurosis?" (1978) 2 *British Medical Journal* 76.

Leading Article, "Kleptomania" (1991) 337 *The Lancet* 1090.

Lehmann, H, "Schizophrenia: Clinical Features" in Freedman, A, Kaplan, H and Sadock, B (eds), *Comprehensive Textbook of Psychiatry – II*, Baltimore: The Williams & Wilkins Company, 1975.

Link, B, Andrews, H and Cullen, F, "The Violent and Illegal Behavior of Mental Patients Reconsidered" (1992) 57 *American Sociological Review* 275-292.

Lipkowitz, M and Idupuganti, S, "Diagnosing Schizophrenia in 1980: A Survey of US Psychiatrists" (1983) 140/1 *American Journal of Psychiatry* 52-55.

Lonie, I, "Borderline Disorder and Post-Traumatic Stress Disorder: An Equivalence?" (1993) 27 *Australian and New Zealand Journal of Psychiatry* 233-245.

Lucas, W, "Review for Release: The Use and Misuse of Psychiatric Opinion" in Gerull, S and Lucas, W (eds) *Serious Violent Offenders: Sentencing, Psychiatry and Law Reform*, Canberra: Australian Institute of Criminology, 1993.

Mack, A Forman, L, Brown, R and Frances, A, "A Brief History of Psychiatric Classification From the Ancients to DSM-IV" (1994) 17 *Psychiatric Clinics of North America* 515-523.

Maddison, D, Day, P and Leabeater, B, *Psychiatric Nursing*, Edinburgh: E & S Livingstone, 1965.

Magrinat, G, Danziger, J, Lorenzo, I and Flemenbaum, A, "A Reassessment of Catatonia" (1983) 24/3 *Comprehensive Psychiatry* 218-228.

March, J, "The nosology of posttraumatic stress disorder" (1990) 4 *Journal of Anxiety Disorders* 61-81.

Marcus, E, "Psychiatric Disability Evaluations: Plaintiff and Defence Perspectives" (1986) 7/2 *American Journal of Forensic Psychiatry* 11.

May, R (ed), *Existential Psychology*, New York: Random House, 1969.

May, R, Angel, E and Ellenberger, H (eds), *Existence: A New Dimension in Psychiatry and Psychology*, New York: Simon and Schuster, 1958.

Mayer-Gross, W, Slater, E and Roth, M, *Clinical Psychiatry*, London: Cassell and Company, 1960.

McConaghy, N, "Pseudopatients and Evaluation of Medical Practice" (1974) 2 *The Medical Journal of Australia* 383-385.

McElroy, S, Hudson, J, Pope, H and Keck, P, "Kleptomania: Clinical Characteristics and Associated Psychopathology" (1991) 21 *Psychological Medicine* 93-108.

McElroy, S, Pope, H, Hudson, J, Keck, P and White, K, "Kleptomania: A Report of 20 Cases" (1991) 148 *American Journal of Psychiatry* 652-657.

McGorry, P, "The Clinical Boundaries of Posttraumatic Stress Disorder" (1995) 29 *Australian and New Zealand Journal of Psychiatry* 385-393.

McGuffin, P and Thapar, A, "The Genetics of Personality Disorder" (1992) 160 *British Journal of Psychiatry* 12-23.

McLaren, N, "Is Mental Disease Just Brain Disease? The Limits to Biological Psychiatry" (1992) 26 *Australian and New Zealand Journal of Psychiatry* 270-276.

McNiel, D and Binder, R, "Predictive Validity of Judgments of Dangerousness in Emergency Civil Commitment" (1987) 144/2 *American Journal of Psychiatry* 197-200.

Mendelson, G, "The Rating of Psychiatric Impairment in Forensic Practice: A Review" (1991) 25 *Australian and New Zealand Journal of Psychiatry* 84-94.

— "The Scope and Limitations of Psychiatric Expert Testimony" (1990) 10 *Australasian Forensic Psychiatry Bulletin* 10-18.

Miller, R, "Hidden Agendas at the Law-Psychiatry Interface" (1990) Spring-Summer, *The Journal of Psychiatry and Law* 35-58.

⚡Milte, K, Bartholomew, A and Galbally, F, "Abolition of the Crime of Murder and of Mental Condition Defences" (1975) 49 *The Australian Law Journal* 160-172.

Modestin, J and Ammann, R, "Mental Disorders and Criminal Behaviour" (1995) 166 *British Journal of Psychiatry* 667-675.

Mollica, R, "Mood Disorders: Epidemiology" in Kaplan, H and Sadock, B (eds), *Comprehensive Textbook of Psychiatry* (5th ed), Baltimore: Williams & Wilkins, 1989.

Monahan, J, "Limiting Therapist Exposure to Tarasoff Liability Guidelines for Risk Containment" (1993) 48 *American Psychologist 242-250.*

— "Mental Disorder and Violent Behaviour" (1992) 47 *American Psychologist* 511-521.

— "The Prediction of Violent Behaviour: Toward a Second Generation of Theory and Policy" (1984) 141/1 *American Journal of Psychiatry* 10-15.

Monahan, J and Steadman, H, "Crime and Mental Disorder: An epidemiological approach" in Morris, T (ed), *Crime and Justice: An Annual Review of Research*, Chicago: University of Chicago Press, 1983.

— (eds), *Violence and Mental Disorder*, Chicago: The University of Chicago Press, 1994.

Montandon, C and Harding, T, "The Reliability of Dangerousness Assessments: A Decision Making Exercise" (1984) 144 *British Journal of Psychiatry* 149-155.

Mora, G, "Historical and Theoretical Trends in Psychiatry" in Freedman, A, Kaplan, H and Sadock, B (eds), *Comprehensive Textbook of Psychiatry – II*, Baltimore: The Williams and Wilkins Company, 1975.

⚡Morse, S, "Excusing the Crazy: The Insanity Defence Reconsidered" (1985) 58 *Southern California Law Review* 780-836.

Mortimer, A, "Phenomenology: Its Place in Schizophrenia Research" (1992) 161 *British Journal of Psychiatry* 293-297.

Mowry, B and Levinson, D, "Genetic Linkage and Schizophrenia: Methods, Recent Findings and Future Directions" (1993) 27 *Australian and New Zealand Journal of Psychiatry* 200-218.

Mullen, P, "Mental Disorder and Dangerousness" (1984) 18 *Australian and New Zealand Journal of Psychiatry* 8-17.

— "Morbid Jealousy and the Delusion of Infidelity" in Bluglass, R and Bowden, P (eds), *Principles and Practice of Forensic Psychiatry*, Edinburgh: Churchill Livingstone, 1990.

Nash, M, "Memory Distortion and Sexual Trauma: The Problem of False Negatives and False Positives" (1994) XLII *International Journal of Clinical and Experimental Hypnosis* 346-362.

Nemiah, J, "Depressive Neurosis" in Freedman, A, Kaplan, H and Sadock, B (eds) *Comprehensive Textbook of Psychiatry – II*, Baltimore: The Williams and Wilkins Company, 1975.

Noble, P and Rodger, S, "Violence by Psychiatric In-patients" (1989) 155 *British Journal of Psychiatry* 384-390.

Noyes, A and Kolb, L, *Modern Clinical Psychiatry*, Philadelphia: WB Saunders Company, 1958.

O'Callaghan, E, Sham, P, Takei, N, Glover, G and Murray, R, "Schizophrenia after Prenatal Exposure to 1957 A2 Influenza Epidemic" (1991) 337 *The Lancet* 1248-1250.

O'Reilly, R, "Viruses and Schizophrenia" (1994) 28 *Australian and New Zealand Journal of Psychiatry* 222-228.

Ofshe, R and Singer, M, "Recovered-Memory Therapy and Robust Repression: Influence and Pseudomemories" (1994) XLII *International Journal of Clinical and Experimental Hypnosis* 391-408.

Owen, A and Winkler, R, "General Practitioners and Psychosocial Problems An Evaluation Using Pseudopatients" (1974) 2 *The Medical Journal of Australia* 393-398.

Owen, M and McGuffin, P, "The Molecular Genetics of Schizophrenia: Blind Alleys, Acts of Faith, and Difficult Science" (1992) 305 *British Medical Journal* 664-665.

Owens, D, "Imaging Aspects of the Biology of Schizophrenia" (1992) 5 *Current Opinion in Psychiatry* 6-14.

Parker, G, Hadzi-Pavlovic, D, Boyce, P, Wilhelm, K, Brodaty, H, Mitchell, P, Hickie, I and Eyers, K, "Classifying Depression by Mental State Signs" (1990) 157 *British Journal of Psychiatry* 55-65.

Parker, G, Hall, W, Boyce, P, Hadzi-Pavlovic, D, Mitchell, P, Wilhelm, K, Brodaty, H, Hickie, I and Eyers, K, "Depression Sub-Typing: Unitary, Binary or Arbitrary?" (1991) 25 *Australian and New Zealand Journal of Psychiatry* 63-76.

Parker, N, "The Garry David Case" (1991) 25 *Australian and New Zealand Journal of Psychiatry* 371-374.

Pathe, M and Mullen, P, "The Dangerousness of the DSM-III-R" (1993) 1 *Journal of Law and Medicine* 47-51.

Pato, C, Lander, E and Schulz, S, "Prospects for the Genetic Analysis of Schizophrenia" (1989) 15/3 *Schizophrenia Bulletin* 365-372.

Philipsborn, J, "On Firm Ground? A Discussion of the Current Law of Foundation for the Expression of Opinions by Psychiatrists and Psychologists" (1994) 15 *American Journal of Forensic Psychiatry* 53-66.

Plutchik, R and van Praag, H, "A Self-Report Measure of Violence Risk, II" (1990) 31/5 *Comprehensive Psychiatry* 450-456.

Pollock, N and Webster, C, "The Clinical Assessment of Dangerousness" in Bluglass, R and Bowden, P (eds), *Principles and Practice of Forensic Psychiatry*, Edinburgh: Churchill Livingstone, 1990.

Poythress, N, Jr, "Avoiding Negligent Release: A Risk-Management Strategy" (1987) 38 *Hospital and Community Psychiatry* 1051.

Prins, H, "Besieged by Devils – Thoughts on Possession and Possession States" (1992) 32/3 *Medicine, Science and the Law* 237-246.

— "Dangerous People or Dangerous Situations? – some Further Thoughts" (1991) 31/1 *Medicine, Science and the Law* 25-37.

— "Dangerousness: a Review" in Bluglass, R and Bowden, P (eds), *Principles and Practice of Forensic Psychiatry*, Edinburgh: Churchill Livingstone, 1990.

Quality Assurance Project, "A Treatment Outline for Depressive Disorders" (1983) 17 *Australian and New Zealand Journal of Psychiatry* 129-146.

— "Treatment Outlines for Antisocial Personality Disorder" (1991) 25 *Australian and New Zealand Journal of Psychiatry* 541-547.

Raifman, L, "Problems of diagnosis and legal causation in courtroom use of post-traumatic stress disorder" (1983) 1 *Behavioral Science and the Law* 115-130.

Rappeport, J, "Differences Between Forensic and General Psychiatry" (1982) 139:3 *American Journal of Psychiatry* 331-334.

Ray, J, "Is the Ned Kelly Syndrome Dead? – Some Australian Data on Attitudes to Shoplifting" (1981) 14 *Australian and New Zealand Journal of Criminology* 249-252.

Resnick, P, "Assessment of Psychic Harm" (1995) *Presentation Notes for Annual Meeting* of The Royal Australian and New Zealand College of Psychiatrists Section of Forensic Psychiatry, Article 6, 1-26.

— "Court Testimony as An Expert Witness", Article 4, 1-35.

— "Malingering" and "Guidelines for Courtroom Testimony" in Rosner, R (ed), *Principles and Practice of Forensic Psychiatry*, New York: Chapman & Hall, 1994.

— "Psychiatric Prediction of Violence" (1995), Article 9, 1-46.

Rice, M and Harris, G, "A Comparison of Criminal Recidivism Among Schizophrenic and Nonschizophrenic Offenders" (1992) 15 *International Journal of Law and Psychiatry* 397-408.

Rofman, E, Askinazi, C and Fant, E, "The Prediction of Dangerous Behaviour in Emergency Civil Commitment" (1980) 137/9 *American Journal of Psychiatry* 1061-1064.

Rogers, R, "Ethical Dilemmas in Forensic Evaluations" (1987) 5/2 *Behavioral Sciences and the Law* 149-160.

Rogers, R, Bagby, R and Chow, M, "Psychiatrists and the Parameters of Expert Testimony" (1992) 15 *International Journal of Law and Psychiatry* 387-396.

Rogers, R, Gillis, J, Turner, R and Frise-Smith, T, "The Clinical Presentation of Command Hallucinations in a Forensic Population" (1990) 147/10 *American Journal of Psychiatry* 1304-1307.

Rogers, R, Nussbaum, D and Gillis, R, "Command Hallucinations and Criminality: A Clinical Quandary" (1988) 16/3 *Bulletin of the American Academy of Psychiatry and the Law* 251-258.

Rollin, H, "Nineteenth Century Doctors in the Dock" (1981) 283 *British Medical Journal* 1176.

Rosenhan, D, "On Being Sane in Insane Places" (1973) 179 *Science* 250-258.

Rosner, R (ed), *Principles and Practice of Forensic Psychiatry*, New York: Chapman & Hall, 1994.

Roth, M, "Psychopathic (Sociopathic) Personality" in Bluglass, R and Bowden, P (eds), *Principles and Practice of Forensic Psychiatry*, Edinburgh: Churchill Livingstone, 1990.

Royal Australian and New Zealand College of Psychiatrists Section of Forensic Psychiatry, The, *Presentation Notes for Annual Meeting*, 1995.

Sainsbury, M, "Psychiatry in the People's Republic of China" (1974) 1 *Medical Journal of Australia* 669-675.

Sainsbury, M and Lambeth, L, *Sainsbury's Key to Psychiatry*, Wentworth Falls: Social Science Press, 1988.

Schulz, S and Pato, C, "Advances in the Genetics of Schizophrenia: Editor's Introduction" (1989) 15/3 *Schizophrenia Bulletin* 361-363.

Schwartz, D, "Some Problems in Predicting Dangerousness" (1980) 52/2 *Psychiatric Quarterly* 79-83.

Scott, P, "Assessing Dangerousness in Criminals" (1977) 131 *British Journal of Psychiatry* 127-142.

Shaffer, D, *Developmental Psychology*, Monterey: Brooks/Cole Publishing Co, 1985.

Shaw, J, *Golden Rules of Psychiatry*, Bristol: John Wright & Co, 1899.

Shea, P, "A danger to themselves and others" (1995) 11 *Open Mind* 17-18,24.

— Commentary in *Proceedings of the Institute of Criminology* No 57 "Shoplifting", Sydney: Institute of Criminology, 1983.

— "Mental Disorders and Dangerousness" (1993-1994) 22 *International Journal of Mental Health* 71-79.

— "Psychiatrists and Psychologists: Use and Usefulness of Their Evidence in Criminal Cases" (1995), paper delivered at the Thirteenth Biennial Conference of District and County Court Judges of Australia, Melbourne.

Slovenko, R, "Posttraumatic Stress Disorder and the Insanity Defence" (1994) 151 *American Journal of Psychiatry* 152.

— "The Lawyer and the Forensic Expert: Boundaries of Ethical Practice" (1987) 5/2 *Behavioral Sciences and the Law* 119-147.

Sparr, L and Atkinson, R, "Posttraumatic Stress Disorder as an Insanity Defense: Medicolegal Quicksand" (1986) 143 *American Journal of Psychiatry* 608-613.

Spiegel, D and Scheflin, A, "Dissociated or Fabricated? Psychiatric Aspects of Repressed Memory in Criminal and Civil Cases" (1994) XLII *International Journal of Clinical and Experimental Hypnosis* 411-432.

Stafford-Clark, D, *What Freud Really Said*, Harmondsworth: Penguin Books Ltd, 1967.

Stanley, R, "The Psychiatrist as Expert Witness: A Legal Perspective" (1989) 9 *Australasian Forensic Psychiatry Bulletin* 2-7.

Starobinski, J, *History of the Treatment of Melancholy from the Earliest Times to 1900*, Basle: J R Geigy, 1962.

Steadman, H and Cocozza, J, "Selective Reporting and the Public's Misconceptions of the Criminally Insane" (1978) 41 *Public Opinion Quarterly* 523-533.

Strachan, C, *Assessment of psychopathy in female offenders*, unpublished doctoral dissertation, University of British Columbia, Vancouver, Canada, 1993.

Sutherland, E and Cressey, D, *Principles of Criminology*, Chicago: J B Lippincott Company, 1960.

Szasz, T, *The Myth of Mental Illness*, New York: Dell Publishing Co, 1961.

Taylor, P, "Victims and Survivors" in Gunn, J and Taylor, P (eds) *Forensic Psychiatry Clinical, Legal and Ethical Issues*, Oxford: Butterworth-Heinemann, 1993.

Tennant, C, "Life Events and Schizophrenic Episodes" (1985) 19 *Australian and New Zealand Journal of Psychiatry* 327-329.

Teplin, L, "The Criminality of the Mentally Ill: A Dangerous Misconception" (1985) 142/5 *American Journal of Psychiatry* 593-599.

Tidmarsh, D, "Schizophrenia" in Bluglass, R and Bowden, P (eds), *Principles and Practice of Forensic Psychiatry*, Edinburgh: Churchill Livingstone, 1990.

Tienari, P, "Implications of Adoption Studies on Schizophrenia" (1992) 161 (supplement 18) *British Journal of Psychiatry* 52-58.

Torrey, E, "Are We Overestimating the Genetic Contribution to Schizophrenia?" (1992) 18/2 *Schizophrenia Bulletin* 159-170.

Van der Kolk, B, Herron, N and Hostetler, A, "The History of Trauma in Psychiatry" (1994) 17 *Psychiatric Clinics of North America* 583-600.

Walker, N, "Dangerous Mistakes" (1991) 158 *British Journal of Psychiatry* 752-757.

Warner, C, "A Study of the Self-Reported Crime of a Group of Male and Female High School Students" (1982) 15 *Australian and New Zealand Journal of Criminology* 255-272.

Weiner, H, "Schizophrenia: Etiology" in Freedman, A, Kaplan, H and Sadock, B, *Comprehensive Textbook of Psychiatry – II*, Baltimore: The Williams and Wilkins Company, 1975.

West, D and Walk, A (eds), *Daniel McNaughton His Trial and the Aftermath*, Ashford: Gaskell Books, 1977.

Winfield, R (ed), *The Expert Medical Witness*, Sydney: The Federation Press, 1989.

Winkler, R, "Research Into Mental Health Practice Using Pseudopatients" (1974) 2 *The Medical Journal of Australia* 399-403.

World Health Organization, *International Classification of Diseases: Manual of the International Statistical Classification of Diseases, Injuries, and Causes of Death, Volume 1*, Geneva: World Health Organization, 1977.

— *The ICD-10 Classification of Mental and Behavioural Disorders: Clinical Descriptions and Diagnostic Guidelines*, Geneva, World Health Organization, 1992.

Zilboorg, G, *A History of Medical Psychology*, New York: W W Norton & Company, 1967.

Zusman, J, "Primary Prevention" in Freedman, A, Kaplan H and Sadock, B (eds), *Comprehensive Textbook of Psychiatry – II*, Baltimore: The Williams and Wilkins Company, 1975.

NEWSPAPER ARTICLES.

New York Times Magazine, "Staring Into the Heart of the Heart of Darkness", 4 June, 1995.

Sydney Morning Herald, "Girl psychotic, court told", 14 November 1992.

— "Mother's 3 murder convictions quashed", 16 February 1993.

— "My syndrome made me do it. . . the latest US defence", 11 June 1994.

— "The children who live in no-man's land", 1 July 1995.

— "Why an abuse excuse is the ultimate ruse", 23 February 1994.

INDEX

Alcohol dependency, 16
Anti-psychiatry, xii, xvi
Antisocial personality disorder, 61, 65
Antisocial reaction, 63
Aversion therapy, 17-18
Baxstrom, 156
Behaviourism, 16-18
Bestiality, 119
Bleuler, Eugen, 28-30, 62
Biochemical abnormalities, 14-15
Bipolar (affective) disorder, 47-48, 54
Butler Committee Report, 117-118, 145, 156
Byrne, 75, 76
Cognitive-behavioural school, 16-18
Compulsive behaviour, 129
Compulsive gambling, 16
Crimes Act 1900 (NSW), 119
Cyclothymia, 47, 54
Dangerousness, 141
David, 72, 76-77
Defence mechanisms, 18, 20, 107
Delusion, 39, 52, 53, 127
Depression, 15, 45, 120
    unitary and binary, 49-51
Depressive disorders, 45
Depressive episode, 48, 53
Depressive neurosis, 6, 54
Depressive personality, 54
Depressive psychosis, 47, 49
Depressive reaction, 47, 49
Diagnostic and Statistical Manual of Mental Disorders (DSM)
    DSM-I, 3, 36, 37, 46, 51, 55, 63
    DSM-II, 37, 65
    DSM-III, 2, 11, 31, 36-37, 55, 65-68, 78-79, 81, 126, 150
    DSM-III-R, 2, 5, 6, 11, 31-33, 36-40, 68-69, 78-79, 82, 105, 111-112
    DSM-IV, 2, 4-9, 11, 33, 36, 38, 40-41, 48-49, 51, 53-54, 56, 70, 72-73, 78-80, 83, 96, 105-107, 109, 119-120, 128-131

Diagnostic categories, 6-8
Dissocial personality disorder, 69-70
Dissociation, 19, 107
Dissociative amnesia, 105-109
Dissociative fugue, 106
Drive theory, 19
    sexual drive, 19
    aggressive drive, 19
Drug dependency, 120
Dyssocial reaction, 63
Dysthymia, 6, 47, 54-55
Ego, 20, 21
Endogenous depression (depressive reaction), 47, 49
Epidemiologic catchment area (ECA) survey, 150
Existential school, 21-24
Exogenous depressive reaction, 49
Expert witnesses, xi
Freud, Sigmund, 18
Genetic causes of mental disorder, 12-14
Hallucination, 12, 127
    command hallucination, 110-112
History-taking, 102
Id, 19
Impulsive behaviour, 129
International Classification of Diseases (ICD)
    ICD-9, 4, 36, 46, 51, 55, 65, 128
    ICD-10, 4-6, 9, 32-33, 37-38, 47-48, 51, 53-56, 69, 71, 73, 80, 96, 106-107, 119-120, 128-129, 131
Involutional melancholia, 47
Involutional psychotic reaction, 46
Kleptomania, 128-131
Kraepelin, Emil, 28-29, 35, 50, 62
Language of psychiatry, xii, 1
Major depression (depressive episode), 48, 51-53
    melancholic subtype, 53
Major schools of psychiatry, 11
MacArthur risk assessment study, 152
Mania, 15, 59

Manic-depressive psychosis (illness, reaction), 47, 48, 54
Memory, 103
Mental disorder
    and criminal behaviour, xiii, 118
    and dangerousness, 149
Mental Health Act 1958 (NSW), 9, 143, 144
Mental state examination, 104
Monopolar depression, 47
Moral insanity, 61-62
Necrophilia, 119
Neurasthenia, 6
Neurosis, 2-5
Neurotic depression, 47, 49-50, 56
No mental disorder, 133
Objectivity, 23-24
Organic school, 12
Pedophilia, 119
Person referred for assessment, 96
Post-schizophrenic depression, 48-49
Post-traumatic stress disorder, 78-87, 131-133
Prediction of dangerousness, 155
Pseudopatients, 97
Psychiatric evaluation, 90
Psychiatric reports, xi-xiii
Psychodynamic school, 18-21

Psychogenic amnesia, 19, 105
Psychogenic depressive psychosis, 47
Psychopathic personality, 20, 61, 64, 67
Psychopathy checklist, 70
Psychosexual disorders, 17, 119
Psychosis, 2-5
Psychotic depression, 46-47, 49, 50
Reactive depressive psychosis, 47
Repressed memories, 109
Repression, 18, 107
Risk assessment, 158
Risk management, 158
Role of the psychiatrist, 90-96
Schizo-affective disorders, 48
Schizophrenia, 12-14, 27, 44, 125-128
    and homicide, 127
    and violence, 151
    signs and symptoms, 39-41
    simple, 37-38
    subclassifications, 35-37
Shoplifting, 121-125
    and depression, 121-125
Simulated amnesia, 108-109
Social learning theory, 20
Super-ego, 20
Twin studies, 12-14
Unconscious mind, 18, 19, 21
Zoophilia, 119